Educational Technology: Implications for Early and Special Education

Alan Cleary
Department of Psychology,
University of Newcastle upon Tyne

Terry Mayes
Department of Psychology,
University of Strathclyde

Derek Packham
Department of Psychology,
University of Newcastle upon Tyne

JOHN WILEY & SONS

London · New York · Sydney · Toronto

Library of Congress Cataloging in Publication Data:

Cleary, Alan.
  Educational technology.

  Bibliography: p.
  Includes indexes.
  1. Educational technology. I. Mayes, Terry, joint
author. II. Packham, Derek, joint author. III. Title.

LB1028.3.C62   371.3'078   75–1239
ISBN 0 471 16045 8

Photosetting by Thomson Press (India) Limited, New Delhi
and printed in Great Britain by Pitman Press, Bath, Avon.

Educational Technology:
Implications for Early
and Special Education

Preface

The scope of the book is interdisciplinary and we have tried to offer solutions as well as to pose problems. We find it difficult not to have preconceptions and prejudices about early and special education and no doubt these will be more apparent to the reader than we realise. One which we will acknowledge is that educational technology is undervalued; its development has been accompanied by inaccurate and emotive claims from both supporters and opponents and it has not yet weathered the storm of opposition which met initial proposals to use programmed texts and teaching machines in the early 1960s.

Another problem concerns the extent and level of description appropriate for a readership from different disciplines. It is not likely that most readers will be equally well-versed or interested in all the subject matter. Obviously the requirements of, say, an early education specialist lacking technical expertise and a computer scientist wishing to apply his skills to early education are very different. Yet we hope both would find this book a useful starting point; of course it is also intended for the increasing number of students and practitioners of educational technology.

Throughout we have faced the need to impose some structure on disparate approaches and techniques. The final arrangement is made explicit on the contents pages and there is substantial cross-referencing in the text; a technical glossary is included. For most chapters one author produced a complete first draft, which was subsequently rewritten by the other two working together; they had the final decision about chapter content. Other tasks were equally shared and so we are jointly responsible for any merits or shortcomings of the book. In the absence of any better alternative, the order of authors' names was determined alphabetically. We wish to thank the organisations who have supported our research and enabled us to gain experience of the problems at first hand. These are principally the Social Science Research Council; Science Research Council; Prudhoe and Monkton Hospital, Northumberland; Audiology Research Unit, Royal Berkshire Hospital, Reading; Behavioural Research and Development Ltd., and the Spastics Society. We are especially grateful to Professor J. E. Merritt, Faculty of Educational Studies, Open University, for his comments on the first draft of the book and to our publishers for their editorial help throughout. Val Glendinning and Thel Larby deserve special mention for their ability to transform poor manuscript into accurate typescript and Penny Nolan was of great help with copyright permissions, indexes and references.

AC/JTM/DP

Acknowledgements

We wish to express our appreciation to the following individuals, institutions, journals and publishers who have granted permission to reproduce figures, illustrations and tables.

Fig. 1.2 H. Kay from Kay, Dodd and Sime (1968); Fig. 1.4 Fearon Publishers, Inc.; Fig. 1.5 B. F. Skinner and American Association for the Advancement of Science from *Science*, Vol. 128, pp. 969–977, 24 October 1958; Fig. 1.6 Harper & Row, Publishers, Inc. from W. N. Tavolga, *Principles of Animal Behavior* (1969); Fig. 1.7 Lawrence & Wishart Ltd. from Pavlov (1927); Fig. 1.8(a) Pfizer International, Inc.; Fig. 1.9(b) B. F. Skinner; Figs. 1.8(c), 4.13(a) Department of Photography and Teaching Aids Laboratory, University of Newcastle upon Tyne; Fig. 3.1 D. V. Moseley; Fig. 3.2 Association for Educational Communications and Technology from Hively (1960); Fig. 3.3 W. Hively; Fig. 3.4 I. P. St. James-Roberts; Fig. 3.6 M. S. Jackson; Figs. 3.7, 3.11 Prentice-Hall Learning Systems, Inc.; Fig. 3.10 Bell & Howell A-V Ltd.; Figs. 4.2, 4.29 Behavioral Controls, Inc.; Fig. 4.3 Kodak Ltd., Fig. 4.4 Counting Instruments Ltd.; Fig. 4.5 La Belle Industries, Inc.; Figs. 4.6, 4.10(a) Philips Electrical Ltd.; Fig. 4.8 Digital Equipment Co. Ltd.; Fig. 4.9 Tektronix UK Ltd.; Figs. 4.10(b), 6.1, Tables 7.1, 7.2 Association for Programmed Learning and Educational Technology; Fig. 4.11(a) Willi Studer Elektronische Apparate; Fig. 4.12 Gates Division, Harris-Intertype Corporation; Fig. 4.14 W. Hively and *Journal of the Experimental Analysis of Behavior*, Copyright 1964 by the Society for the Experimental Analysis of Behavior, Inc.; Fig. 4.17 W. H. Freeman & Co.; Fig. 4.21 Psychonomic Society Publications; Fig. 4.22 Enfield and Southgate Gazettes; Fig. 4.28 D. M. Bear and The Society for Research in Child Development; Fig. 4.30 BRD (Electronics) Ltd.; Fig. 5.1 Data Dynamics Ltd.; Figs. 5.2, 5.4, 5.5, 5.6, Tables 5.1, 5.2 R. C. Atkinson and the American Psychological Association; Fig. 5.3 R. C. Atkinson; Figs. 5.7, 5.8 D. Bitzer; Fig. 5.9 W. W. Cooley, R. Glaser and American Association for the Advancement of Science; Fig. 5.10 The Mitre Corporation; Fig. 5.11 Digital Equipment Co. Ltd. based on figures from their publication *Introduction to Programming* (1969); Fig. 5.12 Digital Equipment Co. Ltd. from their publication *Introduction to Data Communications* (1971); Figs. 6.2, 6.3 Kogan Page Ltd.; Figs. 6.4, 6.5, 6.6, 6.7 P. Hodge; Fig. 6.8 Organisation for Economic Cooperation and Development; Fig. 7.1 D. R. Olson and Academic Press, Inc.; Table 2.1 McGraw-Hill Book Co.

Contents

CHAPTER 1

Traditions within Educational Technology

1.1 Introduction

A popular joke amongst educational technologists is that the only piece of technology ever to be really effective in education is the school bus. This joke, like most good ones, encapsulates some serious arguments about its subject matter. Firstly, of course, it questions assumptions about what constitutes educational technology. Is the school bus really a component in what Kay, Dodd and Sime (1968) have called 'the quiet revolution'? Not so quiet, one might think. Similarly Stolurow (1966) has remarked, 'The transition from the little red schoolhouse to the computer-based school system is one of the more dramatic and significant developments taking place in the shadow of the space race and in the climate of the cold war'. An extravagant claim for the school bus, surely? The suspicion is raised, then, that educational technology is an area in which old ideas and well-established techniques have been repackaged in elusive new terminology. On the other hand it could be that some educational technologists in attempting complex, even spectacular, demonstrations of automated teaching have significantly reduced their effectiveness.

Secondly, the joke implies that whatever their intrinsic value and despite their capacity for arousing enthusiasm, the new techniques have had no serious impact in the classroom or the training school: or worse, that in some way they have seemed to underrate the complexity of the educational process and to disregard the need for face-to-face interaction. Thirdly, one is forced to ask what is meant by really effective? The school bus certainly performs the job it is intended to perform, namely to transport children to and from their formal place of learning. How can we say whether a teaching machine performs its allotted task as well? Clearly we ought to be able to state objectives and criteria precisely before we begin evaluation of effectiveness.

There is, however, little agreement even about the term educational technology. According to its practitioners the term cannot be taken to refer exclusively to the hardware employed in education. And, if it is accepted that a definition should cover all techniques, then educational technology has a wide meaning indeed. We see no advantage at this point in offering a comprehensive definition and will attempt to reach an understanding of present-day educational technology by examining the way in which the separate approaches have developed and merged.

In our view educational technology is concerned with the overall methodology and set of techniques employed in the application of instructional principles. The teacher, who rewards a child by smiling and saying 'well done' when the child performs some act that conforms with the teacher's intention, is employing educational technology just as if the child was responding to a fully automated system. That is to say, the teacher is himself acting as an instructional tool to carry out a technique (in this case for increasing the likelihood that the child's response will recur) designed to achieve the teacher's goal for the child's behaviour. In this example the means of implementing the technique is clearly of less importance than the use of the technique itself and its immediate or long-term effect. Confusion about the logic of this system may arise simply because the human instructor is so well suited to perform this role. Such confusion hardly exists in other applied disciplines where human beings are manifestly unsuited to act as tools for applying scientific principles.

Although comparatively few devices employed in education are designed to operate in a way entirely beyond the capabilities of the human operator, it would be quite incorrect to suppose that educational technology consists solely of aids for the teacher. The advent of educational technology has made possible many types of training which have hitherto been difficult for the human instructor to accomplish, or even impossible. In some cases the speed and scale of the response required from the training system is beyond the ability of a human instructor, e.g. in flight simulators. Other forms of training frequently require detailed analyses of responses either to provide students with feedback on their performance, for example in microteaching by videotape replay, or to allow the teacher to modify his course by reference to statistics derived by processing responses through a computer.

Sometimes educational technology is concerned with very subtle interplay between human and non-human resources, as illustrated by some attempts to teach emotionally disturbed children, but increasingly it is involved in the allocation of these resources within a system. What has been termed the systems approach to educational technology consists of four main activities, outlined by Silvern (1968) as follows: (i) analysis of system components and inter-relationships; (ii) synthesis of these elements together with others previously unrelated; (iii) model building to show the structure and relationships with a view to possible quantification and (iv) simulation of the system model prior to implementation in real life and modification of the model where necessary in the light of evaluation. This approach is discussed in more detail in Section 6.1.

Finally, it does emerge very clearly that educational technology can be interpreted as threatening traditional styles of teaching. In a sense this is true and it arises incidentally, given the shift of emphasis from the teacher's to the learner's viewpoint. The teacher's role may alter in the light of an analysis of the needs and the resources available but hopefully the outcome should allow the teacher more scope to exercise his talents.

1.2 The audio-visual aids tradition

This tradition in educational technology can be distinguished from the other two as it has been largely pragmatic in its approach. The lack of clearly defined scientific principles and the difficulty of their application have led to those directly involved with practical problems of communication to use their own personal or group experience as a basis for utilising certain techniques and equipment in an educational setting. Inevitably they have had to make their choice within the limits of existing technology and other dominant factors, such as the physical location of their work and financial constraints. Yet it is important to realise that, even in very fortunate circumstances, sophisticated tools of the trade cannot supplant the need for a science-based technology. An individual today with a magnetic chalkboard is basically operating at the same level of communication as his predecessor several thousand years ago. In comparison, new possibilities for conveying information in a more efficient way could result if research on the particular requirements is undertaken and specialised hardware developed. In this context it is easy to see why mass entertainment with its enormous market has produced most of the developments, many of which are in the process of being adapted for use in education. Indeed it is as well that the refusal to acknowledge the educational benefits which can be derived from mass entertainment has declined over the past ten years and allowed more cooperation between the two sectors. Chapter 4 describes specific equipment but it is worth noting that young children today are likely to gain rapid acquaintance with the media and will therefore be far more discriminating than children of previous generations. It would be surprising if they were not dissatisfied with formal attempts to communicate information by their parents and teachers in comparison with, say, television broadcasters. The latter must seem to be endowed with quasi-magical abilities derived from the facility with which they are able to supplement their spoken message by sophisticated graphics. This form of competition, together with the increasingly technical aspects of teaching, may have discouraged parents from participating informally in their children's education. In addition it has probably contributed to a rather defensive attitude among teachers who may have felt, quite rightly, that they could not compete with the mass media.

It would be most unfortunate if negative attitudes should block progress, particularly in educational television, which is one of the most promising developments in early education at present. Later in the book we will consider further refinements such as interactive television (Section 5.4); here we wish to point to recent innovations and research issues.

The most ambitious is based on the American children's television programme, *Sesame Street*, and organised by Children's Television Workshop. The objective of this project is to promote the intellectual and social and cultural growth of pre-school and young schoolchildren. Specific goals include symbolic representation, problem solving and reasoning, and familiarity with the physical and social environment. The target population consists of all children, three to five years old, with emphasis on the disadvantaged child. The stimulus material, presented principally in the form of cartoons, has included: (i) letters, numbers and geometric forms; (ii) problem solving and reasoning, consisting of recognition of parts of the body, visual discrimination among objects and pictures and understanding of relational concepts such as size, shape, position and distance; and (iii) natural environment, with concepts differentiating city and country, objects and people, rules of behaviour and fair play.

The effects of the first year's work have been evaluated by the Educational Testing Service (Ball and Bogatz, 1970) and further assessments are under way. It is difficult to summarise briefly the results involving the multiplicity of factors studied, e.g. age, sex, socio-economic class, encouragement to view, type of material presented and former achievement level. Yet it seems worth noting that children who viewed most often show the highest gains (independently of normal growth, class, IQ and previous achievement) and that younger children (3 year olds) gained at least as much as older children (5 year olds). The mother's behaviour also seemed to be important in that the children who viewed more and learned more came from homes where both mother and child viewed together and where the mother discussed the programme with the child. It is conceivable that training the mothers, as in the Sesame Mother pilot project, would have produced greater gains and/or more children who showed learning gains from pre-test to post-test. In this project volunteer mothers were trained to conduct viewing sessions in their own homes. Following the viewing of each programme the Sesame Mother directed activities to reinforce specific aspects of the programme and relate the programme to the children's experiences. Effectiveness tests (including cognitive and attitudinal measures) indicated that in most cases the Sesame Mother intervention improved the children's skills and that more child involvement resulted in more improvement. In a similar fashion other volunteers have been recruited for high-viewing Spanish-speaking children from a disadvantaged community, and in general high-viewing children with low pre-test scores show the greatest gains. Of course the advantages of intervention of this kind have to be weighed against their costs; educational television by itself is cheap in terms of cost per viewer but unless additional help is provided, mainly in terms of unpaid volunteers or better utilisation of existing interaction between adults and young children, the cost could become prohibitive.

In comparison with *Sesame Street*, there are few British television programmes with obvious educational objectives and none attracting research on a scale comparable with the evaluation of Educational Testing Service. Evans (1971) has analysed children's television programmes during one week in 1969 and discussed the various functions they serve. His comment, 'there is a rather random quality about most of it', still seems apt five years later and, without funding for an organisation in this country analogous to Children's Television Workshop, the same state of affairs is likely to continue.

However some interest in *Sesame Street* itself has been shown in this country. The Primary Extension Programme of the then National Council for Educational Technology produced a report based on monitoring reactions to ten programmes from the American series during a short period in 1971 (Blackwell and Jackman, 1971). Children watched in a wide range of locations, at home, at play groups, in nursery and infant schools and special schools; a variety of field observers commented on their own and the children's reactions. Not surprisingly the comments are very mixed and the report consists mainly of samples presented without any attempt to draw general conclusions. Broadly, the reaction was positive with some criticisms raising real problems, e.g. the optimal length of time for a programme, while others were trivial, e.g. dislike of the American accent. These trials obviously provide useful information but they can offer no evidence on the more importat cumulative effects of viewing television programmes which have explicitly stated educational objectives. Small-scale research, though it can contribute in exploratory studies or to the development of particular techniques and aids, is quite inadequate in relation to the long-term effects of a mass medium.

A second innovation with wide implications for early and special education is growing out of the need to classify and disseminate information about audio-visual materials or the materials themselves. Resource centres have been set up, mainly in schools or in higher education and often in collaboration with libraries; these centres can loan both the necessary equipment and the learning materials. So far there are few comparable arrangements, whereby nursery group leaders or individual mothers can borrow from a centralised agency, yet it would seem particularly appropriate for a target population which has not yet learned to read. The relatively low cost of widely used materials, together with the ease and reliability of operation of replay equipment, should at least bring these facilities within the reach of nursery groups if a free service cannot be provided. A similar development can be seen in the growth of toy libraries for mentally and physically handicapped children and in the increasing concern to provide stimulating environments for children in hospital. It is to be hoped that these kinds of outlet for audio-visual materials, toys etc. will continue to expand, through both public and voluntary efforts, and that some systematic evaluation of materials will also take place.

Turning to more abstract issues, it is apparent from even a cursory glance at educational technology that there has been little contact between those theorising about learning behaviour and specialists in the use of audio-visual aids. Smith and Smith (1966) identify two major problems in the current discussion: firstly they suggest that a particular audio-visual device does not have invariant properties as an aid to learning and must be studied as a function of the system within which it operates; and secondly they consider that principles based on animal learning (see Section 1.4) have not been adequately extended to human audio-visual communication. In both respects a more fruitful source of work may develop from current research by experimental psychologists who are attempting to develop detailed models of a variety of cognitive processes (see Section 7.3).

Another prevalent but misleading assumption in assessing the effects of introducing audio-visual aids, whether automated or not, is that only objective measures of learning produce satisfactory evidence. It is difficult to assess the effect of a set of slides, a tape recording or a film when it is often unclear how the researcher should measure ensuing performance. The emotional or intellectual impact can be considerable and may even have decisive consequences on the subsequent behaviour of the child without it being possible to place such consequences under experimental investigation. Take a simple problem: assuming the availability of some kind of test, when should it be administered? Results may appear encouraging at a given instant (immediately afterwards, the following day etc.) but less satisfactory over a longer period or vice versa. One suggestion, put forward by Mialaret (1966), is to make observations while the psychological processes are taking place, that is during the actual teaching situation. He claims that it has been possible to observe the emotional reactions of children quite precisely using physiological measures such as skin resistance (GSR) and electroencephalograms (EEG).

It is conceivable that, although in traditional terms no change may have taken place, the child may still have been subjected to the effect which the educator intended, especially if it is of an emotional kind. Here audio-visual techniques play the role of catalyst, perhaps preparing the child for a new area of knowledge by inculcating a favourable attitude. The distinction might equally be made in terms of intentional and incidental effects. If a questionnaire is used after a film is shown, then part of the intended effects of the film may be studied, such as the content of the factual information or the relative advantage of one mode of presentation against another, but any unintended side-effects on the subsequent behaviour of the child will normally remain unknown. The latter are no less strong or valid because they remain unmeasured, for a wide and reliable body of evidence outside an educational setting indicates that our behaviour is the result of many influences amongst which incidental, unnoticed factors are not the least.

A final point concerns terminology. Waite (1971a) has complained that many items of equipment described as audio-visual aids are not aids but in fact provide valid learning experiences in themselves. We would agree that continued usage could promote the misconception that the use of audio-visual materials is in some way peripheral to learning and teaching. However, in trying to characterise one of the historically separate components of educational technology which have gradually merged, we have retained the rather outdated term, audio-visual aids.

1.3 The cybernetics tradition

The role assigned to errors that arise during learning is a principal source of difference between the traditions reviewed in this section and the next. Whilst the psychology tradition has placed emphasis on rewarding correct responses and avoiding or eliminating incorrect ones, within the cybernetics tradition errors have been accorded an important redirecting function. The precise origins of this discipline are as unclear as those which led to the development of programmed instruction, but they appear to stem from the comparison of living and non-living control systems which arose during the Second World War.

Much of cybernetics is concerned with how stability can be maintained in control systems. One of the earliest systems which was explicitly designed using concepts of this kind was Watt's invention of the rotating governor for the steam engine, the theoretical analysis of which was due to Maxwell (1867). The development of a general theoretical treatment of both control and communication systems is, however, usually attributed to Wiener (1948) and it was with his book on cybernetics that the science was really founded. Wiener and other engineers and mathematicians who had worked on guidance and control systems during the war were impressed by the similarities between the behaviour of electromechanical systems and many living organisms.

The term cybernetics is derived from a Greek word meaning steersman and relates to the way the steersman regulates the rudder so as to keep a ship on course. This is termed the feedback principle. A feedback control system has three main functions:

(i) it controls some aspect of the system in relation to its environment (i.e. it has an output);
(ii) it can compare the state of its output with a target or objective (its input) to detect a difference signal or error;
(iii) it can use the error to redirect the output.

If the output is redirected so that it moves towards the target the error will be reduced and the feedback is termed negative. This is the type which is always used in control systems as shown in Figure 1.1.

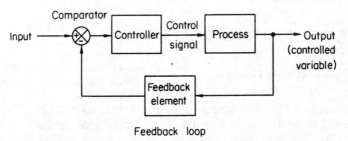

Feedback loop

Figure 1.1 A diagrammatic representation of a feedback control system. If the input or reference is steady, the system is termed a regulator; if, however, the system is intended to follow a changing input, then it is termed a servomechanism or error-corrected servo system

Systems which monitor their outputs and take corrective action are termed closed loop; such systems reduce the effects upon the output of changes in the process itself and in the state of the environment. Watt's steam governor, for example, kept the speed of the engine (the output) fairly constant despite changes in steam pressure (the process) and load upon the engine (the environment). Before the advent of the governor the system was open loop and engine

8

speed varied markedly with pressure and load, so much so that a man was needed to effectively close the feedback loop. It is worth referring to Figure 1.1 again and noting the vital part played by the error signal in a feedback control system. It directly controls the output and thus for any case requiring output such a system must always have some residual error, but this will be less than for the open loop case.

Let us now see how this work may be related to the training process. An application would involve comparing the student's responses with the requirement and, when an error is detected, providing further training so as to reduce the incorrect responses. This is, of course, just a formalisation of the ideal of individualised teaching.

Crowder (1959) devised a form of programmed instruction which was based on principles of feedback control, i.e. the emphasis was on using information from errors to eliminate incorrect responses, rather than on designing the system to produce mainly correct responses and then reinforcing them. Crowder's system was designed to meet the needs of technical military training and differs from linear programs* (see Section 1.4) in two important respects: (i) the student is presented at the end of each frame with a multiple choice question from which he selects an alternative before being allowed to proceed, and (ii) the system checks his answer and branches to an appropriate frame. Thus the path the student takes depends on his previous knowledge of the subject matter and his individual responses. Consequently a branching program is usually suitable for a wider target population than an equivalent linear program and, because of the feedback control included in the system, it can also achieve the required terminal behaviour with fewer responses.

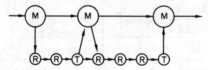

Figure 1.2 A form of skip branching. M = main sequence frame; R = non-specific remedial frame; T = test frame containing equivalent problem to previous main sequence frame

Crowder (1960) devised a range of simple and complex branching techniques, but skip branching (Figure 1.2) is the most widely used method. In this case the main program consists of diagnostic frames and a correct response will cause the student to be directed to a frame further on in the program. If he is incorrect he will be presented with one or more intervening frames containing remedial help before reaching that point. Originally branching programs were designed for presentation in teaching machines (see Figure 1.3) but later the system was adapted to produce what have been called scrambled texts. Here the sequence of items depends on the responses made by the student. Figure 1.4 shows some frames from one type of branching program.

In educational technology the term feedback is often used loosely to refer to both the reinforcing effects of knowledge of results in linear programming

*We have used the spelling 'program' to denote the technical term and retained the spelling 'programme' for non-technical usage.

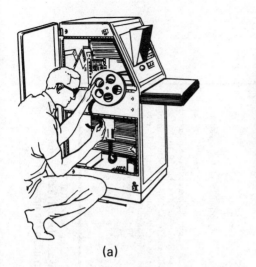
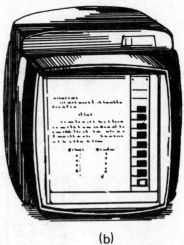

(a)   (b)

Figure 1.3 Crowder's teaching machines which were designed for presenting branching programs; (a) shows the Autotutor Mk I which was very sophisticated and could even present cine sequences; (b) shows the Autotutor Mk II, a simpler production version. (Based on F. F. Kopstein and I. J. Shillestad: A survey of auto-instructional devices, USAF Aeronautical Systems Division, *Technical Report No. 61–414*, 1961)

and to the knowledge of results given to the student about his previous response at the head of a frame in a branching program. In fact from the point of view of the training system neither of these represent feedback in the sense discussed above. A training system using a branching program does allow for error correction on the basis of the student's responses and it is these which close the feedback loop not the material presented to the student. If we were to consider the student as a system with an objective it would have feedback from its environment, including the teaching machine or program, but that is a different matter. Educational technologists are not able to design the student!

Though most effort has been put into the application of programmed instruction for individual use, feedback devices for group use are a promising development. Glynn, Pearce and Willott (1969) have reviewed three simple devices: (i) coloured cards, marked with identifying letters to allow students to indicate their responses; (ii) the Cosford Cube, developed by the R.A.F., which provides for up to four choices plus a 'help' or 'more time required' response via the remaining two faces; and (iii) battery-operated devices which would flash green or red lights as the students progressed through a series of multiple choice questions. In a more sophisticated example, the Pennant feedback classroom, the teacher presents a multiple choice question to the class and each student responds by pressing one of the response buttons. A display on the teacher's console indicates the number and distribution of the correct responses. The program may be prepared for presentation by overhead projector or automatic slide projector using any of the established programming techniques,

19

You said "To be able to repair a radio" is stated in behavioral terms. Good for you! This objective meets the first criterion of a useful statement, because it tells *what the learner will be doing* when demonstrating his achievement of the objective. He will be "*repairing a radio.*"

Let's try just one more example. Which of the following is stated in performance terms?

To be able to write a summary of the factors leading to the depression of 1929 ....turn to page 21.

To understand the rules of logic...........turn to page 22.

To know the rules of football...........turn to page 23.

21

You said "To be able to write a summary of the factors leading to the depression of 1929" was stated in performance terms.

Absolutely correct! Apparently you applied the key question to this objective and correctly concluded that the learner should be "writing a summary." He wouldn't be reciting a summary, or recognizing factors in a long list of factors, or even dictating a summary. The learner would know that in order to demonstrate achievement of his objective he would have to write a summary of factors of some sort.

And speaking of summaries, turn to page 24.

22

You said "To understand the rules of logic" is stated in performance terms.

Well, let's ask the key question of this statement. What will the learner be DOING when he is *understanding* the rules of logic? Will he be reciting them? Will he be listing them? Will he be solving problems in logic? If so, what kind of problems? This objective doesn't say. You must decide what you will accept as evidence of "understanding" and then describe this intent in your objective.

Return to page 19 and select another answer.

23

You said "To know the rules of football" is stated in performance terms.

Well, once again, let's ask of this statement the key question. What will the learner be DOING when he is showing that he has reached this objective? Will he be reciting rules? Will he be writing a list of rules? Will he be playing the game without breaking any of the rules? Will he be watching others play the game and pointing out errors as he sees them? The objective does not tell us.

Now return to page 19 and select another answer.

Figure 1.4 An example of frames from a branching programmed text (Mager, 1962). Note that the head of each frame gives knowledge of results, the main body of the frame presents new material and the end of the frame presents a multiple choice test which routes the student by intrinsic programming to the next frame but clearly the teacher can interrupt the program at any stage where further explanation or comment is required. The students' responses may be recorded to allow the program to be revised for future presentations. All these devices originated and have been tested in secondary and further education but, in principle, they could be used in early education; probably they will remain too intricate to be of much value in most fields of special education.

Although feedback control provides a powerful method for keeping a variable at a required value, there still remains the question as to what this value should be. In training a particular skill the requirement should be raised as the student gains competence. It is a basic feature that the system continually exerts a forward pressure on the student. There is a requirement to increase difficulty along a particular dimension as learning progresses within a specific skill and ideally this should relate to the individual student's responses. This facility is excluded by the nature of linear programming, but does occur to some extent with branching programming. Here the limitation is due to the absence of a store of information on the student's previous responses. The decision as to what material is next presented is based entirely on the student's current response to the particular frame which is being presented. It is also possible that training could be made more effective if the system were able to analyse the responses made by the student so that remedial training could be given where required subskills were found to be lacking. Systems of this kind, which modify their immediate requirements in the interests of higher order objectives, are termed adaptive systems and are being found increasingly in the control of industrial processes; their use in education has not been widespread. However, there are practical problems in ordering cognitive material for difficulty and in analysing subskill requirements. Lewis and Pask (1966) have reviewed the theory and practice of adaptive teaching systems and have achieved some success in training keyboard and other simple skills.

The second mainstream within the cybernetics tradition is computing. Although the history of computing may be traced to Babbage (1792–1871) or earlier, it was only with the advent of the solid state, general purpose, digital computer in the late 1950s that the computer began to have any widespread impact. The data and communications industry is likely to have an increasing effect on educational technology, not so much within the limited area of what is generally termed computer-assisted instruction or CAI (see Section 5.2), but more from the availability of a wide range of automated information display and retrieval devices, resulting from the increased use of computers and general acceptance that systems analysis, design and management are effective.

The majority of CAI systems currently being operated are research projects, although a significant number of students in the USA are now receiving some of their instruction under CAI from such systems as the IBM 1500. The ideal CAI system, as Zinn (1967) has pointed out, would be one in which each student could type, in everyday language and unconstrained format (free-form input), questions and statements to the computer which would then construct and display suitable replies to the student and continually update its instructional programme. Seltzer (1971) states that the two crucial questions concerning CAI are, firstly, what can the computer do that more traditional instructional methods cannot and, secondly, are there less expensive ways to effect the same instructional goals? On the latter point Seltzer concludes, 'if one is to judge for the adoption or nonadoption of CAI on the basis of cost alone then it is clear that CAI should not achieve widespread use in any mode'. On the first issue there is clear evidence for the effectiveness of CAI in drill-and-practice and tutorial modes (see Section 5.2), but it is unlikely that CAI can actually improve the quality of learning with these paradigms. The most exciting possibilities for CAI undoubtedly lie in the dialogue mode. A few pilot systems, such as that developed by Suppes, Jerman and Brian (1968), have approached this level of sophistication but none has yet been fully implemented. Seltzer points out that this is mainly because information processing models capable of dealing with natural language input are non-existent and apparently little is being accomplished at present.

Atkinson and Wilson (1968) have listed some of the technical problems still limiting the development of CAI. These mainly concern terminal hardware and in particular the use of the cathode ray tube (CRT) as a display device. The difficulty of maintaining the image and of extending the distance between the computer and the CRT limits the number of terminals that may be maintained on a given system. In addition, random access audio-tape units present a problem in resolving the conflict between the access time for each message and the capacity for storing items. The PLATO IV (Section 5.2.2) system recently installed at the University of Illinois incorporates a specially developed plasma display tablet and uses random access sheet-film and audio-discs loaded by the student to overcome these problems.

Further computer-based influences have come from the field of artificial intelligence. Clearly if an automated teaching system is to be effective it must exhibit many of the features which would normally be expected from a human teacher. If we are successful then we have, by Turing's test (1950), created artificial intelligence. From this point of view the relationship between student and teaching system is seen as symbiotic; the teaching system seeks to understand the student just as he tries to understand the teacher. It is therefore important that the two should be effectively coupled. This raises a further relevant discipline, that of ergonomics or the study of man–machine systems. Ergonomics has grown jointly from psychology and engineering and is particularly concerned with effective display and control systems designed for the human operator. It is therefore highly relevant to much of educational technology. As yet its application has been limited mainly to the design of display systems in conventional teaching, such as lecture theatres and classrooms, but, given a large-scale production of automated teaching systems, ergonomics would play an increasing role in the design of both display and response systems.

A last influence related to the general area of cybernetics is gaming and simulation, which was mentioned as one of the main activities in the systems approach. Simulation refers to a group of activities in which direct observation of the real situation may be difficult or even dangerous. Hence an artificial situation which models the original is created. Games have a well established place in traditional teaching, but their serious use in training high level skills, such as business management, is fairly recent and has been made possible by the use of computers to simulate the environment in which the participants are required to operate. In this context it is worth noting that young children essentially adopt simulation techniques in their play and indirectly reveal the level of their intellectual functioning. Observation of this form of simulation can obviously provide useful descriptive evidence but as yet no techniques to initiate the process in a particular direction have been devised. This illustrates a problem common to many apparently powerful techniques derived from cybernetics. They are not applied because of the difficulties in defining educational objectives and carrying out an analysis of the prerequisite skills.

1.4 The psychology tradition

Until recently psychological experiments had, for several decades, remained comparatively isolated from educational needs. The arguments for and against such a separation are outside the scope of this book. Nevertheless an impressive body of scientific data about instruction and training has emerged from controlled experimentation on factors affecting animal and human learning in the laboratory. Much of the opposition raised to the application of a science of behaviour has confused the empirical questions, as to whether the techniques will be effective in practice, with issues as to whether it is desirable to control human behaviour in this way. The elegance and precision of operant conditioning experiments with pigeons fails to impress the educator who regards pigeon and human behaviour as even further apart than the laboratory and the classroom. The argument often centres on whether one is justified in generalising from one situation in which variables are carefully controlled to another in which less control is possible. Experiments have been conducted in the field to settle this question but given the inevitable lack of control clear-cut results are hardly to be expected.

Applications arising out of the psychology of learning have developed in an essentially unplanned, haphazard way. It has normally been the case that individuals have found applications for their research work rather than that technologists have designed systems to meet specified objectives. The history of programmed instruction provides a good illustration. Though Thorndike (1913) set out the principles for a linear teaching machine, it is with Pressey (1926) that the modern development of this approach is generally assumed to have commenced. Pressey devised a testing system that provided automatic scoring of multiple choice tests (see Figure 1.5). The machine only advanced to the next test after the student had chosen the correct alternative and Pressey argued that by providing information to the student about the correctness of his response the device was in fact teaching. Pressey's work was somewhat in

14

Figure 1.5 Pressey's self-testing machine. The student is directed to a particular item in the multiple choice test. He makes a response by pressing the appropriate key and, if he is correct, the machine advances to the next item. The machine keeps a count of errors

advance of the formulation of a systematic learning theory on which to base an extension of the technique. Nevertheless he appreciated the importance of the main principle on which all subsequent work has been based, namely knowledge of results. More recently Pressey (1963, 1964) has argued for more widespread use of self-testing in conjunction with other methods of instruction, as for example embodied in current work at the University of Surrey (Elton, 1970; Hills, 1971).

Classical learning theory was derived almost exclusively from studies of animal learning and its value within educational technology has probably been overrated. However, certain basic concepts should be mentioned, the most relevant being secondary reinforcement. Stated simply, the assumption was that animals would act in order to reduce the strength of an internal physiological need (primary drive). Primary reinforcement (defined in Figure 1.9), it was postulated, directly reduced primary drives (e.g. hunger or thirst) while secondary reinforcers were stimuli closely associated with this process. A classic demonstration was by Cowles (1937) who trained chimpanzees to use tokens in a vending machine to obtain food and subsequently to solve discrimination problems in order to obtain the tokens alone. It is still generally argued that most human learning is governed by secondary rather than primary reinforcement and in the next section we will discuss behaviour modification in early education using token systems, which operate essentially in the same way as in the classic demonstration just described.

Skinner's (1953) position was based on a rejection of the kind of model-building previously attempted. The inferred, intervening variables were, Skinner suggested, no concern of the psychology of learning. Skinner's position allowed only observable stimuli and responses. Accordingly no hypothetical constructs, such as internal stimulus–response bonds, were permissible and reinforcers were defined solely in terms of their effect on the probability of recurrence of a response; the distinction between primary and secondary reinforcers was of no interest.

Despite Skinner's disregard for theory many of the developments to be described later in this book are derived from techniques originated by him for controlling and recording behaviour. Since Skinner's influence far exceeds that exerted by any theorist it is worth while considering his work briefly. In the first place Skinner has laid emphasis on the importance of applying the knowledge gained from laboratory experiments to the educational setting. His rejection of theoretical model building encouraged psychologists to apply established laboratory findings to real-life situations rather than to concentrate exclusively on their refinement in the laboratory. Nevertheless, Skinner also played an important role in his clarification of the theoretical principles themselves. For example, he clarified the distinction between classical conditioning (Pavlov, 1927) and escape from Thorndike's puzzle box (see Figures 1.6 and 1.7). If an organism operates on its environment without an eliciting stimulus

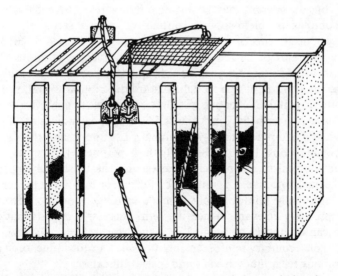

Figure 1.6 Thorndike placed a cat in a puzzle box such that the cat could open the latch and get to its bowl of milk by stepping on a treadle and pulling a string. By chance the cat pressed the treadle and thereafter other non-rewarding movements became fewer, with the cat eventually learning to press the treadle and open the latch (after E. L. Thorndike, *Animal Intelligence*, The Macmillan Co., 1911)

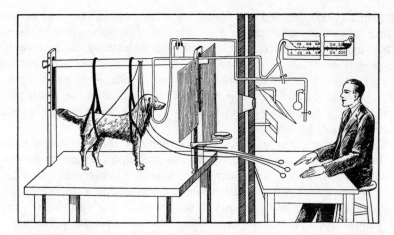

Figure 1.7 Pavlov's procedure for conditioning salivary responses. At the outset of a typical experiment the animal produces a salivary response (unconditioned response) to the presentation of food (unconditioned stimulus) but not to a neutral stimulus such as a tone. If the tone and the food are repeatedly represented to the dog a salivary response (conditioned response) will be obtained to the tone presented without food. The tone has become a conditioned stimulus

controlled by an experimenter, then in Skinner's terms it has produced an operant. Thus an operant may be a simple motor response such as pressing a lever, a complex problem-solving routine, or even a series of words. The probability of occurrence or the strength of an operant is raised by an immediate reinforcing stimulus or by the withdrawal of an aversive stimulus. This probability is measured simply by the rate or frequency of occurrence of the operant.

Now the implication of this straightforward description is that, provided an experimenter can find an effective reinforcer, he is able to achieve a remarkable degree of control over behaviour. Figure 1.8 gives some indication of the range of experimental equipment used with animals. Let us consider the shaping of a lever pressing response by a rat. Basically the experimenter attempts to arrange that the rat is reinforced on each occasion that its behaviour approximates towards the final objective, e.g. initially by turning or moving in the direction of the lever. Gradually reinforcement is made contingent on movements which are more precisely relevant, hence the term successive approximation. This procedure can obviously be applied to many forms of learning and, together with the use of secondary reinforcement, it has had a wide influence in development of training techniques in early and special education.

Although an operant is not in the first place elicited by a stimulus it can nevertheless be brought under stimulus control. If the operant is, say, pecking a key in a Skinner box in the presence of a light, then the light may be regarded as a discriminative stimulus. If pressing the lever is only reinforced in the presence of the light, then that stimulus becomes the discriminative stimulus. By employing appropriate reinforcement procedures it is possible to bring an operant under the control of a stimulus that is finely differentiated from other, similar stimuli by, for example, reinforcing responses to a green light but not reinforcing responses to a red light. A major problem for the application of stimulus control procedures is the question of which reinforcement schedule is most appropriate for a particular purpose. Here it is important to distinguish between the occasions when a new response is being trained and others when the aim is to increase the frequency of an already established response. For the former purpose Skinner proposes that a one-to-one relationship (continuous reinforcement) is necessary and it is this phase which normally predominates in learning since, as soon as one goal is reached, a new objective is set. Adaptive systems, which were discussed in the last section attempt to maintain the same level of difficulty as the learning progresses by effectively keeping the student at the same point in the shaping process. They thus avoid the problem of boredom when new material is too easy or discouragement when it is too hard. In contrast the requirement for increasing the frequency of an established response seldom arises in an educational setting, except partially in the case of drill-and-practice. Here the use of intermittent schedules of reinforcement (i.e. providing reinforcement after a number of responses or after an interval since the last reinforcement) could be appropriate.

A common technique for developing complex stimulus control is the matching-to-sample paradigm which is further discussed in Chapter 3. A sample stimulus (e.g. a circle) is presented together with response alternatives (e.g. a circle, or square and a triangle), one of which must be chosen as matching the sample on the relevant dimension. Only the correct response is immediately reinforced. An incorrect response may be followed either by repeated presentation of the same display or by a short delay before displaying the next items. The correct item may be identical to the sample on one or more dimensions, or it may be related in more complex ways. Matching-to-sample is a particularly useful procedure for developing control of stimuli which are related by abstract properties, such as larger/smaller or above/below.

From the framework provided by his work on operant training Skinner (1954) devised his system of linear programming. In its usual, written form a linear program looks like a series of incomplete sentences, each containing a blank, see Figure 1.9. The student constructs his response, by writing a word or words in the blank, then turns a page, moves a masking device or advances a teaching machine and the correct answer is revealed. The program is linear because all students are presented with the same frames in the same order, in contrast to a branching program where the student's responses determine the sequence of frames presented. A correct response is reinforced by providing an indication that it was a correct response. From Skinner's point of view, then, a response has to be seen to be correct before reinforcement occurs; an incorrect response is simply not reinforced, although the student is, of course, shown the correct response. It is important, therefore, to construct a linear program in such a way that as few errors as possible will occur. Conventionally a 10% error rate is the maximum acceptable before progression to new material, otherwise the student

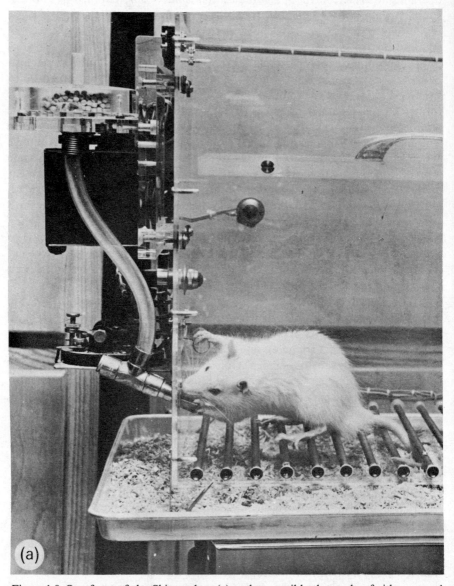

Figure 1.8 One form of the Skinner box (a) makes possible the study of either reward conditioning through food pellets dropped into the receptacle, or aversive conditioning, through shock delivered to the floor grid. In a form of the apparatus designed for use with pigeons (b), there is a key to peck instead of a lever to press. In either case, complex electronic equipment (c) may be used to program the schedule of reinforcement and other special conditions and to record the subjects' behaviour thus making it possible to run many subjects simultaneously

(b)

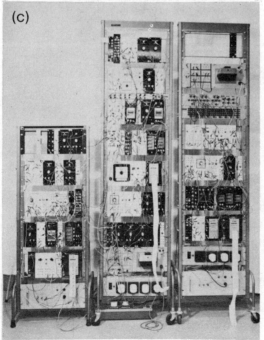

(c)

1.31 When an organism's hunger is reduced by the attainment of food, the food is a *reinforcer* which is said to *reinforce* the particular *response* that immediately preceded the presentation of the food.

1.32 The food _____ the response which immediately precedes its presentation, and it becomes more likely or more *probable* that the same response will recur when the organism is again placed in that situation.
reinforces

1.33 If a rat deprived of food for forty-eight hours is placed in a box containing a lever and discovers that when the lever is pressed it will receive a food reward, the rat will *learn* to press the lever repeatedly. This is probably because the food _____ the response of pressing the lever.
reinforces

1.34 It is generally agreed that *reinforcement* occurs whenever an event following a response increases the *probability* that that response will recur in that situation. This statement is called the *empirical law of effect*. Thus, when the rat's bar-pressing response increases in probability following presentation of food, it can be said that _____ has occurred.
reinforcement

1.35 An event which increases the probability of a particular response in a given situation is a *reinforcer*. When a water-deprived rat learns to press a bar for water, the bar-pressing response is _____ by water, which is a _____.
reinforced
reinforcer

1.36 Reinforcement involves an increase in the _____ of occurrence of a particular response.
probability

1.37 The statement that _____ will increase the probability of occurrence of a response is called the _____ _____ _____.
reinforcement
empirical law of effect

1.38 Most reinforcers can be conveniently divided into *positive* and *negative* reinforcers. A *positive* reinforcer is one which the animal *approaches;* a *negative* reinforcer is one which the organism will learn to avoid or escape. Both types increase the _____ of a response.
probability

Figure 1.9 This example of a linear programmed text is from R. C. Teevan and B. D. Smith, *Motivation*, McGraw-Hill, 1967. The student is required to complete the frame by inserting a word for each blank. A mask should be used to cover the answers so that they are only displayed one at a time after completing the frame

is recommended to repeat the program. The step between successive frames must always be small and this may lead to long and rather boring programs.

The principles derived from Skinner's work which form the basis of linear programmed instruction, have been formulated by Holland (1960) as follows:

(i) immediate reinforcement of student responses;
(ii) student emission of responses;
(iii) gradual progression to establish complex repertoires;
(iv) fading or gradual withdrawal of stimulus support;
(v) control of the student's observing behaviour;
(vi) discrimination training, abstraction, and concept formation through controlled variation of examples;
(vii) revision or modification of the program to fit the student.

The successful application of these principles requires careful analysis of several aspects of reinforcement. The most serious problem, both theoretical and technical, is the search for reinforcers that are effective, appropriate and ethical. This represents no problem in the case of mature students of normal intelligence motivated by factors outside the immediate instructional situation. It is by no means clear, however, that such factors are in any measure effective for shaping and maintaining a response from an immature or retarded child. Extrapolating from animal research an obvious choice would be the use of a period of deprivation prior to giving food as a reward, or less directly the use of sweets or trinkets. The former implies a large-scale restructuring of the child's environment (as illustrated in the next section) whilst the latter is subject to rapid satiation. Bijou and Baer (1966) in their discussion of the operant responses studied in children draw attention to the fact that the responses which qualify as representative of operant behaviour in general are most subject to satiation and adaptation effects. In a later section in the same contribution they give a useful list of reinforcers specifically for use with children. In practice the nature of the learning situation usually forces the experimenter to sacrifice elements of technical control which are theoretically available to him and typically the careful management of weak reinforcers such as a sound, light or social approval has been used with young children. Olson and Bruner (1974) comment on the constrained circumstances necessary for reinforcement to be effective and emphasise that a child may obtain no information unless he is attending to the relevant aspects of the learning situation. They list three techniques which should tend to clarify the consequences of a response, namely (i) providing for immediacy of reinforcement, (ii) placing it in a context which differentiates possible alternatives and thus avoids the formation of incorrect hypotheses and (iii) attempting to stress the necessity and regularity of the relationship.

Assuming that effective reinforcement is possible it is necessary to consider what is actually being reinforced in what Bloom (1956) has termed the cognitive and affective domains. Not only correct discriminations or constructed responses may be reinforced but also some forms of anxious behaviour. The question of eliminating incorrect responses or negative attitudes arises in this respect. The techniques employed in the animal laboratory, in which incorrect responses are followed by direct punishment or loss of all reward, are inappropriate when it is necessary to maintain a high rate of responding. Therefore punishment is ruled out not only on ethical grounds but also because of practical problems. To achieve sufficient control for the punishment to be effective there would be a substantial risk of the child ceasing to respond at all or even attempting to leave the learning situation. Even if punishment were effective the weight of experimental evidence suggests that the response may not be permanently weakened by punishment but merely suppressed in the presence of the aversive stimulus. It is evident that any general solutions to these kinds of difficulties will have to be flexible in relation to the particular learning situation and quite probably the particular child.

We can now review the advantages common to both linear and branching programs:

(i) there is improved control in the learning situation;
(ii) the student is required to respond actively and construct or manipulate information;
(iii) he is able to proceed at his own pace and so individualised instruction is possible;
(iv) he is only presented with information for which he has the prerequisite skill or knowledge.

One further point should be noted. Once a program has been constructed the teaching has, in a sense, already been done. All that is required is that the student should learn from it. Thus the role of the human instructor is only usurped in a very limited sense by the use of a teaching machine.

1.5 Behaviour modification—an emerging technology

Deriving directly from Skinner's work, described in the last section, are specific attempts to modify behaviour. Initially most studies were concerned to demonstrate under laboratory conditions that it was possible to use operant training procedures for establishing stimulus control in infants and retarded children: they have been successful both in terms of simple intermittent schedules (e.g. Weisberg and Fink (1966)) and combinations of schedules (e.g. Bijou and Orlando (1961)). Recently attempts at behavioural control have been made which are clearly relevant to problems encountered in starting formal education. In particular, it has been necessary to show that certain operant techniques can be applied effectively outside the artificial conditions created for the experimentally isolated child. In a group situation it is not normally practicable to control continuously response contingencies for each individual. One solution is to sample individual behaviour systematically, for instance, Bushell,

Wrobel and Michaelis (1968) analysed the study behaviour of a group of pre-school children. Examples were attending quietly to instructions, working independently or cooperating with others as appropriate: counter-examples included disrupting others, changing from an uncompleted task or escape behaviour, such as leaving the room or looking out of the window. Tokens, which could be used to buy a ticket for a special event and also for ice-cream, drinks etc., were given out for appropriate behaviour while the children worked and were accompanied by statements of approval. The teacher did not mention any specific task requirement and avoided a set pattern in dispensing tokens. The results showed that study behaviour could be controlled in this way and the authors suggest that management via a token system was likely to be more effective than one relying only on verbal praise and attention. Similar studies on retarded children with attentional deficits are more difficult to assess owing to the variability in the diagnosis of the children and also in the findings themselves. Zimmerman, Zimmerman and Russell (1969), who achieved some measure of control over instruction-following, point out that in two unsuccessful cases the use of these procedures provided objective information about the children's behaviour that could be useful in planning their further education. This criterion is likely to be more important in the case of handicapped children than the rapid success of a particular training procedure.

The most ambitious projects attempt to structure the total environment and their goals extend well beyond the range of early education. The Learning Village at Kalamazoo, Michigan, was established (Ulrich, Alessi and Wolfe, 1971) as an experimental educational programme. Its declared ideals have been stated as follows:

(i) education (in the broad sense of organised experience) can never begin too early;

(ii) when children fail in school, the fault lies with the educational system, not with the children;

(iii) education, to be effective in the twentieth century must include much more than the traditional '3-Rs'. Our children must learn a compassion for fellow man, a respect for the environment, an understanding of human behaviour, a knowledge of the need for social change, a love of learning and a respect for one's self;

(iv) education should not involve physical punishment nor the constant threats, reprimands and general unpleasantness encountered in schools and homes. Learning can be, and is, fun when educational systems are so devised that children often experience success and a joy of accomplishment;

(v) the only way our present generation can constructively contribute to the future of mankind is through proper emphasis on the education of our youth.

These ideals seem worth emphasising since it is obvious that the techniques of behaviour modification could be used for less worthy ends. The day-to-day operation of the Village is based on the assumption that immediate reinforcement is the means by which the specified educational goals may most efficiently be attained. Children from various socio-economic backgrounds and from age two months to eleven years are taught according to the Premack principle: this states that a behaviour which has a high probability of occurrence can be used to reinforce a behaviour which has a lower probability of occurrence (Premack, 1959). A token economy is instituted, whereby specific responses are immediately reinforced with tokens, these being exchanged later for a reinforcer selected by the child from a reinforcer menu which he himself has helped to construct. Spates and coworkers (1974) have defined the prerequisites for entry into the nursery programme, which correspond to the goals of the infant programme of the Learning Village. These are differentiated under the headings of self-care skills, motor skills, social skills including play skills, interactions and self-control, and language skills. Instructional procedures in the infant programme principally consist of using the method of successive approximation, and reinforcers are usually social or edible; appropriate behaviours which occur spontaneously are reinforced. Test results are rather limited at present and obviously comprehensive and repeated evaluation is necessary. However, on the current evidence the authors are optimistic.

The disparity between this approach, with its emphasis on careful contingency management, and the discovery methods favoured by some educators may be more apparent than real at least for this age and ability group. One argument is that discovery learning should lead to increased competence in personal management, not mindless conformity to principles decided by a teacher; yet in a sense society does require conformity over the range of skills specified above, which in turn leads to increased competence and freedom to act as an individual.

1.6 Summary

From an overview of the main developments in educational technology it can be seen that work from a number of different fields has converged. For convenience we have considered similarities and differences under three main headings (i) audio-visual aids tradition, (ii) the cybernetics tradition and (iii) the psychology tradition. In the final section, techniques of behaviour modification currently under investigation with young children were reviewed. Throughout, the assumption adopted is that for some crucial skills the most effective environment will involve controlled presentation of stimulus events and that the most effective control can often be provided by automated or programmed techniques.

CHAPTER 2

Objectives, Needs and Target Populations

2.1 The present dilemma

In general terms our objective is to explore the potential of educational technology for pre-school children between the ages of three and five (extending downwards to the toddler group and upward to the primary school group where appropriate) and in certain areas of special education, where the solutions offered by educational technology may be similar. Over ten years ago Leith (1963) proposed that programmed learning research in these areas should be mutually supportive and in the wider context of educational technology we would still endorse this view. There is as yet too little known about the potential of educational technology or the classification of learning deficits to justify the exclusion of any useful developments by rigidly drawing boundaries at certain points on the continua of age, learning ability, extent of handicap etc.

One obvious line to pursue is to review work with older children and adults with a view to simplifying it; this is superficially attractive because relatively little work by educational technologists has been directed specifically at the pre-school or special education group. Clearly it is possible to gain useful ideas or approaches in this way but straightforward extrapolation from complex to elementary is precluded by the particular characteristics shared by this population. Compared with older children or adults, they are not socially competent and they cannot read or write; they are subject to a wide range of experience, often acquired in a piecemeal fashion, within the family, at informal play groups, nurseries etc. These environments generally differ from schools in several respects (e.g. they are outside the formal education system, they are less didactic and less structured and perhaps most important, there is relatively more parental influence) and exhibit much variability within themselves.

We are not convinced that simply lowering the age of starting school will make a significant contribution to the problems of improving early education and wish to examine the part that sophisticated physical technology (linked unfortunately at present with rudimentary behavioural technology) can play in the future. At one extreme this can involve fully automated systems (probably computer-controlled), or semi-automated systems requiring intelligent student participation, through to simple, but carefully designed, educational toys or instructional techniques that are independent of a particular device. At the time of writing there are two widely held views which bear directly on the question of the implementation of the kind of techniques we are to discuss here.

26

Firstly there exists a general approval for the view that early education should be injected with a considerable increase in resources. This reflects the realisation that experience in the first few years of life can critically determine a child's subsequent development and that if we permit inequities of experience at that stage then we have little chance of breaking the cycle which results in a sizeable proportion of our population experiencing life-long social and intellectual deprivation. In this connection the study by Bloom (1964) is often quoted, especially the conclusion that 'in terms of intelligence measured at age 17, at least 20% is developed by age 1, 50% by age 4, 80% by age 8 and 92% by age 13'. However it is legitimate to challenge these results on the grounds that the tests were only representative of a rather restricted type of intelligence related to school performance. More substantial evidence can be found in the second report of National Child Development Study (Davie, Butler and Goldstein, 1972), in which a broad range of attainments of nearly 16,000 children in England, Scotland and Wales are described.

A second view, perhaps more radical, is expressed as opposition to the continuing development of technology. A number of disparate strands come together here but the essential argument is that the pursuit of new technology, for whatever worthy short-term goals, will lead eventually to the creation of conditions worse than those which the technology was intended to ameliorate. Apart from the obvious fact that some technology is creating a dangerous imbalance in the global ecology it is now beginning to be widely felt that the long-term effect of almost all technological advance is a dehumanising one, resulting in alienation and loss of individuality. In addition it is appreciated that technology implies control. It is reasonable then that the development of educational technology might be resisted by those with an interest in radically changing our educational system since it may serve only to consolidate the status quo. We cannot refute this view; we merely point out here that educational technology is not in itself an educational philosophy. The techniques for attaining behavioural changes do not themselves help us to specify the direction and nature of those changes.

There are of course some perfectly reasonable grounds for caution in educational innovation. The first concerns decisions about our educational goals. There is obviously some temptation to hand over responsibility for specifying these objectives to technologists and scientists or for the latter to assume them, but, as Bruner (1966) points out in his essay on education as social invention, such people often lack the kind of follow-up commitment that is the requisite of wise social policy. 'The political process—and decisions about the aims of education must work their way through that process—is slow, perhaps, but is committed to the patient pursuit of the possible.'

A further issue is also discussed by Bruner and relates to the rate of change in developed countries. A property of tools and techniques is that they spawn more advanced versions of themselves at an ever increasing speed. In parallel with such a development, the role of education should be expanded to enable society to adapt more readily to the consequences of rapidly changing technology.

At the present time it seems clear that far too few resources are being allocated for the design of educational systems to meet current requirements, not to mention future needs.

It would appear to be wasteful, if not pointless, to proliferate various educational techniques without also trying to formulate a theory of instruction. What features should a theory of instruction have? According to Bruner, it should specify (i) the experiences which most effectively implant in the individual a predisposition towards learning, (ii) the ways in which a body of knowledge should be structured so that it can be most readily grasped by the learner, (iii) the most effective sequences in which to present the materials to be learned and (iv) the nature and pacing of rewards and punishments in the process of learning and teaching. A theory of instruction thus differs in important ways from theories of learning and development. Whilst the latter seek to describe, summarise and predict relationships between classes of behaviour, a theory of instruction is prescriptive in that it provides rules for achieving knowledge of skills which have been derived from a general framework and not merely formulated in an *ad hoc* fashion. In other words the emphasis in a theory of instructions is on improving rather than describing learning.

2.2 Origins of current demands

It is not our concern here to trace all those factors which have influenced the development of social and political thinking about the role of early education in our society. We will restrict our interest to a consideration of the scientific evidence which has accumulated from various sources to support the demand for early education. Whether the uncovering of this evidence has stimulated or been stimulated by social and political pressures is of little interest here. We wish to draw attention briefly to psychological research on animal and child development and to sociological studies of the effects of variables such as social class and family structure. Each of these sources has provided evidence that supports the now widely accepted notion that the learning experiences during the first four or five years of life are of the utmost importance in determining later development and in fulfilling potential.

2.2.1 Animal studies

Data from naturalistic studies on animals lend strong support to the view that at certain stages during an animal's early life a critical interaction occurs between genetic potential and experience. The notion of imprinting (see, for example, Sluckin (1964)), based on Lorenz's observations of the following response of young ducklings, was important because it seemed to indicate the operation of a special mechanism whereby stimuli presented during a critical period became attached to certain responses in a manner that was completely resistant to subsequent modification. Later work has suggested that some modification of the initial effects is possible by appropriate manipulation of environ-

mental stimuli but the existence of certain sensitive periods for the acquisition of a variety of stimulus–response links and for the development of general organisational processes has now been established for several species. A further feature of this work is the tendency displayed by many animals, once imprinting has occurred, to subsequently avoid novel stimuli. Early experience will apparently determine certain kinds of inhibition just as it will determine certain kinds of activity; the nature of later behaviour is a function of both.

In laboratory studies on animals an essential feature is the precise control that can be exercised over the individual's environment throughout its life history and, if necessary, over its genetic inheritance. As operant conditioning studies have already been described, let us briefly consider studies involving deprivation or additional experience. Denenberg (1970) states that research is at a point where it is possible to take an animal and within broad limits specify the 'personality' of that animal, as well as some of its behavioural capabilities, by the appropriate manipulation of experiences in early life. Several experiments have confirmed Hebb's original (1947) demonstration that enriching the environment of laboratory rats enhanced their learning capacity. In general there is now much evidence to support the view that animals which receive additional stimulation during infancy will become less emotional, more curious and investigatory, more efficient at learning and problem solving, and less susceptible to the effects of environmental stress. Among non-human primates the work of the Harlows on the development of affectional systems supports similar general conclusions. One striking conclusion from many studies of different types of deprivation (Harlow and Harlow, 1965, 1969, 1970) is that female monkeys who fail to develop affection for members of their species in their first year of life are ineffective, inadequate and brutal mothers toward their first-born offspring. In one experiment two of the seven infants born to 'motherless mothers' did not survive although the maternal brutality did become gradually less violent. All of the infant monkeys would have died had not the experimenters intervened and fed them by hand.

2.2.2 Human developmental studies

The interest aroused by the data from both observational and experimental studies of young animals has stimulated certain attempts at an extrapolation to man. The validity of these attempts (e.g. Lorenz (1966) and Morris (1967)) has however recently come under serious attack. As Smith (1969) has pointed out, wherever some processes in children resemble those identified in other species this should not be regarded as satisfactory evidence of evolutionary continuity. Tinbergen (1972) has commented thus, 'professional students of human behaviour have, in rejecting some of Lorenz's and Morris' claims, thrown away the baby with the bathwater, and so the Ethology of Man finds itself at the moment in a false position: over-acclaimed by many, shrugged off by others'. Whilst animal experiments present a fairly clear picture of the effects of experimental intervention, it is of course the case that equivalent

studies of child development cannot be undertaken for ethical reasons. In human developmental psychology, therefore, a more complex relationship exists between the empirical evidence and its interpretation. Thus studies of, say, maternal deprivation (Bowlby, 1953; Rutter, 1972) have to take into account a multitude of factors other than separation from the mother, which might produce disadvantageous effects on a child's current behaviour or subsequent development.

Despite these problems of collecting adequate data the accumulation of evidence points clearly to the crucial role of early human experience both in terms of the specific skills acquired and perhaps more importantly in non-specific learning, such as the maintenance of attention and confidence in attacking new problems. We are not yet able to identify very clearly the critical periods in human learning although we are able to point to at least two stages of special importance. Firstly it seems that the stage of initial physical independence when the child develops the ability for walking and independent locomotion is of importance for the development of exploratory behaviour in general. Secondly the age at which language and other cognitive functions are rapidly acquired is probably crucial for the development of what one might term cognitive strategies. The study of human intellectual development has, like many areas of human psychology, undergone a recent change of emphasis in the recognition of the importance of covert, as well as overt, cognitive operations during this stage.

There is now increasing recognition that the educational needs of young children differ from those of children who are ready to participate in formal academic education. Schaefer (1970) has even proposed the development of a new discipline of 'Ur-education' which would cover the earliest and most fundamental education of the child. In Schaefer's view the young child is able to function autonomously only after successful completion of a process of parent–child interaction and the joint exploration of an object or a common activity. This is compatible with our general conclusion that some degree of enrichment of the early environment, including intervening experiences such as peer group contact within a play group, may be not merely beneficial but an essential prerequisite for successful participation in more formal education.

Theoretically, by far the most significant contribution has been that of Piaget (Flavell (1963) provides a comprehensive review). His theory is descriptive of the child's development of intelligence and has obvious implications for a theory of instruction, although this is not its objective. Inevitably, different people draw different conclusions; some regard it as evidence for the gradual unfolding of cognitive abilities; others believe that appropriately structured learning experiences will accelerate development. Surprisingly it has taken a long time for Piaget's contribution (some studies date back fifty years or more) to become widely known. This may be due to technical problems of communication but more probably it is because until recently his work could not be integrated into prevailing theoretical positions. Now it seems that there will be many fruitful lines of development. We will draw attention to one that links

0395148

it to the work of Bloom and his colleagues on the taxonomy of educational objectives (Bloom, 1956; Krathwohl, Bloom and Masia, 1964), namely the Ypsilanti Early Education Program directed by Kamii. She has recently specified the objectives for pre-school education (see Table 2.1) and has contrasted the extent to which a Piagetian, cognitively-oriented pre-school meets these objectives as compared with traditional nursery schools. With some provisos she concludes that only the Piagetian pre-school can meet all the objectives, whereas traditional nursery schools usually cover objectives *B–J*. In addition, Kamii (1971) gives detailed examples of evaluation procedures, such as developmental tests of perception and motor coordination, and it is clear that much of this material could be presented in a programmed form either with or without automated devices.

Table 2.1 Specifications for pre-school education: socio-emotional, perceptual-motor and cognitive objectives

OBJECTIVES

CONTENT	Socio-emotional								Perceptual-motor		Cognitive								
											Physical knowledge	Social knowledge	Logical knowledge				Representation	
	Dependence on the teacher	Inner controls	Interaction: quantity	Interaction: quality	Comfort in school	Achievement motivation	Curiosity	Creativity	Gross motor coordination	Fine motor coordination			Classification	Seriation	Number	Space	Time	Symbols	Language: signs
	A	B	C	D	E	F	G	H	I	J	K	L	M	N	O	P	Q	R	S
1. The self																			
2. Body parts																			
3. Members of the class																			
4. Members of the family																			
5. Community roles																			
6. Playground equipment																			
7. Foods																			
8. Clothes																			
9. Furniture																			
10. Houses and buildings																			
11. Tools																			
12. Kitchen utensils																			
13. Vehicles																			
14. Animals																			
15. Plants																			
16. Art materials (e.g., paint)																			
17. Toys (e.g., balls)																			
18. Colors																			
19. Sizes																			
20. Shapes																			

2.2.3 Sociological studies

Sociological research too has attempted to elucidate factors affecting the child's cognitive functioning. Hindley (1965) found substantial relationships between social class and mental test scores by the age of three years, though no clear differences existed at eighteen months. Difficulties for successful working class mother–child interaction probably did exist even if their effects were not apparent at an early age. However, the major source of difficulty which working class children experience at school has been most fully expounded by Bernstein (1971a, 1971b). In general terms he postulates that two types of speech code exist, the restricted and the elaborated code. The difference between the two is concerned primarily with structures that define and explain relationships to the listener. Children from low socio-economic classes mainly communicate on concrete matters, opinion, states of feeling; in contrast, abstractions are more important in the environment of the middle class child. As Bernstein links his codes to the development of thought processes, he believes that use of the restricted code leads to low levels of conceptualisation and causation which in turn affect what is learned and how it is learned. If this is true, and it is still a matter of controversy, then the working class child using such a code will not only be at an initial disadvantage but will be at an increasing disadvantage as he moves into secondary education where more complex and formal levels of thought are required.

Even so, social class should not be considered as having clearly distinct levels nor does it necessarily operate to produce discrete effects. This can be illustrated by reference to the survey of Douglas (1964) which includes evidence on the variable of family size. The finding here was that the larger the family in excess of four children the lower the intelligence of the children: this effect was independent of social class, since Douglas was unable to find a social level at which family size had no effect upon intelligence. A possible line of explanation is that children in large families are more subject to peer group pressure than adult pressures; whereas the converse might obtain for singletons.

By systematic studies of this kind it is possible to identify geographical areas of deprivation in which children are severely disadvantaged by their home conditions. The Plowden Report (HMSO, 1967) advocated a policy of positive discrimination in favour of schools in these educational priority areas so that the school could compensate by providing the stimulus and support for learning that the home fails to supply. This leads us on to consider how intervention may be achieved successfully.

2.3 Problems of intervention

Although most schemes for intervention are concerned with the period of normal schooling, it is of course quite feasible to start earlier with the pre-school environment or even with the mother–child relationship. The question here is whether it is possible to compensate during schooling for some kind of prior disadvantage the child may have suffered or whether such early disadvantages tend to produce crucial deficits and should be prevented as early as possible.

Looking back at the facilities for early education in this country over the past fifty years or so, it can be seen that the state has had a history of interest in the provision of facilities but full implementation is still awaited. Expansion in this part of the educational system has owed more to economic necessity than the belief that provision for the under-fives was of great value in itself. For, although local authorities have been empowered to support pre-school facilities since 1918, there was only something approaching an adequate supply of nursery schools during the Second World War, when they were established mainly to free women for war work: when the women were no longer needed to supplement the labour force, many of the nurseries were closed down. It is the result of voluntary effort that attendance at a play group or a nursery school is a common feature in the lives of so many children, often those least in need of it (Packham, 1974). Many play groups function only because of the availability of voluntary unpaid labour and cheaply rented accommodation. There are indications that the situation may improve. Educational facilities in educational priority areas were expanded following the recommendations of the Plowden Report (HMSO, 1967) and more recently (HMSO, 1972) the government has announced a general programme of nursery school education.

Here may exist a clue towards a constructive solution to the difficulty. Given that pressure on government and local authorities is desirable, it is virtually certain that sufficient financial aid will not be forthcoming from public funds. If this point is accepted, it then becomes necessary to examine the human and non-human resources available free of charge or cheaply. Let us consider three examples:

(1) A venture called the Children's Caravan was started some ten years ago by Schindel and is described in detail by Weisblat and Weisblat (1966) and Waite (1971b). A school bus was converted into a mobile theatre and used for educational and entertainment purposes. An additional vehicle housed a cafe and display area for books etc. Mothers were encouraged to participate and the sites chosen were shopping areas or other focal points in the community. Recently the possibility of adopting this non-formal approach in certain educational priority areas in this country has been explored.

(2) In an effort to bring pre-school training opportunities to economically disadvantaged young children in rural areas, the Appalachia Educational Laboratory has devised a programme using educational television, weekly home visiting by paraprofessional school personnel and mobile classrooms (Alford, 1971). Evaluation of the programme indicates that children who have participated in the programme have increased language development and cognitive learning, and greater psychomotor and social skills development. The cost of the programme was found to be approximately half of that of the standard kindergarten programme.

(3) The mother–child home programme reported by Levenstein (1971) was

planned as a home-based, two-year cognitive intervention method. Women with varied incomes and education, both volunteer and paid, made thirty-minute home visits twice weekly to help mothers become cognitive trainers of their own toddlers (starting at age 2). Mother–child verbal interaction was stimulated with gifts of attractive, self-motivating materials, chosen because of their suitability to the child's developmental level and their potential for verbal interaction when used in play between mother and child. The visitors guided mothers to use the materials in an atmosphere that was spontaneous, relaxed and, more importantly, non-didactic. Most mothers seemed to welcome intervention designed to help their children do well at school; others were resistant, yet appeared cooperative because it was difficult for them to make verbal face-to-face refusals.

In the light of these illustrative projects, a productive form of pressure on government agencies would consist of requests for direct or indirect assistance in organising voluntary help and ensuring maximum use of existing facilities.

Another difficult problem for intervention programmes concerns the selection of appropriate criteria against which to judge their success. Project Head Start in the USA provides an illustration. This is a child and family development programme which is generally considered to have produced disappointing results (see, for example, Smith and Bissell (1970)). It highlights the problem that isolated short-term intervention is unlikely to be successful if other aspects of the child's surroundings contain many elements that are counter-productive. The involvement of parents seems to be a central issue here. Given such involvement in Head Start, frequently expressed attitudes were to the effect that parents approved of the programme: they wished to contribute to its development and administration and to control it at all levels. At a purely intuitive level, it seems odd that a programme deemed to have failed should have so much parental support and it raises the question whether intervention programmes should be expected to prove themselves with a high degree of certainty or precision. This should not be taken as justification for continuing to support work which has little chance of success but is intended to make clear the balance of difficulty between originators and critics. It is always easier to pose problems than to solve them; enthusiasts for early education can play into the hands of opponents by promising too much. Within the field of educational technology the advent of programmed learning and teaching machines in the early 1960s fits this paradigm and perhaps the lesson has now been learned.

The current status of intervention programmes has been summed up concisely by Pringle (1974), 'those devised so far have all been too short-term; they have been further handicapped by too narrow a framework, too late a start, too limited a methodology and insufficient theoretical knowledge about early learning'.

2.4 Areas of application

Before discussing the application of educational technology to subsets of the target population, a general note of caution seems appropriate. The evaluation of novel techniques will normally be carried out in a teaching situation and the experimenter certainly has no right to initiate procedures which could conceivably harm the children taking part; sometimes extreme care is needed to avoid causing some emotional disturbance. Many children when faced with unusual equipment, a strange adult and possibly unfamiliar surroundings will be rather apprehensive and may even be initially unable to carry out quite simple instructions. The problem is made more intractable because most sophisticated equipment is bulky, requires special facilities of one sort or another and therefore cannot be readily transported to the child's home. In this case the presence of one of the child's parents at the first testing session, and subsequently if necessary, is an obvious precaution, not only to reassure the child but also to satisfy themselves that the child is not being placed under unreasonable stress. Even if the actual presence of the parent prevents the experiment proper being carried out, it should be possible to arrange dummy sessions which are representative of what will be taking place later so that the parent may be present until the child will happily go into the experimental room without the parent.

At the beginning of the chapter we specified three groups, toddler ($1\frac{1}{2}$–3), pre-school (3–5) and primary (5–8). It may be useful to the reader if we now indicate those applications which in the light of current knowledge are likely to be most suited to these groups and the special education population. It does not necessarily imply that a particular application has little or no value for any other group. The long-term prospects are dealt with in Chapter 7.

2.4.1 Early education population

For the toddler group, the systematic design and testing of educational toys is likely to be fruitful. Though we have no firm evidence, we suspect that the care exercised in the design and construction of toys is directly proportional to the age of the child. Labelling toys to indicate their function rather than an age range would represent a substantial step forward and assist adults in ensuring that the toy is used appropriately.

There is already evidence that educational television projects, such as *Sesame Street* (Section 1.2), can be effective with the pre-school group, especially if there is maternal involvement or other voluntary help. In this country it seems certain that coverage would be universal rather than selective, but in areas of particular need it may be important to provide additional facilities, e.g. mobile theatres. For the primary group we would support the development of multi-media learning kits, incorporating especially tape, tape-slide and film-loop presentation with traditional materials. Programmed texts have been seldom used with this group but techniques could be modified to adjust to the ability level, e.g. tape recorded instructions and pictorial presentation on cards for those who had not yet learned to read.

2.4.2 Special education population

Apart from the socially disadvantaged, whom we considered in Section 2.3, this population can for convenience be divided into the physically handicapped, the mentally handicapped and the emotionally disturbed. These categories should not be considered as mutually exclusive but they do allow us to point to three characteristic contributions of automated systems.

With modern techniques it should be possible to interface automated educational equipment so that it can be operated by physically handicapped children. For example a spastic child may be unable to turn the pages of a book or draw, but may be capable of responding to large touch detecting panels on a display (Thompson and Johnson, 1971) and POSSUM devices (Oldfield, 1971) can be used to allow physically handicapped children to operate a wide variety of equipment, such as electric typewriters, slide projectors, teaching machines etc. If systems of this kind are used early enough they may be able to offset to some extent the additional educational disadvantage resulting from the basic handicap.

To the extent that mentally handicapped children can be viewed as requiring more time to reach equivalent learning criteria of normal children, devices and materials that provide repetition without inducing boredom are at a premium. Simplicity of operation, coupled with frequent opportunities to experience success, is essential. Several of the systems described in the next chapter have sought to meet this need. Finally emotionally disturbed children may profit, temporarily at least, from an impersonal mode of presentation and source of reward. Some of their learning difficulties could have arisen through failure of human interaction and accordingly they would feel less threatened by a predicatable machine, which operates only under their control.

2.5 Summary

It has been our intention in this chapter to provide an orientation to some of the issues surrounding the potential role of educational technology in early and special education. We have traced the origin of current demands by sampling from studies on animal behaviour, human development and sociological factors. Yet because there has been much concern regarding the uncritical expansion of physical technology and its harmful side-effects, such as environmental pollution on one hand and dehumanisation of society on the other, there might be a danger that an emotional reaction to this state of affairs could lead to a generalised rejection of all technology.

We then examined some problems of intervention and will consider them again in the final chapter (Section 7.2). Finally examples were given of the type of applications appropriate to different subsets of the target population under review.

CHAPTER 3

Automated Systems: Past and Present

3.1 Comparative overview

In this chapter we will examine some of the automated systems that have been designed primarily for use in early and special education and consider some of the attempts to evaluate their effectiveness. There are several dimensions along which it is possible to categorise systems which have been commercially produced and/or used extensively for research purposes. Table 3.1 is intended to provide a convenient summary and comparison of the more important aspects. The eight developments listed are not completely exhaustive but are typical of the types of device produced and the target populations tested. To attempt classification on the basis of their programs would probably be confusing, but the reader is asked to bear in mind the broad distinction between linear and branching programs. The preparation of programs has in fact been highly specific to the particular system, unlike applications in more advanced fields of education where programming techniques have been generally applied. At the present time there is insufficient agreement in early and special education, (i) on the relationship between training and stages of intellectual development and (ii) on the relative merits of alternative methods of structuring material, to allow separation of hardware and software in our discussion.

For the present purposes, however, we feel it will be helpful to retain the division between the three traditions specified in the first chapter, viz., psychology, cybernetics and audio-visual. Looked at in this way some of the considerable differences between these developments seem less surprising and arbitrary and, given that there is still little attempt to integrate different traditions within the emerging technology, our classification may remain appropriate for some time to come. We are deferring the consideration of two issues which on balance are more relevant to later chapters. Firstly the potential of computer-assisted instruction (see Section 5.2) and, secondly, the problems of organising the commercial production of new systems (see Sections 6.3 and 6.5). In passing we note the commonplace observation that several systems have been produced commercially without having the support of adequate empirical evidence, while several ingenious research devices have failed to emerge from the laboratory in which they were designed.

Psychologists, perhaps because of their longstanding interest in early childhood, have contributed easily the largest number of developments, though they have had the least success in implementing them beyond the laboratory stage.

Table 3.1 Summary of eight major developments

Name	Originating tradition	Mode of presentation	Response required	Nature of feedback	Flexibility of programming		Cost	Main groups tested	Main reference
					Preparation of materials	Mode of operation			
ERE (Figure 3.7)	cybernetics	audio, slide words on card	keyboard, record and replay of child's voice	keyboard locking, audio	a job for a specialist, but very varied subject matter can be programmed	wide range of modes—almost CAI	high	normal pre-school, dis-advantaged and handi-capped	Moore (1966)
HANSEL (Figure 3.1)	psychology	rear illu-minated paper sheet	pushbutton multi choice	visual	wide range and easy to prepare, can be done in classroom	restricted	medium	handicapped adults	Hansel (1971)
HIVELY* (Figures 3.2, 3.3)	psychology (operant)	visual slide	press panel	auditory bell	wide range of subject matter, but difficult to prepare	restricted	medium	pre-school and first grade (US)	Hively (1964a)
LANGUAGE MASTER (Figure 3.10)	audio-visual	audio, words or pictures on card	none re-quired, cards manually inserted	passive presentation device	wide range of subjects and easy to prepare	depends upon ins-tructions and basically uncontrolled	low	elementary school	Experimental Development Unit, NCAVAE (1970)
ST. JAMES-ROBERTS* (Figure 3.4)	psychology (operant)	audio, slide, tactual	lever pull	cumulative visual cartoon story	limited applica-tion intended, difficult to prepare	restricted—special objectives	medium	deaf and language-disordered children	St. James-Roberts (1973)

Table 3.1—*Contd.*

Name	Originating tradition	Mode of presentation	Response required	Nature of feedback	Flexibility of programming		Cost	Main groups tested	Main reference
					Preparation of materials	Mode of operation			
TALKING PAGE (Figure 3.11)	audio-visual	audio record, book	items manually selected	audio, but knowledge of results requires interpretation by student	wide range of subject matter possible, but must have professional preparation	restricted	low	elementary school	Salisbury (1971)
tm 1024/ts 512 (Figure 3.8)	cybernetics	visual filmstrip	pushbutton two choice	visual	wide range possible but needs professional preparation	branching capability	medium	elementary school upwards; handicapped ts 512	Gedye and Miller (1970)
TOUCH-TUTOR (Figure 3.5)	psychology (operant)	visual slide	touch panel	auditory pre-recorded words	wide range possible but difficult to prepare	restricted	medium	normal pre-school handicapped	Cleary and Packham (1968)

*These systems have only been used in research by the originators. The others have been commercially available at some stage and have, therefore, been used by workers other than the originators.

In most cases it is possible to detect the influence of operant conditioning techniques, though the extent to which they are employed solely or in conjunction with other techniques is variable. In general, developments have been undertaken with limited objectives in mind and consequently a narrower range of facilities have been offered to the learner as compared with developments from the cybernetic tradition. In particular the consequences of making errors and the related scope for remedial training represent a major source of difference between the two. They are similar in that the learner is frequently required to make responses to the material presented and is given immediate information related to the response. In contrast, the audio-visual tradition has been notably less concerned with the active process of learning and many developments have involved passive presentation only.

These broad comparisons between the different developments will now be examined in further detail in relation to individual devices.

3.2 Developments from the psychology tradition

The Hansel Training Machine, which is discussed first, differs fundamentally from the remainder because it is neither clearly based on the principles of operant conditioning nor does it follow the conventions of linear programming by using specific techniques such as prompting to reduce the number of errors made. Secondly, we consider Hively's continuation of Skinner's original work: this extension into the field of early education in the early 1960s has led to the development of other specialist and general purpose devices, which are subsequently described.

3.2.1 Hansel Training Machine

Presentation of material to the student is via a display panel (see Figure 3.1). The various sections of a paper matrix, covered by a translucent screen, are selectively illuminated by back lighting. A keyboard of 30 buttons, labelled by a template placed over the keyboard, allows a single correct response to be constructed from a sequence of button pressings. Originally the machine was programmed by plugging in pre-wired panels which required a particular sequence of buttons to be pressed for each item, but subsequently a new memory feature has been incorporated which allows the machine to be programmed by pressing the correct answer buttons. It can present items from the matrix in various sequential combinations and a remedial subroutine may follow an error. Items may be written, typed, traced or stuck onto the visual matrix. The ease of preparing the visual material (both as stimuli and as response alternatives), the possibilities for varying presentation order and for programming particular sequences contingent either on correct responses or on errors, and the facility for allowing sequential responses to be constructed (such that the pupil may be required to spell words) all combine to offer a degree of flexibility to the programmer.

Figure 3.1 Hansel Training Machine

Hansel (1971) argues that a learner is generally aware whether or not he knows the answer to a question and may only make errors when he is forced to make a choice. He considers that it may be equally effective when the learner is uncertain of the correct answer to allow him to check on the answer rather than to force him to guess. This solution may well be appropriate for the categories of adult handicapped tested by Moseley and Sowter (1972) at a training centre and for normal school children. However, for the pre-school child, much of whose learning may be incidental, some form of shaping and prompting techniques is probably necessary, at least in the initial stages of learning.

The most promising application seems to be in the sequential processing of symbols, which has often been a source of difficulty for subnormal trainees. Moseley and Sowter showed that progress was sustained for a period of up to three months in tasks such as learning to count and telling the time. Evaluation of this machine is still at an early stage and further projects are planned.

3.2.2 Hively's visual discrimination apparatus

Hively's work started as a study of concept formation in children using the technique of matching-to-sample, which had previously been developed in work on animal discrimination learning. The technique was subsequently applied to

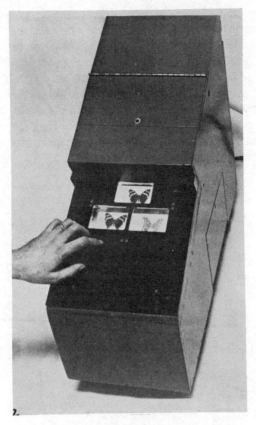

Figure 3.2 Two choice apparatus for teaching
visual discrimination

the training of skills associated with elementary reading behaviour based along
the lines of Skinner's analysis of verbal behaviour (Skinner, 1957). There are
published accounts of two versions of the apparatus (Hively, 1960, 1964a).
Figure 3.2 shows the two choice matching-to-sample apparatus and Figure 3.3
the more sophisticated version, which allows for multiple choice discrimination,
dispensing of rewards and tape recording of conversations between experimenter and child.

In the former, a series of cards is automatically presented in a triangular
display: a sample appears in the top window and a match to it in one of the lower
windows. An incorrect alternative or distractor appears in the other window. All
are hinged and spring-loaded so that by pressing a window the child can actuate
programming contacts. The sequence of operations is that at first the top
window only is illuminated, while the lower ones are dark. The child should
now make a response to the sample, which causes the choice windows to be
illuminated and to become operative. A correct matching response makes a
bell ring and a new sample stimulus is presented after a short delay. An incorrect

response stops the sequence of operation and another response to the sample is necessary before a further matching response can be made.

Given fairly modest objectives, this apparatus was successful with the preschool children (aged 3 to $5\frac{1}{2}$) who were tested. From the 27 children tested 25 returned for as many sessions as were available and took between 4 and 13 minutes to work through a set of 40 cards. However, there were some problems associated with the operation of the machine and accidental reinforcing of inappropriate responses. Perhaps also the requirement for making an orienting response to each sample would only be advantageous in the early stages of training and would become frustrating later on.

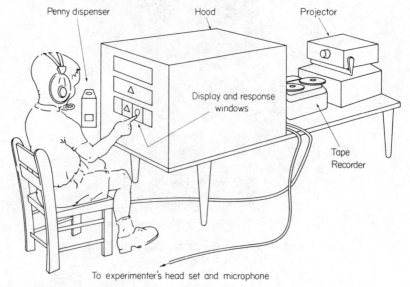

Figure 3.3 Apparatus for multiple choice visual discrimination·

The multiple choice apparatus is more sophisticated in several ways. The stimuli are projected as slides onto the front panel and the correct alternative is coded photoelectrically. The child can operate the machine by pressing windows in the same way as before, though in some experiments a response to the sample was not required. In its most complex mode the experimenter communicated with the child by means of a two-way intercommunication system and their conversation was recorded. Initially the child was asked to press a window and to speak the word. For these responses the experimenter gave verbal approval. Later, when the child made correct responses without being prompted, a muffled chime sounded and he received a penny from the automatic dispenser. At a subsequent stage consecutive correct responses were required in order to receive a penny.

Hively and his colleagues at the Harvard Teaching Machine Project report studies with pre-school and first-grade children using coloured stimuli (Hively, 1962) and word discrimination (Hively, 1964b).

The coloured stimuli differed also in size and shape and children were trained on a series of increasingly difficult discrimination tasks, leading up to matching-to-sample. This procedure was more efficient than simply training the final discrimination. It may be, as Hively points out, that a sequence of successive discriminations tends to make children attentive to relevant stimulus properties and therefore less likely to adopt incorrect hypotheses, which may be inter-mittently reinforced. The more errors the children made during training, the more they continued to make.

The word discriminations required were between minimally different pairs of three-letter words. Children were trained under different conditions which varied in the extent to which the experimenter presented the task and whether pennies were given as additional extrinsic rewards. Training was effective and the performance of all groups was similar. This raises a point to which we shall return from time to time, that is the use of material rewards. Extrapolating from studies of animal discrimination learning, material rewards would seem to be a necessity. However, it is important to remember that students using teaching machines are not under equivalent conditions of food or water deprivation and so they are more likely to be motivated by material that is intrinsically interesting.

3.2.3 St. James-Roberts's operant audiometry system

One line of development from Skinner's and Hively's early work has been the use of automated devices for specialist diagnostic purposes. Such a device was used by St. James-Roberts (1973) to administer audiological tests to deaf and language-disordered children. The traditional method of testing is to instruct the testee to respond when he detects the test stimulus. Thus, by presenting a range of audio frequencies at different intensities, the audiologist is able to construct an audiogram which shows the variation of the testee's hearing threshold with frequency. Such a procedure is clearly very difficult to administer in the case of children who do not comprehend the spoken instructions. Accord-ingly St. James-Roberts used operant conditioning to establish a lever pull response to a visual or tactual cue. Having trained the child to make this res-ponse to a stimulus, which he could be expected to detect without difficulty, the cue was gradually changed to the audiometer test tone.

Pilot experiments had shown that traditional operant conditioning tasks, involving colour matching with flashing light reinforcement for the training phase, failed to maintain responding for the number of sessions necessary to establish an audiogram and so a motivating procedure was adopted. This allowed the child to participate in the construction of a cartoon-style story, the additional frames of the story being added as reinforcers for responding correctly to the cue stimulus. The apparatus (Figure 3.4) presented a stimulus slide depicting a scene from the story on the upper rear-projection screen and a

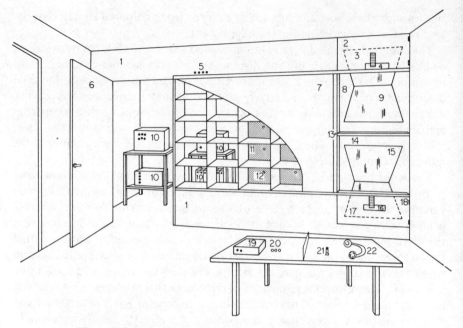

Figure 3.4 St. James-Roberts's operant audiometry apparatus.
Exploded view showing (1) plywood wall; (2) door permitting access to projector I; (3) upper mirror projector I; (4) projector I; (5) start and override buttons; (6) door permitting access to control apparatus; (7) reinforcer screen (shown cut-away to allow matrix boxes to be seen; (8) upper response sample screen; (9) lower mirror projector I; (10) control apparatus; (11) reinforcer matrix cube (some of these cubes have been drawn cut-away to show control apparatus normally hidden from view); (12) reinforcer matrix cube bulb; (13) visual cue bulb; (14) lower response sample screen; (15) upper mirror projector II; (16) projector II; (17) lower mirror projector II; (18) door permitting access to projector II; (19) audiometer; (20) cue selection switches; (21) response lever; (22) headphones

series of three plausible alternatives for the next scene on the lower rear-projection screen. If the child responded with a lever pull while the alternative which was deemed to be correct was being presented the corresponding box in the reinforcer matrix was illuminated. The correct alternative was accompanied by a visual or tactual cue during the training phase and gradually changed to the audiometer tone for the testing phase. The responses made during the testing phase were analysed and thresholds calculated.

Clearly the rear-projected stimuli formed a dummy task, the crucial stimuli being the visual, tactual or auditory cues. The additional stimuli served to provide an entertaining game within which a weak reinforcer, the rear illuminated matrix, could be used for many sessions without satiation. St. James-Roberts found that the apparatus worked well in this respect and would maintain responding in children as young as three years, providing an interesting and enjoyable task. The panels and slides could easily be changed so that a variety of stories could be used to cover the many sessions needed for the testing program.

This ingenious use of formally irrelevant cartoon material to maintain motivation is somewhat similar to the approach adopted by the Children's Television Workshop in the educational television programme, *Sesame Street*. It is also an indication of the difficulties involved in providing an acceptable and durable reinforcer for operantly based training systems.

3.2.4 Touch-Tutor

The Touch-Tutor (Cleary and Packham, 1968) was originally designed to train reading and other visual discrimination skills in young pre-school children although its most extensive use to date has been with mentally handicapped children. At the outset it was realised that a machine aimed at the young pre-school population required certain essential design features. It must be extremely simple to operate, it should involve the child's sensory system as completely as possible and it must require no ability from the child to understand sophisticated verbal instructions.

The Touch-Tutor has undergone a series of redesigns. The original prototype was constructed with the control and presentation units housed separately. It was similar in some respects to Hively's visual discrimination apparatus but differed in important features such as electronic touch detection, the type of auditory feedback and the automatic computation of performance. Subsequent versions have all been built as a single unit but have incorporated a variety of experimental features.

The developed version of the Touch-Tutor, which is available commercially, houses all parts of the system in a single unit. Figure 3.5 illustrates the form of

Figure 3.5 Touch-Tutor

display presented to the child. The screen has an upper panel displaying the stimulus sample and below this are three response panels. The child's task is to decide which of the response panels is displaying material which correctly relates to the stimulus sample. If he responds by touching the correct panel then an auditory stimulus follows. Typically a correct match to the sample would be followed by the machine 'speaking' the stimulus name thus giving immediate auditory knowledge of results. If an incorrect alternative is chosen then the auditory stimulus is absent. In either case, however, a new display appears within a few seconds and remains displayed until a new response is detected. Hence any response is rewarded to some extent by the presentation of a new visual display.

The basic presentation unit is a slide projector which will accept a rotary magazine holding 100 35-mm slides. This means that the machine is able to employ programs which can recirculate without breaking the sequence. A novel feature of the Touch-Tutor system is involved here as the programs are not linear in the usual sense since they have no start or end points. The material presented in each program of 100 frames is not sequentially ordered but is intended to represent a constant level of difficulty. The child responds to as few or as many frames as is necessary for him to attain the criterion level of performance which indicates that he has mastered the material at that particular level of difficulty. Thus sequencing is between rather than within programs.

The slides are displayed on a rear-projection ground-glass screen. The front surface of the glass has three electrically conducting areas corresponding to the three picture panels of the multiple choice test. This is achieved by the evaporation of a thin conducting layer of chromium in these areas, each of which is connected to a high impedance electrical supply. This conducting layer is transparent and only slightly reduces the brightness of the display. Together with some associated electronics this arrangement acts as a touch detecting system for the child's responses (see Section 4.3).

A tape cartridge is used to replay the auditory material. The slides are synchronised with items recorded on endless loop tape so that the recirculating system is maintained. The spoken items are recorded on one channel of the tape with synchronising pulses on the other. When the synchronising pulse is replayed the control circuit stops the tape player and advances the slide projector one frame. When a response is detected (and this requires only the merest touch on one of the response panels) the tape advances one item. The loudspeaker is muted for an incorrect response. The stimulus slide remains displayed during the auditory knowledge of results.

The basic programs on the Touch-Tutor involve matching-to-sample of colours, shapes or pictures and are intended to lead on to the matching of symbolic material. The pre-reading programs introduce words whilst retaining the matching-to-sample requirement. These progress to the more difficult reading programs requiring the child to choose which picture correctly relates to the word or phrase presented as the sample. It is possible to vary the difficulty of the material in several ways: for example the number of incorrect alternatives and their similarity to the correct one, and the frequency with which new material is introduced.

Each visual presentation is projected from the central portion of a standard 35-mm slide. The remainder of the vertical format of the slide is allocated to optical codings. The codings indicate the correct alternative and the blank panels and are decoded by photocells mounted above and below the viewing screen. Thus the slides themselves convey the information necessary for the system to give appropriate knowledge of results. Some versions of the Touch-Tutor have incorporated further programming facilities. Detection of responses made to blank panels, for example, may be inhibited by the presence of the appropriate photocell code for that panel.

The principles used in constructing Touch-Tutor programs are mostly those developed as a result of research on discrimination learning sets in primates and children, especially the work of Harlow (1959) and Reese (1963) respectively. Sequences are generated, technically similar to Gellermann series, such that incorrect strategies result in chance-level knowledge of results. This is the case for strategies such as position perseveration, position alternation, win-stay lose-shift and win-shift lose-stay. Similarly, placing blanks in particular response positions can be used to counteract error factors associated with position, since a response to these fails to produce a new display. On the question of stimulus perseveration, all items used as correct alternatives also appear elsewhere in the program as distractors.

An important feature of the Touch-Tutor is its facility for automatically computating each child's ongoing performance level. The characteristics of this measure are described in Section 4.6. An analogue computing circuit continuously displays the performance level in the form of a weighted moving average on the monitor panel of the machine. Computer simulation of chance responding has enabled both the weighting and a criterion level to be set at values which clearly differentiate true improvement from chance variations. The criterion level of performance required for mastery of a particular program should be set at a level which strikes a balance between, on the one hand, allowing for large differences in the speed of learning individual items and, on the other hand, boring the student who has adequately grasped the principle or material being presented. When this level of 0·9 is reached a light comes on to indicate that a new program is required.

To summarise, then, the Touch-Tutor differs from most other teaching machines in the simplicity of the required response, in the fact that no instructions are necessary at the commencement of training, in the continuous and automatic computation of individual performance and in the structure of its programming.

Huskisson, Packham and Cleary (1969) reported three studies with pre-school normal children (aged between 3 years 10 months and 4 years 10 months). Eighteen of these children received initial training on a matching-to-sample program containing colours, shapes, pictures, and picture–word combinations. Initially no instructions were given and the children were left to explore the front of the machine for themselves. As an aside here it is worth noting that, although it is tempting to reduce the time taken to learn by verbally instructing the child, as proposed by Fellows (1968), this can pose greater difficulties than it solves. Children may interpret verbal instructions in a manner far removed from that intended by the experimenter. In their examination of the use of reinforcers with young children Bijou and Baer (1966) point out that children may feel that they have to obey even a permissive statement in their desire to please the adult experimenter, who in turn may unwittingly dispense social reinforcers. In the study by Huskisson and coworkers all except one of the children reached criterion performance on the matching-to-sample program within four short sessions. These children were then transferred to a reading program with frames consisting of a picture as the stimulus item and words as response alternatives. The hypothesis tested was that those words the children (i) preferred and (ii) learned, would be those which were maximally different from each other. A significant preference was obtained for unpaired words (e.g. dog, lip, sun) over minimally paired words (e.g. bat, cat, hat). A further variable investigated was the efficiency of two types of auditory knowledge of results. On a simple reading program the naming of the stimulus item was compared with 'non-specific' words and phrases such as 'well done', 'very good' etc. In terms of learning (the ratio of correct to total responses) subjects receiving specific knowledge of results did best although in terms of motivation (taking total number of responses as a measure) no difference emerged between the two groups.

The analysis of errors made in these experiments revealed a variety of hypothesis-testing strategies adopted by the children at various stages. For example a clear preference for the centre response panel emerged and confirmed Lombard and Stern's (1967) observation of this tendency. It is reasonable to expect a child who has not yet mastered the material to tend to respond on the basis of an inappropriate hypothesis and if this can be clearly identified it serves as an indication that the child is not under appropriate stimulus control. This, of course, requires a response-by-response analysis of the data and for this purpose an event recorder or tape punch may be connected to the Touch-Tutor for automatic recording of such information.

A practical observation arising from these experiments was that the presence of parents or other adults during the learning sessions tended to provide an uncontrolled source of social reinforcement, the children looking at the adults after responding rather than attending to the knowledge of results from the machine. For sustained responding to the machine it is also deemed desirable to incorporate sessions with the machine into a regular part of the child's routine.

For various reasons most of the evaluation of the Touch-Tutor has been conducted in the general field of mental subnormality. Harper, Cleary and Packham (1971) employed this machine in an investigation of the training of matching-to-sample in severely subnormal children. An assumption here was that pretraining on an easy discrimination would facilitate later performance on a difficult one (Spiker, 1959) and the intention was to minimise failure and the resultant frustration during the crucial stages of early learning. It was suggested that the lack of curiosity which has been noted in retarded children may be a direct consequence of early failure. Thus, as before, an easy matching task was learned to criterion before the more difficult program was presented. The latter consisted mainly of matching the letters b, d, p and q which are known as a source of confusion in early reading (Dunn-Rankin, 1968).

On the simple program three of the children reached criterion performance in their first session, an encouraging result for children classified as severely subnormal. Nine of the remaining 13 children reached criterion, taking between two and ten sessions to achieve this level. The children found the matching of pictures to be least difficult, followed by colour, shapes and finally the matching of words as the most difficult task. Harper and coworkers suggested that the superior performance on picture matching results from the larger number of discriminative cues available combined with the increased attention which complex stimuli attract. On the second and more difficult program in this experiment three of the children reached criterion. An analysis of all errors showed that most difficulty was created by left–right reversals (b–d)(p–q), less with inversions (b–p)(d–q), and least difficulty with rotations (b–q)(d–p). This result confirmed previous findings and demonstrated the usefulness of the Touch-Tutor as a research tool with severely subnormal children. Thus auditory knowledge of results had been effective for 12 of the 16 children tested in reinforcing matching-to-sample behaviour and in maintaining it over many sessions. Several of these severely subnormal children were observed to interact in a social manner with the machine and appeared to gain satisfaction from self-instruction and success on the task. It was considered that the control they were able to gain over the machine ('by being able to make it talk') was especially valuable for these children to whom success was uncommon. Some of these children could not be satisfactorily assessed by conventional procedures but they responded to this automated system. The experimenters also regarded as encouraging the fact that discrimination training with the Touch-Tutor on highly confusable letters resulted in similar errors to those made by normal children.

On the basis of the above studies the Touch-Tutor has received favourable support as a training and research device for pre-school and retarded populations. Two recent studies (Beasley and Hegarty, 1970; Hegarty and Beasley, 1971) have drawn somewhat less enthusiastic conclusions from experiments on the training of matching-to-sample skills in severely subnormal children using the Touch-Tutor. These studies were based on the authors' observation that severely subnormal children 'seem to find the slide-change a more rewarding event than the machine speaking, and that allowing children to respond first to the easier slides with only one response choice led them to respond more enthusiastically and correctly on later slides with two and three response choices'.

In the first of these studies the efficiency of progressing from one to two to three choice presentation was examined as well as a condition in which correct responses were followed by an immediate slide-change, with no auditory knowledge of results at all. The conclusion from this experiment was that neither arrangement of the sequences nor the modification of the correct response contingency led to better performance. Only 17% of the children were able to successfully match to the sample although it should be noted that Beasley and Hegarty gave these children only very limited training on the Touch-Tutor and introduced the task with an initial demonstration of one choice presentations. In the second experiment a videotape analysis of the various patterns of responding to the machine was undertaken and this again revealed the systematic nature of incorrect responses. These children responded most commonly to position, often systematically responding to a particular panel, although some responded on the basis of the outcome of previous responses to a particular position. Hegarty and Beasley suggest, 'it is clear that continued practice is not helping to teach the principle of matching to those children with rigid position habits of responding. On the other hand, practice does help those children who are undecided about which hypothesis to adopt'.

Although these experimenters conclude, 'it does not seem that the optimism generated by the makers of this machine and by other research workers who have used similar machines has been fulfilled in practice', it is worth noting that they also report that 'approximately 30% of a hospital school are likely to be able to operate the machine in a fairly short space of time', a conclusion which on the face of it would seem capable of supporting a moderate optimism at least.

Several other studies employing the Touch-Tutor in a subnormality setting have also been reported. For example Thompson and Johnson (1971) reported an evaluation with children attending a Spastics Society Assessment Centre. They concluded that children with an IQ higher than 55 on the Columbia Scale could successfully learn the skill of matching words to pictures on the Touch-Tutor and that this training could successfully be transferred to other classroom situations. They also emphasised some incidental advantages which seem to follow from the use of a teaching machine with physically handicapped children, such as an increase in their span of concentration. This kind of observation has also been made by Levinson (1970) in a summary of the progress made in a long-term programme evaluating the Touch-Tutor for use with children in a mental subnormality hospital. 'An unanticipated bonus was provided by our clinical observations of the children in this situation. We were frequently surprised by the extent of their capacities, as they frequently showed skills which had never been demonstrated during conventional methods of assessment.'

A number of modifications of the Touch-Tutor have been tried out in attempts to meet the special needs. Pilot experiments have been conducted using the system for the diagnosis of perceptual difficulties in the skills associated with learning to read (Huskisson, 1971) and programs covering elementary principles of seriation have also been tested on pre-school normal children and cerebral palsied children of school age. Modifications have also been made to the display-response system (larger response panels, foot-switches, headpointers etc.) for cerebral palsied children and to the knowledge of results system (a flashing light rather than an auditory stimulus) for the deaf.

An experiment by the present authors employed an initial response training program which had no stimulus samples (i.e. the upper panel always remained blank) and only one response alternative was presented on each frame, although this could be presented in one, two or all three response panels. Auditory reinforcement thus followed every response, except those to blank panels, and was non-specific ('good', 'well done' etc.). A response-rate criterion was adopted for the first program change. The rationale for presenting no stimulus sample at the response training stage was based on the notion that information should only be presented in the stimulus panel when the child is required to use it in order to select his response. The data indicated that several severely subnormal children who had failed previously to make any progress on a simple matching-to-sample program performed well on this program in terms of response rate. Unfortunately the indications are that this procedure gives negative transfer when the discrimination task is subsequently introduced. This problem of how to train most effectively the response and attentional skills needed by mentally handicapped children for such situations would seem to be the major empirical question facing further research in this area. An important factor here will be the identification of appropriate and manageable reinforcers for these children.

3.2.5 Other variants using matching-to-sample

The Touch-Tutor has been considered at some length as it is representative of a whole range of related devices which employ matching-to-sample techniques, although to our knowledge no others incorporate all the features discussed above.

One example is the Behavioural Controls, Stimulus–Response Programmer (Figure 4.2), which employs a display with five press-panel response areas and can be used with a tape player and a coin/sweet dispenser. Another is HUMID, a research device developed by Karlsen (1966) at the University of Minnesota. This machine, which resembled the Touch-Tutor in several aspects although no auditory system was included, used a visual knowledge of results system involving the illumination of response panels. If the correct panel was depressed the other two panels were illuminated in green whereas if an incorrect response was made, then that panel was illuminated in red.

A third related device is the Association-Teaching Module developed by Jackson at Monash University, Australia. This device, while technically quite different from other matching-to-sample machines, still employs the principle of requiring the child to perform an active discriminative response to displayed information followed by immediate knowledge of results. The Association-Teaching Module (Figure 3.6) consists of a display panel, a feedback window and a number of response keys which also display information. The child's task

Figure 3.6 Association-Teaching Module

is simply to choose the appropriate response key and use it to open the feedback window thereby receiving visual knowledge of results. An incorrect choice of response key will fail to open the feedback window. Modules may be used in combination to achieve increasingly complex discriminations.

3.3 Developments from the cybernetics tradition

The influence of the cybernetics tradition is demonstrated by two devices. The first of these is a sophisticated multimodality device controlled by a special purpose computer. It represents an attempt to control the total environment. The second is a fairly standard branching filmstrip teaching machine, which because of its simple two choice pushbutton response has been adapted for use by handicapped and geriatric subjects.

3.3.1 Edison Responsive Environment

There can be little doubt that the most ambitious, best known and most expensive special purpose system aimed at the kinds of population we are considering is the Edison Responsive Environment designed by Moore (1966) and commonly known as the Talking Typewriter. Basically this system consists of a booth inside which the child sits at a keyboard (Figure 3.7). A booth assistant operates a control panel outside the booth and exercises supervisory control over the machine, the detailed machine operation being under the control of a special purpose digital computer. The booth assistant can observe the child through a one-way viewing screen.

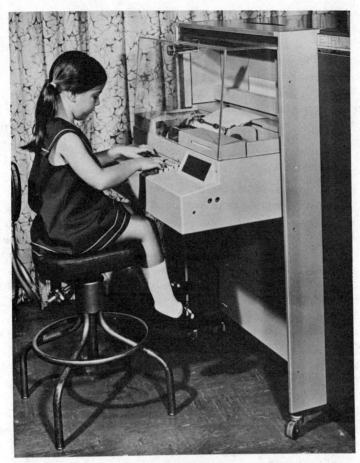

Figure 3.7 Edison Responsive Environment or Talking Typewriter

A typical procedure with the Talking Typewriter would be as follows: the child sits at the keyboard on which each key is one of nine different colours, to assist with correct fingering on the keyboard. Moore painted the children's fingernails in correspondence with the key colours. If the child presses one of the keys, the letter is typed on the paper roll in the usual manner, except that the paper roll is behind a transparent cover. In the second phase of programming, in addition to typing the letter, the sound of the letter is heard through a loud-speaker beside the keyboard. The letters may be identified in this way either phonetically or by name. As six different voice tracks can be selected by a switch outside the booth it is possible to use even foreign languages.

After the child has explored the keyboard for himself, he is expected to res-pond to audio commands from the machine, his task being to find the appro-priate key. If the child fails to locate it, the sound of the letter will be repeated at regular intervals and eventually other cues will be introduced to narrow down the area of search, such as giving the colour of the key. During this phase a keyboard locking device is brought into operation in order to prevent the operation of any but the correct key.

In this third phase of programming, printed material may also be presented in a window above the typewriter. A small red pointer directs attention to individual letters in the display, which can be of single letters, words or up to four lines of text. A rear-projection screen to the right of the window may be used for the presentation of slides containing any suitable material at appropriate points in the program. Recorded messages may also be replayed through the loudspeaker under program control and, in addition, the child may be allowed to record his own voice and have it replayed for comparison with a master track.

The Talking Typewriter is controlled by signals which are recorded on one face of a magnetic program card. This card, which looks rather like a record sleeve, has printed on the other face the letters and words which are to be displayed through the window. The machine has two magnetic pick-up heads; one for the program codes and another for the audio messages. The cards are coded by means of the special code panel, located alongside the keyboard. This panel is normally covered and so is not accessible by the child. Hill (1970a) has described the Talking Typewriter and has also developed some programming strategies (Hill, 1970b) and given a detailed account of its programming.

Moore's (1966) description of the Talking Typewriter stresses five features:

  (i) it allows the learner to explore freely;
 (ii) it immediately informs the learner of the consequences of his actions;
(iii) it is self-pacing;
 (iv) it allows the learner to use his capacity for discovering relations;
  (v) it is structured to encourage the learner to make a series of interconnected discoveries about the physical, cultural or social world.

Despite the large number of reports published on the Talking Typewriter its effectiveness is extraordinarily difficult to assess. Although the Response Environments Corporation has listed over a hundred publications only a handful of these are anything other than anecdotal. The Brooklyn project (Israel, 1968) employed 18 machines in an extensive study. The report of this project describes significant advances for children of various ages and abilities in alphabet recognition and reading comprehension tests. It concludes that the Talking Typewriter is effective with young children partly because of its motivational qualities in getting them interested in language activities, but that once the child has acquired the basic skill necessary for reading it may be an inefficient system for producing advanced comprehension and speed of reading performance.

Moseley (1969) used the Talking Typewriter with educationally subnormal children and Hill (1971) used the system with illiterate adults. Both Moseley and Hill used control groups without the Talking Typewriter and in each case their results were inconclusive. In a later study Moseley (1971) used severely subnormal children and adults and concluded that the system was less effective than a teacher equipped with flash cards. He considered that the main problem in using the Talking Typewriter with this population was that they found difficulty in remembering the sequences of letters required to type a response on the keyboard. It would be possible to program the Talking Typewriter for rapid word-matching by sacrificing the typing facility but, as Moseley remarks, word-matching games and less expensive machines, such as the Touch-Tutor and Hansel Training Machine, are able to perform this function perfectly well. Hill and Cavanagh (1968) in reporting a study in which the Talking Typewriter was used with illiterate adults, also commented on some of the unfortunate constraints involved in the programming of the machine.

Nevertheless, much publicised opinion has supported the claims for the effectiveness of the machine. At Freeport public school in New York (Martin, 1964) for example, 20 kindergarten and mentally handicapped children were taught to read better, by the Talking Typewriter, than 20 children (carefully matched in terms of various criteria) who were taught by traditional methods. At Rosewood State Hospital (1970), Maryland, 23 retarded children showed, in 6 months with the Talking Typewriter, an average mental age increase of 11 months. Morgenstern (1969) has summarised similar findings from a number of sources.

In the present authors' view it seems likely that the main problem with the Talking Typewriter, apart from its cost, is that the use of a keyboard response presents young or retarded children with a much greater initial difficulty than a touching or button pressing response in a simple matching-to-sample task.

3.3.2 tm 1024/ts 512

Newman and Scantlebury (1967) at the Autonomics Division of the National Physical Laboratory investigated the use of teaching machines as devices for amplifying human intelligence. Their idea was that, given machine aid in dealing with a complicated logical structure, people might be able to perform tasks which would otherwise be beyond their intellectual capacity. The task could be reduced to a program of elementary instructions and the individual guided through the task by a machine which presented him with instructions and responded to information obtained by him as a result of carrying out the instructions. Thus the man would provide pattern recognition and motor skills whilst the machine dealt with the logical structure of the task. Newman and Scantlebury devised such a machine and wrote a program which enabled completely unskilled people to diagnose and repair faults in an audio amplifier, thus demonstrating the feasibility of the approach.

A commercial version of the device was marketed by Educational Systems Limited as the ESL tm 1024 (Figure 3.8). The 35-mm film was loaded onto spools mounted in a retractable drawer in the lower part of the machine and was projected onto the rear-projection screen. In addition to the visual material each frame contained two ten-bit binary coded numbers, one being selected when the

Figure 3.8 tm 1024/ts 512. (Based on Gedye and Miller, 1970)

NO button was pressed and the other when the YES button was pressed. The number represented by the code determined the number of frames the film would move and also the direction of travel. Any frame in the film could thus be programmed to branch to any two out of 1024 frames according to which button was pressed.

Although the tm 1024 was an essentially simple device, it was electronically controlled and therefore allowed a variety of modifications for experimental purposes. Remote response detectors were readily attached because the standard machine was fitted with an extension socket to allow the use of foot operated controls in an industrial situation. Gedye and Miller (1970) developed an extended and modified version, which was known as the ts 512. This allowed control of the display presentation time and the inter-presentation interval, and also collected data on the response mode and the time taken to make it.

At the time of its development the ts 512 represented a most advanced system for testing and the collection of data. Because this method of data collection is still representative of modern techniques we will describe it in some detail. The data logger was designed to be compatible with teletypewriter equipment and therefore used ASCII code (Section 5.5.2). The termination of each frame caused a series of eight ASCII characters to be generated. The first of these characters was chosen from a set which defined the type of response made (e.g. left button correct response, right button incorrect response and so on) or indicated the beginning or end of a testing session. The next five characters were normally used to record the response latency in milliseconds, the final two characters being carriage return and line feed which allows listing on the teletypewriter printer and normally signals end of record for computer input. The logger could either drive a teletypewriter directly, producing both a print-out of the responses and a punched paper tape for computer analysis, or in the more usual mode its output could be recorded silently during the testing session on an integral tape recorder for subsequent replay into a teletypewriter.

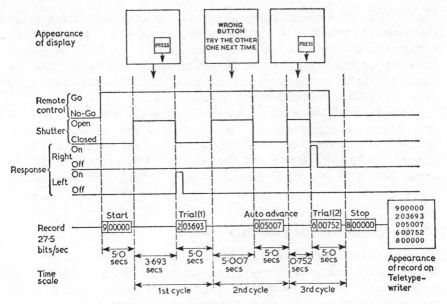

Figure 3.9 tm 1024/ts 512 operating cycle. (Based on Gedye and Miller, 1970)

Figure 3.9 shows the detailed time relationships of three operating cycles of the system, in which the subject is presented with a program frame demanding a right response, makes an incorrect left response, is presented with a frame giving knowledge of results and not requiring a response, and is finally re-presented with the original frame and this time makes a correct response.

The squares at the top of the figure indicate the appearance of the program frames which are presented. The top line shows the state in time of the tester's remote control and the three lines below this indicate the state of the shutter and the left and right response buttons respectively, these being active only when the shutter is open. The bottom line shows the successive stages of generation of the data record, the final printed appearance of which is shown at the extreme right.

Before starting the test session the filmstrip is positioned to the appropriate initial frame of the program. The tester then operates the remote control to close the shutter of the visual display. When the subject is ready and the test is to commence, the tester starts the tape recorder and then operates the remote control in order to display the first frame. This action first generates the data word 900000, the symbol 9 in the first position indicating the start of the test and the 00000 that the timer has been reset. When 5 seconds have elapsed the shutter opens and the response buttons become active. When the subject responds to the left button, the data word 203693 is generated, the symbol 2 in the first position indicating a left button incorrect response and the 03693 a response time of 3·693 seconds. When this has been transferred to tape the first cycle is complete. The second cycle is a knowledge of results frame which is displayed for a pre-set interval of approximately 5 seconds and does not require a response. The third cycle is a right button correct response and while the data word generated for this response is being transferred to tape, the tester operates the remote control to end the test. This generates the data word 800000, the symbol 8 in the first position indicating the end of test. This is transferred to the tape at the end of the normal 5-second delay.

A small batch of these machines was built by ESL and were used for assessment of brain damaged and geriatric patients (Gedye, 1967) and for the assessment of learning difficulties in mentally handicapped and normal 5 to 11 year old school children by Davies and Needham (1971) who concluded that the system was not reliable as a diagnostic instrument with children below the age of seven years.

3.4 Developments from the audio-visual tradition

The audio-visual aids tradition has produced a variety of audio-visual presentation devices. The examples given here represent those which have been designed explicitly for primary school children. Although they do not require a specific response to the material presented, in the manner of the other devices we have considered, they do require some active participation on the part of the child and can be programmed to give some knowledge of results.

3.4.1 Language Master

With the Language Master (Experimental Development Unit, NCAVAE, 1970), manufactured by Bell and Howell, the child is required simply to insert a card, listen and sometimes to speak. For some mentally handicapped children, however, even this sequence of responses may prove too demanding. Nevertheless, in terms of the numbers manufactured and in use, the Language Master has enjoyed great success. The machine (Figure 3.10) is a two-channel record-replay device employing a magnetic stripe on cards which display the associated visual material. Two tracks on the magnetic stripe comprise a 'master' track and a 'student' track. The pupil is able both to listen and record on the latter but material on the master track may only be erased and re-recorded by the operation of a concealed switch. A typical use of the Language Master involves the child inserting a card on which is printed a picture of an object and a few words of description. As the card is transported across the child's view, a pre-recorded reading of the words is played through the loudspeaker from the master track. The child can then insert the card again, this time recording his own message which he may then compare with the pre-recorded version. It is evident that this device also offers considerable flexibility of use. It may, for example, present a programmed sequence of cards allowing the student to make a verbal response with knowledge of results given on the master track. Alternatively this track may be used to give direction about which card to be inserted next and (provided the child cooperates) this may be made contingent on the choice

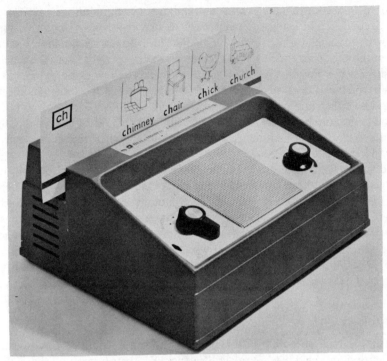

Figure 3.10 Language Master

made from a number of alternatives presented visually on the card. A range of prepared reading (Leedham, 1965) and language teaching kits are available for the Language Master as well as blank cards which allow the teacher, or even the child himself, to prepare his own materials.

Cox and Somerfield (1970) in the final report of the Nuffield Foundation Coventry Primary School Reading Project found that children of all ages were able to use the machine, although some five year old children were initially apprehensive and preferred to have an older child or adult present when using the machine. Teachers appear to have been enthusiastic about the machine and the authors observed that the children enjoyed using the machine but quickly lost interest if the material was unsuitable. The machine was judged to be suitable for the early stages of any educational process. For example in the early stages of reading it

> proved invaluable for word recognition. Children did not have to wait for teacher time to learn a word; by matching the key words in the Language Master set to the required word in the book they could run the card through the machine and get the answer.

The report describes how the teachers and children adapted flash cards and made their own materials for the Language Master and also how the machine was used in second language and mathematics teaching. Crouch (1966) describes experience in using the machine with non-reading and retarded junior school children and Freemont (1968) describes its use in an infant school. Both authors give an encouraging account of their experience with the machine and suggest it would be an advantage to have children working in pairs at the machine. Brown (1972) investigated the effectiveness of the Language Master along with other audio-visual aids in teaching reading to educationally subnormal children. His experimental groups showed significant gains and Brown suggests that the self-confidence brought about by such techniques may be particularly beneficial to these children.

The Language Master and similar devices from the audio-visual tradition have generally not been subjected to the same kind of laboratory-based behavioural evaluation as systems from the psychology and cybernetics traditions. The emphasis has rather been on placing the equipment in schools for subjective evaluation. Although such reports may seem lacking in rigour to academic researchers, it may well be that what is lost due to the absence of quantitative procedures and scientific controls is more than compensated by the reality of the testing situation.

3.4.2 Talking Page

The Talking Page (Figure 3.11) originated with the Responsive Environments Corporation in the USA. Rank-REC, the UK distributors of the Talking Typewriter (Section 3.3.1), manufactured the machine and launched a campaign aimed at selling and hiring the machine and programs in elementary education. The company is no longer in operation and the machine is not at present available in the UK.

Figure 3.11 Talking Page

The Talking Page (Salisbury, 1971) is basically a battery operated record player. The program material is in two parts, a disc and a booklet. The disc is a specially made 7-inch 45 rpm disc, which is thicker and tougher than a normal disc, having a steel plate in the middle. In use the disc is loaded into a slot at the back of the machine and the booklet is slipped onto the front of the machine where it fits over two locating pins. A pointer at the left of the machine can be moved up and down the page to align it with material printed on the page. The pointer is controlled by a lever on the side of the machine which when lifted allows the pick-up to play at a point on the disc corresponding to the position of the pointer. There are 53 predetermined starting positions which are fixed by a series of slots into which the lever can be lifted, but the sound frames do not have to be the same length. When a sound frame has been played a subsonic pulse causes the machine to stop. The child can then repeat the frame or move to a new one as directed by the printed material. Thus, as long as the disc is used with the corresponding booklet, the audio and visual material will be correctly synchronised and the child has random access both to the visual material by turning the pages and to the auditory material by moving the lever.

Such a machine could be programmed after the manner of a branching teaching machine with visual multichoice questions which were to be answered by positioning the lever. The audio could then give knowledge of results and direct the student to the next frame. Trials with this machine in Britain (Cox and Somerfield, 1970) indicated that the machine had potential, but that it would probably have been more suited to a higher age group than was originally intended. On many occasions less able children would accidentally place the selection lever in the wrong slot, thereby moving to an unrelated item and losing their place in the programme. The materials which were originally released for the Talking Page were mainly in the areas of beginning reading and elementary mathematics.

3.5 Summary

In this chapter we have described a number of systems which exemplify the three traditions: psychology, cybernetics and audio-visual aids. The characteristics of the systems are summarised in Table 3.1.

CHAPTER 4
System Components

4.1 New systems for old

Because of the high costs of engineering development and the need for reliable repetitive operation, there is an understandable tendency to use as the components of automated educational systems devices which were originally developed for other, larger markets, particularly the mass entertainment market. This does have some advantage for the user, in that the basic consumable materials, such as tape cassettes and spare parts, are readily available.

Sometimes the process works in reverse. A manufacturer introducing some new audio-visual device, perhaps involving considerable development investment and intended for ultimate use in mass entertainment will, as a pilot exercise, market the device in a restricted area, such as education, where the higher unit costs resulting from limited production may be tolerated. Video cassette recorders were introduced in this way.

Figure 4.1 shows how the basic components of an automated teaching system are related. The whole system may be regarded as a flow of information both from the machine to the student and from the student to the machine. The

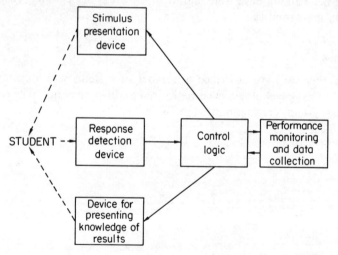

Figure 4.1 The basic components of an automated teaching system.
The device for presenting knowledge of results may be the same as
the stimulus presentation device

student is presented with stimulus information which he must attend to and process and then construct an appropriate response. The machine must, in turn, be capable of detecting the response, processing the information it conveys and feeding back to the student knowledge of results. If each of the machine functions is to be fully automated then in addition to the special devices required to perform these functions it will also be necessary to incorporate a control device capable of determining the correct sequence of operations. If the system is to gain control of the student's rate of progress then it will also be necessary to provide a facility for keeping track of performance.

The sections of this chapter will consider each of the components of such a system in turn. Some of the technical discussion will be in greater detail than elsewhere in the book. This is because the technical details of the system components are rather difficult to unearth from a diverse range of sources and collecting them together may be of practical value to those undertaking research in this field without a background in such matters.

4.2 Stimulus presentation devices

Although on occasions it may be deemed desirable to train appropriate responses to stimulation in other modalities, most effort has been directed towards the presentation of visual and auditory stimuli. This emphasis no doubt reflects the importance of these modalities in human language. It seems unlikely that in the foreseeable future automated teaching will be applied on any significant scale to, say, the olfactory or gustatory modalities. Consequently the remainder of this section is devoted to a review of the main techniques used for the presentation of visual and auditory stimuli. Automated methods for stimulating the other modalities have been developed by sensory psychologists (e.g. Békésy, (1967)) and these techniques could be applied to automated training.

4.2.1 Visual displays

A great variety of devices having widely differing characteristics is available for presenting visual information. The important characteristics for our purpose are:

    (i) still or motion picture capability,
   (ii) speed of frame change,
  (iii) random or serial access,
  (iv) monochrome or colour,
   (v) alphanumeric or full graphical capability,
  (vi) cost of preparation of material,
 (vii) cost of duplication of material,
(viii) capital cost of display device.

Paper is the traditional medium for visual communication and many early

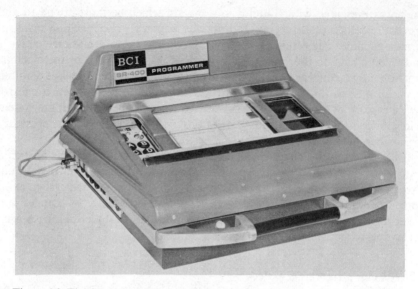

Figure 4.2 The SR paper roll presentation device manufactured by Behavioral Controls, Inc. This device has facilities for coding by holes punched in the paper roll and can also be fitted with transparent response keys

teaching machines used printed material on paper rolls (e.g. Bristol Tutor) or on cards (e.g. Canterbury Teaching Machine). The basic mechanisms used in such devices are not readily available as separate components. They are also rather inflexible and slow in operation. Consequently most experimenters have used photographic or electronic display devices, which can readily be remotely controlled and are faster in operation. However, at least one company, Behavioural Controls, has manufactured a paper roll presentation device (Figure 4.2) for many years. This device is explicitly offered for experimentation in human operant work and educational technology. It has facilities for coding information on each frame in the form of punched holes alongside the stimulus material and can also be fitted with response detecting panels. This company also offers a range of other stimulus presentation and reinforcement dispensing devices which can be interconnected to form a variety of training systems.

Although film has been the most popular visual medium with experimenters, the use of paper or cards should be seriously considered if large-scale production of automated teaching systems for young children is ever envisaged. These media are cheap and readily allow teachers to produce special programmes or to modify commercially produced programmes without recourse to specialised photographic equipment.

The film projectors which have been used in automated systems are usually automatic slide projectors such as the Kodak Carousel or GAF Rotomatic. These are essentially serial access devices, since the order in which the slides may be presented must conform to the physical sequence and therefore must be

Figure 4.3 The Kodak S–RA projector is a special version of the well known Carousel projector, which incorporates electronically controlled random access. The required frame may be selected by using the pushbuttons shown in the photograph or the control may be interfaced directly to a computer or logic system

arranged in advance. In recent years, however, random access versions have been produced (Figure 4.3) mainly in response to the requirements of applications such as information retrieval for operators in process control and military installations. A random access slide projector may present a particular slide at any point in the sequence regardless of its actual location in the slide tray. Although the display may be random access the slide tray still has to be moved serially and in the worst case it may take a few seconds to locate a particular slide. Because the cost of random access projectors is high and the logic involved in selecting the frame is fairly complex, their use in automated teaching systems is still something of a rarity. A radical approach has been made in a few cases to the problem of random access by the use of a sheet film having the visual items arranged in an XY matrix. The now obsolete Philips tm 198 (Philips Industries, 1970) teaching machine used an 11 by 18 matrix on a sheet of microfilm and the new PLATO CAI terminal (Hammond, 1972) uses sheet film loaded by the students themselves. When it is necessary to switch very rapidly from one display to another, multiple projectors, directed at the same projection screen, may be used. The projectors need to be fitted with electrically operated shutters. If the succeeding frame is known in advance, two slide projectors and some suitable control logic may suffice. However, where the succeeding frame is dependent on an external event, such as the nature of the subject's response, then the search time of a mechanically operated random access projector may be unacceptable. If the number of items is small and the resolution required is not great, alphanumeric projection indicators fitted with a specially designed transparency may be suitable (see Figure 4.4). In this case the display is selected by switching on the electrical supply to the appropriate lamp. For experimental

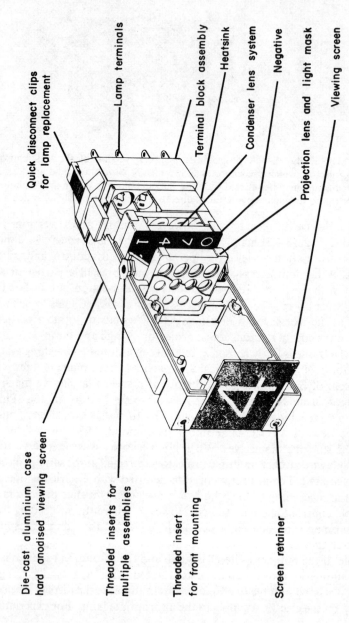

Die-cast aluminium case
hard anodised viewing screen

Threaded inserts for
multiple assemblies

Threaded insert
for front mounting

Screen retainer

Quick disconnect clips
for lamp replacement

Lamp terminals

Terminal block assembly

Heatsink

Condenser lens system

Negative

Projection lens and light mask

Viewing screen

Figure 4.4 A sectional view of a typical projection indicator. Light from the selected bulb illuminates one of the symbols on the transparency: a symbol is thereby projected onto the screen. Projection indicators in common use range from about 1 to 4 inches in height

Figure 4.5 The La Belle Courier 16 sound filmstrip unit features a permanently synchronised audio-visual cartridge. Both the 16-mm film and magnetic tape are in endless loop form. The basic design is for user operation by means of the start, stop and volume controls on the front panel, but remote control is also available

work in visual perception this scheme has been extended to provide an apparatus in which specially designed multiple 35-mm slide projectors are directed onto a single screen and each has as its light source a very fast rise time electronic lamp (Mylrea, 1966). For teaching purposes, however, conventional projection lamps would be adequate.

The filmstrip projector was one of the earliest teaching aids. This device has recently undergone a great deal of redevelopment, primarily aimed at producing a convenient audio-visual sales aid. The modern device is a self-contained automatic filmstrip projector with integral rear-projection screen and synchronised tape player (Figure 4.5). The synchronising pulses are either recorded on a separate track of the tape or use low frequencies which are filtered out of the audio signal on replay. When the tape is played the filmstrip advances as required by the commentary. Recently a number of 35-mm and 16-mm devices, using endless loop films and tapes, have been manufactured. These give the advantage that material is ready for re-use at the end of each session.

Philips have taken the concept a stage further and developed a filmstrip transport which will operate at up to motion picture speeds. This allows a tape filmstrip programme to include motion sequences. The system (Figure 4.6) is known as PIP (Programmed Individual Presentation) and has the audio material on magnetic tape in a standard compact cassette for tape and the visual material on Super-8 film in a specially designed cassette of similar style. All these projectors can readily be adapted for use in automated teaching systems because each frame change is individually initiated by an electrical signal. This is, of course, also the case for the widely used tape-slide units which consist of a conventional slide projector synchronised with a tape player by pulses from one track of the tape. These are particularly suitable for experimental purposes due to the ease of editing and reorganising material. The recently developed 'Sound-on-Slide' projector offers similar advantages provided not more than

68

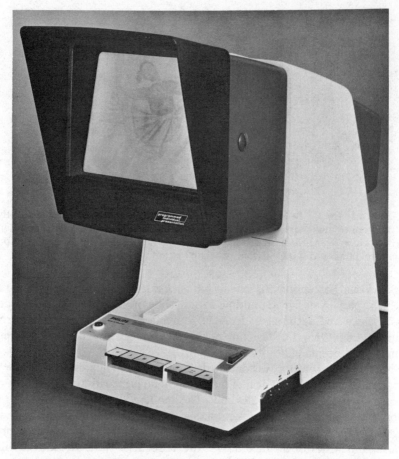

Figure 4.6 The Philips PIP Cassettescope type LCH2020 uses standard
compact cassettes for audio and a similar cassette for Super-8 film. Individual
frames of film can be projected at up to motion picture rates

30 seconds of audio are required to accompany any particular frame. This
projector incorporates a tape recorder, the magnetic sound track being fitted
into each transparency holder. For large-scale production, however, the use of
filmstrip is probably preferable for reasons of cost. Conventional motion picture
projectors are quite unsuitable, even if they incorporate a still-frame facility,
because they cannot be controlled frame by frame.

When selecting projectors for use in automated systems some consideration
should be given to the optical arrangement of the projector and screen. It is usual
to use a rear-projection screen. Traditionally this was made from ground glass.
This material has the disadvantage that the brightness of the image decreases
rapidly as the viewing angle deviates from a right angle to the surface, so much
so that at normal viewing distances the edge of the screen can be quite dim and
the screen appears to have a 'hot spot' of brightness which moves with the

viewer's head position. The problem can be overcome by the use of modern materials, such as Lenscreen manufactured by Polacoat. This material gives a bright image of high resolution with a very wide viewing angle, thus eliminating the hot spot. It is available on glass, acrylic plastic and flexible base materials. The lens–screen distance when projecting is determined by the linear magnification, m, required on the screen and the focal length, f, of the projector lens.

$$\text{lens–screen distance} = m \times f \text{ (approximately)}$$

Space can often be saved by the use of a folded optical path (Figure 4.7) or by the use of projectors which will accept very short focal length lenses, such as the Kodak Carousel SAV-2000 which has been specially designed for audio-visual applications.

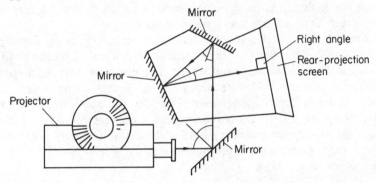

Figure 4.7 A typical folded optical path which may be used to reduce the projector–screen distance. The mirrors should be surface silvered in order to prevent the formation of multiple images on the screen

The limitations of film projection display devices derive mainly from the basic need to transport one frame after another through the projector gate. There is also the time delay and inconvenience involved in using the services of a processing laboratory for the preparation of materials. Both these problems disappear in the equivalent electronic process, television. Television's main limitation, the small screen which makes it suitable for viewing by only a small audience, is not crucial for systems which have been designed for the use of a single student at a time. Television has been widely used as a passive presentation device in education and so it may seem strange that so little use has been made of television picture displays in automated teaching systems. The problem lies in the vast amount of information which is needed to construct a single frame of a television picture. Each frame is equivalent to about 2×10^6 bits of information. At present the only low cost method of storing and retrieving this quantity of data is magnetic tape. Video tape recorders are now manufactured in a wide range of prices, but they are all essentially serial access devices without the ability to step from frame to frame. They are therefore just as unsuitable for use in automated systems as the conventional motion picture projector. Video tape

70

recorders often have a facility which permits manual replay of a single frame by stopping the tape transport and maintaining the helical scan of the replay head, but the use of this procedure on all but the most expensive machines leads to rapid tape wear and gives unsatisfactory picture quality. Recently video disc storage devices have been developed which operate on a random access principle. The disc stores a complete frame of television picture information in magnetic form on each track and a movable head can access each of a hundred or so tracks in any order. At present these devices are still extremely expensive and their use is generally limited to television companies for such applications as special effects and instant replay with motion analysis in sports programmes. If a low cost video disc device is developed it could have many advantages as a programmable source of visual material in automated teaching systems. At present the high capital cost limits the use of such devices to experimental projects such as interactive television (Section 5.4).

A somewhat different type of video disc is currently being developed by Telefunken. This is a flexible pressed plastic disc of rather similar form to the conventional audio gramophone record, but played at very high speed and capable of reproducing video frequency signals. Each disc carries a few minutes of video material. Prototype versions of the disc and player have been demonstrated (Raggett, 1970) which incorporate a manual still-frame facility. In principle it would be possible to have a still-frame remotely programmable, and so if the system goes into production it could form a useful basis for automated television teaching.

Figure 4.8 The DEC VTO5 visual display unit together with a specimen display. Note how the characters are formed by lines in the television picture

At present the only feasible method for generating a still-frame or controlled change in a television picture is restricted to alphanumerical material or very limited graphics derived from a visual display unit (VDU) computer terminal (Figure 4.8). This device stores information in a coded form representing the sequence of characters to be displayed, rather than the detailed structure of the

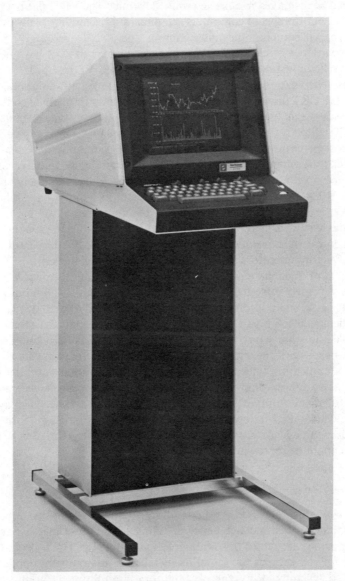

Figure 4.9 The Tektronix 4010 graphic terminal uses a bistable phosphor storage tube. It can display large quantities of flicker-free data, but is unable to present movement. The screen floods with light for a brief period when the display is erased

displayed picture. As each line of the television raster is scanned a pattern of dots is generated in the VDU by reference to an integrated circuit memory which contains data on the dot pattern for each character. By this technique the number of bits needed to specify a frame of the television picture is reduced by a factor of about 100. The penalty is the restriction that only a particular character set can be displayed in a predetermined format. The VDU needs a computer to drive it, but the cost of computers is falling rapidly and it is likely that devices of this type will soon become quite common.

Many varieties of electronic alphanumeric display devices have been developed. We have just considered the television based VDU, but there are other methods of using the cathode ray tube (CRT). These usually employ a computer to drive the CRT directly, rather than generating an intermediate coded character and video signal, and are usually termed computer graphic terminals. When the CRT is directly driven a greater variety of display patterns can be generated at the cost of more sophisticated computer programming and greater use of computer time when displaying. Some graphic terminals are based on the dot matrix principle in which the CRT screen may be addressed at any one of, say, 1024 by 1024 points, thus building up a complete picture. Alphanumeric characters may be generated by a subset of points, usually 7 by 5, or by an additional hardware character generator which may move the spot in a series of straight lines, thus producing a more legible form. Further hardware may provide vector generators which can draw continuous lines on the CRT. The generation of such material without flicker on a conventional CRT screen requires repeated refreshing which is very demanding of computer time. It generally needs an additional mini-computer dedicated to each display. A more economical solution is to use a storage tube type of display. This is a CRT with a bistable phosphor which continues to glow once it has been energised by the electron beam until the whole screen is electronically erased. This allows slow data communication lines to be used between the computer and the terminal. It may take a few seconds to fill the whole screen, but the screen can then be viewed for many minutes without using any computer time. Displays of this kind are widely used in low cost computer graphic terminals (Figure 4.9). The main disadvantage of storage tube displays over refreshed displays is that motion cannot be represented in the display.

4.2.2 Auditory stimuli

The two most widely used methods of storing auditory information are the gramophone record and magnetic recording tape. These media have widely differing properties which are summarised in Table 4.1. The technical features of gramophone records are superior to tape for many likely applications in automated teaching. For example, auditory stimuli are by nature transient, in contrast to visual stimuli. If a subject fails to detect or comprehend a stimulus presentation, he can, in the case of a normal visual display, reattend to it; this is not possible with an auditory presentation. If we wish to provide the possibi-

Table 4.1 A comparison of audio media

	Magnetic tape	Gramophone record
Access	Serial on any one track, but possible to switch between tracks	Manual random access by moving pick-up arm. Programmable random access possible but rare
Remote control facilities	Common on semi-professional machines, e.g. Revox, Uher	Not provided, but possible in principle
Synchronisation with visual media	Specialist machines for motion picture synchronisation and tape-slide	No. Difficult in principle
Number of channels	Up to eight on $\frac{1}{4}$-inch tape	Two, but crosstalk is bad
Cost of preparation of material	Low	High
Cost of duplication	High	Low
Cost of machine	Moderate	Moderate

lity of an auditory representation it is necessary to make specific provision in the replay device. In the case of a tape it is necessary to rewind the tape under some form of logical or manual control. Random access can be achieved with a record player simply by repositioning the pick-up on the record. Although the gramophone record possesses a number of attractive features for automated teaching, they would only be of any practical consequence if a large-scale application were envisaged. The readily available record players are not designed for remote control or programmable random access and they are quite unsuited to modification for such purposes. Also the cost of preparing masters for pressing duplicate records makes the system unattractive for experimental use. Some of the random access features of the gramophone record can be realised for experimental purposes by storing audio information in digital form on a computer with a disc backing store and will be discussed later in this section.

In the present state of the art most automated teaching systems are small-scale and experimental. Consequently, the overwhelming majority of systems have used magnetic tape when auditory stimuli are required. The few systems using gramophone records have typically been designed as large-scale operations, involving considerable engineering effort, for example the Talking Page (Section 3.4.2) and the PLATO CAI terminal (Section 5.2.2).

Tape machines are manufactured in a wide variety of forms. For automated presentation of pre-recorded items on tape the minimum requirements are some means of detecting the end of each item and a means of starting and stopping the tape transport. Although it is technically possible to include synchronising pulses in the same channel as is used for the audio information and to separate them on replay by filtering, such methods are generally not

(a)

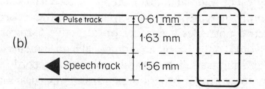

(b)

◄ Pulse track   0·61 mm
                1·63 mm
◄ Speech track 1·56 mm

Figure 4.10 (a) The Philips N2209 slide syn-
chroniser cassette recorder. (b) The track
arrangements used in the recorder are the same
as in the PIP system (Figure 4.6). Tracks 1
and 2 are the mono speech track, track 3 is
unused and track 4 is the pulse track (from
Fletcher (1971))

satisfactory and it is more usual to use a separate channel for this purpose.
Stereophonic tape recorders (two channels) and the more recent quadraphonic
tape recorders (four channels) are particularly useful in this respect. Some
machines (Figure 4.10) have an integral facility for placing synchronising pulses
on a separate recording track. Such machines are designed to operate automatic
slide projectors for tape-slide presentations. When the tape is replayed a switch
contact is made in the tape machine every time a synchronising pulse is detected.
Unfortunately, such machines do not usually have remote control facilities
although, as they are usually compact cassette machines rather than reel to reel
types, the moving mass is so low that it is usually sufficient to switch the supply

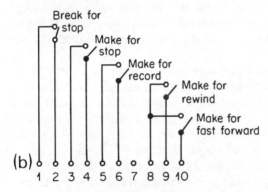

Figure 4.11 (a) The Revox A77 semi-professional tape recorder. All functions of the recorder can be remotely controlled by momentary operation of contacts as shown in (b)

to the drive motor in order to stop and start the machine. It is impracticable to control reel to reel machines in this way and so one is restricted to using those machines which are specifically designed for remote control. Such machines have the brakes and pinch wheel tape drive operated by solenoids (Figure 4.11).

Tape machines using an endless loop cartridge (Figure 4.12) have been developed for radio stations. These machines have provision on one track for the use of coded pulses of up to three frequencies each of which can control different automatic functions. These machines have full remote control facilities

Figure 4.12 The Criterion-Compact II professional cartridge tape unit with 1, 2 or 3 tones for automatic control on a separate track of the tape. Broadcasting industry standards for automatic tape control are: (i) primary cue tone (1000 Hz) used to position the tape for the start of the message; (ii) secondary cue tone (150 Hz) used to indicate the end of message. Generally used to start the next cartridge player in an automatic system; (iii) tertiary cue tone (8000 Hz) used as desired to control auxiliary equipment, such as slide projectors

and are designed so that a prearranged series of broadcasting programmes and advertising messages can be set up. Tape players of this kind are expensive pieces of professional equipment but they are ideally suited to many experimental applications. Where the endless loop feature is required but funds are limited, inexpensive 4- or 8-track car stereo players (Figure 4.13) may be adapted.

Magnetic recording material is sometimes used in a form other than tape. As has been described in Section 3.4.1 the Language Master uses magnetically striped cards, but this machine is only suited to manual operation. The Ricoh Synchrofax is a passive audio-visual presentation device which uses a special writing paper which is magnetically coated on the reverse surface. The student can see the written material on the front surface of the paper while an auditory message is being replayed from the reverse surface. The record/replay head scans a spiral track and it is likely that extensive modification would be necessary to gain random access to individual tracks.

Optical sound tracks are commonly used on motion picture film. In this method of storing auditory information the width or optical density of a track along the film is made to vary with the amplitude of the sound wave. This technique is rarely used in other applications. One device which does so is designed for the random access presentation of pre-recorded announcements, as for example in the speaking clock. A drum contains a series of optical sound tracks each lasting up to a few seconds. In this example a presentation will consist of any combination of (i) an hour in the day, (ii) a minute in the hour and (iii) a 10-second interval. Such devices may be remotely controlled and would be suitable for use in automated teaching except for the limited number of tracks and the need to have the manufacturer prepare the sound tracks on the drum.

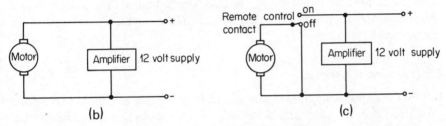

Figure 4.13 (a) A typical low cost car stereo cartridge player. (b) Simplified circuit diagram of player. (c) Modification to provide a remote control switch. In the OFF position the drive motor is short-circuited which gives improved stopping characteristics

So far we have been discussing techniques for the presentation of pre-recorded auditory information. A more radical development, currently receiving a great deal of attention, is the automation of the speech generation process itself. We may distinguish three basic approaches to the computer generation of speech. The simplest is that in which the computer is used merely as a random access digital recorder, samples of the audio waveform being stored every few microseconds. For long messages large computer memories or high speed backing stores are necessary and even very large backing stores cannot deal with messages longer than a few minutes. A second approach is to store information at a higher level, one which specifies the occurrence of certain features of the sound wave, rather than merely sampling the amplitude, thereby reducing the storage requirements for a given message. A commonly used method is to specify the energy present in different bands of the frequency spectrum (Dudley, 1939), a method sometimes used to increase the number of messages which may be transmitted through a long-distance telecommunication link. One disadvantage of these techniques is that highly specialised apparatus is required to analyse and to reconstruct the speech waveform, unlike the first approach which merely requires general purpose laboratory peripherals for the computer, namely an analogue to digital converter for input and a digital to analogue converter for output. A more ambitious approach is to use even more sophisticated hardware in an attempt to simulate the human production of speech. When using this method the computer is programmed with information on the settings needed on the synthesiser for the production of each phoneme. The speech sounds to be generated are then specified in their phonetic form. This last approach is the only one of the three in which the speech is truly computer generated. It is, however, at the present stage of development, still unsatisfactory for the production of connected speech. Many subtle changes take place in the articulation of words depending on their context and unfortunately speech generated on a simple phonetic basis sounds rather artificial and is somewhat difficult to follow. At present the first approach is probably the most suited to the production of a limited vocabulary of short auditory items. It is likely that in the near future reasonably priced devices based on the second approach will become available. The third approach is likely to be limited to large time-shared computer installations for some time because of the complexity and cost of the synthesiser.

4.3 Detection of responses

Ideally the response used in an automated teaching system should correspond closely to the desired terminal behaviour. In many cases this would be a verbal response, but as yet no cheap reliable method of speech recognition exists, the difficulties here being even greater than in speech generation. In some systems the need for speech recognition has been avoided by recording the subject's response and then replaying it to him together with a sample of pre-recorded ideal response, the student being expected to judge if his response was satisfactory. As we have seen these modes of operation are available in the Talking Typewriter (Section 3.3.1) and the Language Master (Section 3.4.1), but most system designers have felt that it is inappropriate to expect young children to operate at a level which assumes that he understands the objective of the training session or to make use of complex feedback modes, as for example, offered by SAID (speech auto-instructional device) used at the University of Michigan, (see Buiten and Lane (1965)).

In most cases the intention has been to train a perceptual skill and the only response required has been a key press or some similar manual selection of an item by the student. This procedure greatly simplifies the problems of interpreting responses, especially when they are restricted to a single key press in a multiple choice task. The interpretation of free-form alphanumeric input from a typewriter keyboard is almost as difficult as speech recognition and will be considered in Section 5.2 on computer-assisted instruction, similarly the use of light pens will be illustrated in Section 5.2.2. In this section we will restrict the discussion to those methods which have been developed for the detection of single touching responses and to an outline of specialised methods for the detection of similar binary responses in physically handicapped children.

The technically simplest method of response detection is, of course, to use a

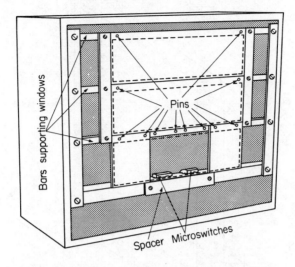

Figure 4.14 Hively's (1964a) apparatus in which response panels doubled as a display screen. The panels were constructed from 1/4-inch acrylic material with a rear-projection coating and hung from steel pins which allowed them to swing slightly. In this figure the two small centre panels have been removed to show how the bottom of each panel rests against the operating lever of a microswitch, the spring of which serves to restore the panel to its original position when the operating pressure is removed. The panels are retained by a faceplate (not shown in this figure) which allows some freedom of movement. Dotted lines indicate the position of the openings cut in the faceplate. The complete apparatus is shown in Figure 3.3

pushbutton switch. This is a spring-loaded button which when depressed actuates a switch and when released allows the switch to return to its normal state. This method is commonly used in conventional teaching machines, such as the Autotutor (Figure 1.3). In the case of young or retarded children, response keys remote from the display may be difficult to use or present a source of confusion, so integration of the display and the response detecting device is usually thought to be important.

One method effectively attempts to incorporate the pushbutton in the display. A multiple choice display would be arranged in a number of discrete areas, each containing a spring-biased transparent panel which operates a switch when it is pushed (Figure 4.14). An improved version of this type of panel uses a reed switch (Figure 4.15) which is operated by a magnet attached to the transparent panel. A read switch has its contacts enclosed by a sealed glass envelope with an inert gas atmosphere and so is protected from contamination. The panel

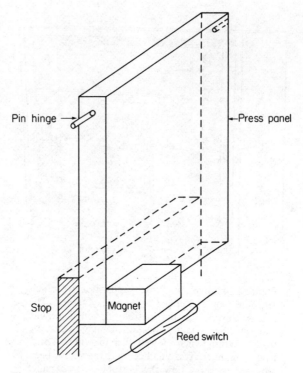

Figure 4.15 A typical arrangement for a press panel which operates a reed switch. When the panel is moved away from the stop the magnet moves near the reed switch and causes the contacts to close. If the panel is operated in a vertical position the mass of the magnet will provide a restoring force, otherwise a spring may be required

requires only a very low force to operate the switch and so if the friction of the hinge is low the force of gravity may be sufficient to restore the panel position.

Response panels with moving parts can give rise to problems. The panels may become jammed with foreign matter, hinges can become stuck and there is the concern that the possible behavioural effect of manipulating the panels themselves introduces an element of uncertainty into the training procedure. It is sometimes argued that the manipulation of such devices, with the characteristic operating feel and sound is in itself reinforcing and therefore desirable in the interests of maintaining responding behaviour. Even so, one may wish to restrict such reinforcement to a specified contingency, such as a correct response, by the use of say an auxiliary solenoid or bell situated behind the response panels. The dual aims of increased reliability and improved control over possible sources of reinforcement have led to the development of a variety of proximity and touch detecting devices.

Proximity detectors operate when the subject's hand is in the vicinity of a sensor, but do not require direct physical contact. Serrell and Kling (1968) used

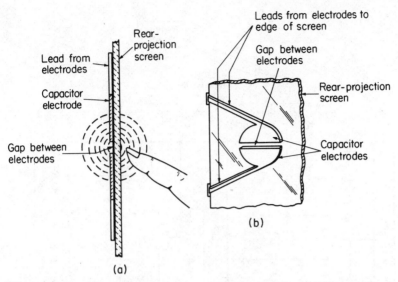

Figure 4.16 A capacitance proximity sensor devised by Serrell and Kling (1968) for use in the rear-projection screen of a teaching machine. (a) is a sectional view and (b) is a rear elevation of the device. The capacitor electrodes and leads are deposited on the glass as transparent conducting films. Because the plates are in the same plane a diffused electrostatic field results, allowing the presence of body tissue near the front surface of the screen to be detected

a capacitor of such a shape that a widely diffused electrostatic field is produced (Figure 4.16). As a hand approaches the electrodes the value of the capacitor changes due to the differing dielectric constants of air and human tissue. Figure 4.17 illustrates a typical circuit for a capacitance proximity detector. Difficulties can arise when a number of such detectors are used in close proximity, as electrical coupling is liable to give rise to spurious operation of the detectors. An alternative approach is to set up a light beam in front of the display and to detect when it is interrupted. Figure 4.18 shows such a scheme. The light source sends a collimated beam of light which is reflected to and fro and eventually illuminates a photocell. If a finger interrupts the light beam the electrical output from the photocell will change. This technique has the advantage that a number of detectors can be used side by side with no cross-coupling between them but it does require the exposed optical surfaces to be kept clean and in reasonably good condition. It is also possible that high ambient light conditions could prevent detection of a response unless special precautions are taken, such as the use of a modulated or infrared light source.

Although proximity detectors have a possible behavioural advantage in that shaping of responses is possible by progressively reducing the sensitivity of the detectors as correct responses are made, it is usually considered that a more precisely defined response is preferable. Thus a touching response is usually required. Although the electronic proximity detectors described earlier could

82

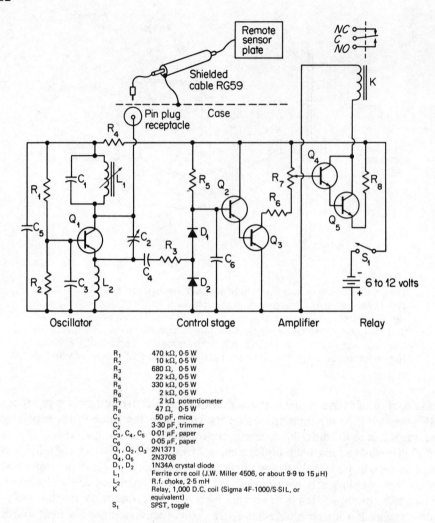

R_1	470 kΩ, 0·5 W
R_2	10 kΩ, 0·5 W
R_3	680 Ω, 0·5 W
R_4	22 kΩ, 0·5 W
R_5	330 kΩ, 0·5 W
R_6	2 kΩ, 0·5 W
R_7	2 kΩ potentiometer
R_8	47 Ω, 0·5 W
C_1	50 pF, mica
C_2	3-30 pF, trimmer
C_3, C_4, C_5	0·01 µF, paper
C_6	0·05 µF, paper
Q_1, Q_2, Q_3	2N1371
Q_4, Q_5	2N3708
D_1, D_2	1N34A crystal diode
L_1	Ferrite core coil (J.W. Miller 4506, or about 9·9 to 15 µH)
L_2	R.f. choke, 2·5 mH
K	Relay, 1,000 D.C. coil (Sigma 4F-1000/S-SIL, or equivalent)
S_1	SPST, toggle

Figure 4.17 A circuit for a typical capacitance proximity detector. Capacitor C2 is set so that the oscillator just functions. When a hand is brought close to the sensor plate the additional loading causes oscillations to cease. The later stages of the circuit detect the output of the oscillator and control the operation of the relay. Potentiometer R_7 adjusts the sensitivity of the circuit. (From *Electronic Circuits for the Behavioral and Biomedical Sciences* By Mitchell H. Zucker. W. H. Freeman and Company. Copyright © 1969)

be degraded so that they function as touch detectors, it is more usual to use circuits which are activated by the electrical leakage path through the subject's body to electrical earth. This leakage path can present a very high resistance and therefore circuits having very high input impedances are required. Early circuits (e.g. Cleary and Packham (1968)) used valve circuits, but the modern field

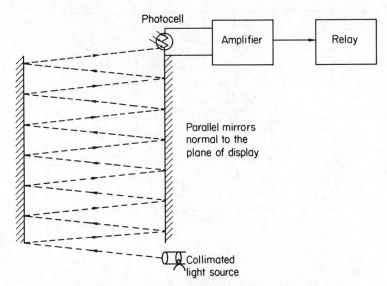

Figure 4.18 Photoelectric proximity detector. When a finger points to the display the path of the light beam is interrupted and the relay operates

effect transistor (Figure 4.19) is much simpler to use. Although touch detectors of this type work quite reliably in carpeted and normally furnished rooms they often fail to work reliably in rooms with rubber or vinyl flooring, such as may be found in institutional buildings. For experimental purposes a convenient solution to this difficulty is to provide the subject with a chair which is electrically earthed to a nearby water or central heating pipe. A safety earth is not necessary for this purpose, merely a method of bypassing the insulating floor. It is equally important to maintain good insulation in the mounting of the touch plate otherwise the changes in resistance to earth which should result from the touching response may be considerably reduced and the performance of the touch detector adversely affected. It is often observed in practice that touch detectors of this type work particularly well in an environment with a high level of electrical noise, for example in the presence of fluorescent lighting, even when the floor covering is of rubber. This is because the subject's contact with the touch plate effectively increases its area and consequently the amount of coupling between the noise source and the input of the detector circuit. This increases the noise picked up and amplified by the circuit and so causes the detector to operate even though the leakage signal is small. This phenomenon may be used to improve the reliability of the touch detector by ensuring that electrical coupling of this kind occurs; for example the touch panels could be encircled by a loop of cable carrying alternating current.

Apart from the question of selecting a suitable touch detector circuit, it is necessary to have a touch panel. This is usually of conducting glass and is incorporated in the visual display. An alternative to conducting glass is the use of small-area opaque conductors mounted in the surface of the display screen,

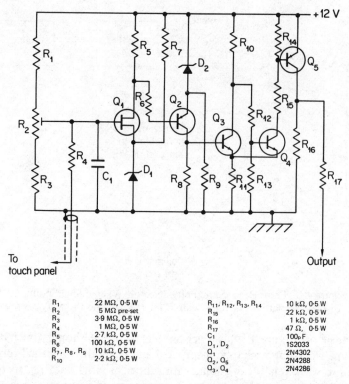

R_1	22 MΩ, 0·5 W	R_{11}, R_{12}, R_{13}, R_{14}	10 kΩ, 0·5 W
R_2	5 MΩ pre-set	R_{15}	22 kΩ, 0·5 W
R_3	3·9 MΩ, 0·5 W	R_{16}	1 kΩ, 0·5 W
R_4	1 MΩ, 0·5 W	R_{17}	47 Ω, 0·5 W
R_5	2·7 kΩ, 0·5 W	C_1	100μF
R_6	100 kΩ, 0·5 W	D_1, D_2	1S2033
R_7, R_8, R_9	10 kΩ, 0·5 W	Q_1	2N4302
R_{10}	2·2 kΩ, 0·5 W	Q_2, Q_5	2N4288
		Q_3, Q_4	2N4286

Figure 4.19 Circuit diagram of a field effect transistor (FET) input touch detector. Potentiometer R_2 is adjusted so that FET Q_1 is just conducting. The other transistors amplify so that the output will be close to zero volts. When the touch panel is operated the resistance between the FET gate and earth is reduced by leakage through the subject's body. This causes a fall in the gate voltage which when amplified will results in the output rising to nearly 12 volts

such as have been used in air traffic control terminals (Orr and Hopkin, 1968). This technique is particularly suited to the selection of one of a number of small elements in a display. However, in displays intended for use by young children responses are generally required to large discrete panels and so conducting glass panels are the usual choice.

Two forms of conducting glass are commonly used for touch panels. Sheet glass can be bought as a stock item with a conducting layer of stannic oxide fused into one surface. Nesa glass, as it is known, has an electrical resistance of about 30–40 ohms per square area and the coating affects the optical transmission only to a very small degree. The second form of conducting glass can be prepared locally by an optical works or laboratory equipped with vacuum coating plant. A thin film of metal is evaporated onto the surface of the glass. Cleary and Packham (1968) have found chromium to be a suitable metallic coating. It has adequate resistance to handling and normal use if the surface has been thoroughly cleansed and degassed before coating. A coating which gives an optical transmission of 60% is satisfactory and has an electrical resistance of approximately 1000 ohms per square area. The slightly greater loss of light with chromium coated glass is not usually important and this minor disadvantage is offset by the ability to coat a specially designed piece of glass in those areas required for use as touch panels. Separate areas can be coated by placing a mask over the glass in the areas to be left clear. Glass of substantial thickness can be used to withstand possible abuse by young subjects. It is even possible to evaporate chromium onto the untreated surface of Lenscreen coated glass, thereby creating a combined rear-projection screen and touch panel. The stannic oxide coating can only be applied to glass in the semi-molten state. If separate coated areas are required on a single sheet the unwanted areas must be removed by acid etching after protecting the wanted areas with lacquer. For a review of coating techniques see Holland (1956).

Whatever form of coating is used it is necessary to make an electrical connection between the coating on the glass and the touch detecting circuits. A simple method is to use a spring contact, set in the mounting frame which holds the glass. If the glass is allowed any free movement trouble can arise due to the edges of the spring making minute scratches in the coating. Although both types of coating are reasonably resistant to rubbing by soft materials, scratches in the coating can produce areas which are electrically insulated from the main body of the coating. Preferred methods of making contact with the coating are either to drill holes in the glass through the coated areas, but beyond the display areas, and to screw a solder tag faced with a soft metal washer to the glass (Figure 4.20) or to flame-spray areas at the edge of the coating with copper so that a conventional soldered joint can be made directly.

Carefully prepared touch panels can give years of service, but should the coated surface become scratched, areas of the panel may immediately become

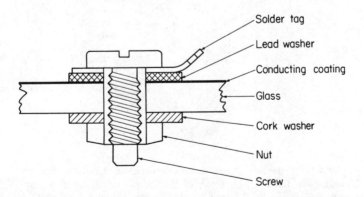

Figure 4.20 Recommended method of making screw contact to a conducting coating. The nut should be sealed with a locking compound

insensitive. Therefore care should be taken to dissuade subjects from taking sharp toys or trinkets into an experimental room when such panels are in use as children tend to move the toys about on the display. It is also a wise precaution to have a completely prepared square panel at hand and to design the mounting system so that replacement can be effected fairly rapidly.

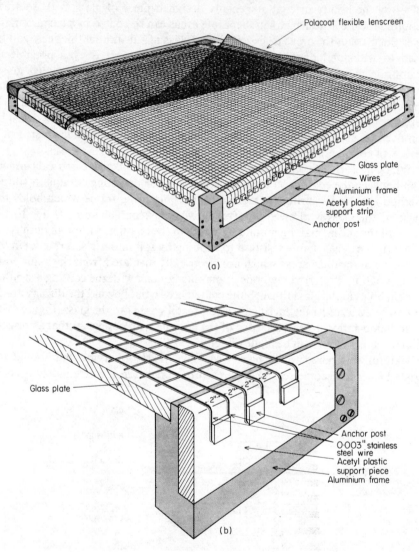

Polacoat flexible lenscreen

Glass plate
Wires
Aluminium frame
Acetyl plastic support strip
Anchor post

(a)

Glass plate

Anchor post
0·003" stainless steel wire
Acetyl plastic support piece
Aluminium frame

(b)

Figure 4.21 A flexible touch screen designed at Learning Research and Development Center, University of Pittsburgh. (a) An overall view of the screen. For clarity, the full number of wires is not shown. (b) A sectional view of the screen. The support pieces are movable to adjust the clearance between the row and the column wires. The anchor posts form part of the support pieces

Considerable development work on a different type of touch panel has been undertaken at the Learning Research and Development Center, University of Pittsburgh (Fitzhugh and Katsuki, 1971). Particularly interesting is their design (Figure 4.21) for a wire–wire touch screen which uses flexible Lenscreen for its front surface and therefore doubles as a rear-projection screen. This screen was so designed that the location of the point of touch on the screen surface could be located, the X and Y coordinates being read by computer to a resolution of 1 in 9 on each axis. This allows considerable flexibility in the location of items on the screen when used as a CAI terminal. A simplified version of such a screen with three fixed response areas in which the groups of wires are connected in parallel was in regular use for two years at the University of Newcastle upon Tyne. This experience confirmed Fitzhugh and Katsuki's claim that their basic design performs reliably.

Finally in this section we shall note an area of development which seeks to widen the range of responses to which training techniques may be applied. Electronic aids are now available for the physically disabled which allow residual responses such as mouth suction and pressure, single finger or chin movements (see Figure 4.22) to be translated into signals which can control various items of technological equipment, such as telephones, tape recorders,

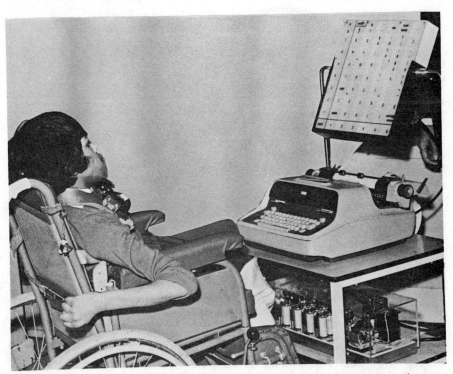

Figure 4.22 A POSSUM selector type 1A/5A with the visual indicator above the typewriter, being controlled through chin operated microswitches

electric typewriters etc. as in the case of the POSSUM selector (Maling and Clarkson, 1963). Most applications of such devices to date have been with adults, but it seems clear that if automated teaching systems were used in conjunction with a POSSUM selector the educational benefits to a severely disabled child could be very great. Once such a child had been trained using matching-to-sample paradigms and introduced to simple written material it would be possible to progress to conventional CAI through an interface which simulated a computer keyboard terminal or, if available, to a two-way cable television teaching system (Section 5.4).

4.4 Control logic

Control of the logical sequence of operations in an automated teaching system may be considered to occur at a number of levels. At the highest level are specified the rules which define the interrelation between the black box components of Figure 4.1. Examples of such rules might be, 'give a reinforcer only im-

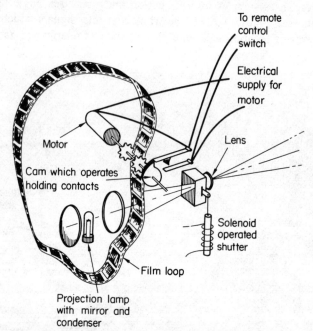

Figure 4.23 Diagrammatic representation of a serial access projection device. The motor drives directly on the same shaft as both the film sprocket wheels and a cam. The number of sprockets are such that each revolution advances the film one frame. When the motor is briefly switched on by closure of the remote control switch, the cam moves allowing the holding contacts to close, thus keeping the motor energised until it has completed one revolution

mediately following a correct response' or 'present a new stimulus display only when an incorrect response has occurred or immediately after the presentation of a reinforcer'. This level of control specifies the fundamental relationship between the hardware and the student, that is the contingencies which follow from the student's responses. At a somewhat lower level of control is the logic which is responsible for operations such as determining whether a response is correct or incorrect by reference to coded information relating to the particular stimuli being presented or determining the next frame number to be presented on the basis of the present frame number and the subject's response. The lowest level of control is the logic which is concerned with detailed operation of the hardware which is specific to a particular implementation of a system. For example, a hypothetical system may have a requirement for the display of any one of 16 items of visual information on demand. This small number is chosen to simplify the description in this example; the principles illustrated would be applicable to a much larger number of items. Let us assume that two different types of frame selection mechanism are available, each requiring quite different types of control logic. Figure 4.23 illustrates one of the devices. It is basically serial access and does not provide any indication of the frame number which is currently being displayed. As our requirement is to be able to display any one of the frames we need some way of keeping track of the frame numbers. One way of doing this would be to have the frame number coded on the film in a machine-readable form. This is usually done in the form of a binary coded number, and to code the numbers 0 to 15 decimal we would need four binary digits. A white patch could be used to represent a 1 and a black patch to indicate a 0 as shown in Figure 4.24. The binary patches could be read by four photocells

Decimal number	Binary number $2^3 2^2 2^1 2^0$	Coded patches
0	0000	■■■■
1	0001	■■■□
2	0010	■■□■
3	0011	■■□□
4	0100	■□■■
5	0101	■□■□
6	0110	■□□■
7	0111	■□□□
8	1000	□■■■
9	1001	□■■□
10	1010	□■□■
11	1011	□■□□
12	1100	□□■■
13	1101	□□■□
14	1110	□□□■
15	1111	□□□□

Figure 4.24 Method of coding frame numbers using binary coded patches

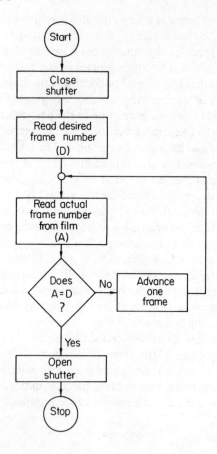

Figure 4.25 Flow chart for control of a serial access film transport with absolute addresses coded on the film

with a light source on the other side of the film or on some part of the mechanism which is positively linked to the frame to be displayed. This is known as absolute addressing. Figure 4.25 shows a typical flow chart for control logic to allow the serial access film transport to be advanced to any specified frame. A more economical but less reliable method of addressing is relative addressing, in which a separate counter keeps a tally of changes in the film position after initial synchronisation of the film and the counter. Figure 4.26 shows a flow chart for a simple form of logical control which provides for the relative addressing of the serial access film transport illustrated in Figure 4.23. In this case only single frame advances are made at a time. The counter which keeps track of the current frame number would be arranged to reset after reaching 15 because the film is in the form of an endless loop. Clearly, if the mechanism were also capable of going into reverse, the control logic could be made more sophisticated and the average random access time reduced. However, the basic situation would still be that a serial access mechanical device is being converted by appropriate logic into a fairly slow random access device. A second type of mechanism which might be used is one in which the transparencies are arranged on sheet film in

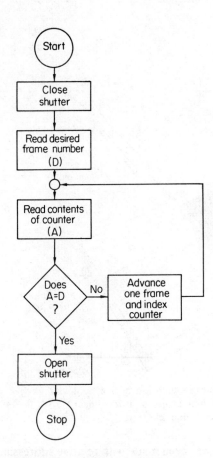

Figure 4.26 Flow chart for control of a serial access film transport using relative addressing

a 4 by 4 matrix and each axis of the transparency holder is fitted with a digital linear actuator which is capable of taking any one of the four positions on demand (Figure 4.27). Frame selection is achieved merely by splitting the four-bit representation of the frame number into two and using each half to drive one of the digital linear actuators. The device will therefore go directly from one frame to another in the matrix. A shutter mechanism may still be incorporated in order to blank out movement from the screen. As will be seen from the foregoing discussion, apart from such considerations as access time and reliability, either form of mechanism would be suitable for our hypothetical system but the forms of logical control required would differ greatly. As has been indicated the use of absolute addressing is fairly rare in automated teaching systems. Its use in a tape player would lead to quite complicated logical control, for the item number would have to be recorded on the tape in serial form and so, on replay, a serial to parallel conversion would be necessary to make a comparison with the desired item number. However, it should be realised that automated systems can be in use regularly, day after day, making hundreds of thousands of operations a year. Even if the engineering is of a high standard failures can arise from external causes, such as temporary loss of

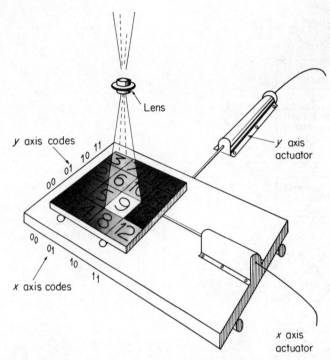

Figure 4.27 A diagrammatic representation of a 4 by 4
matrix random access sheet film projector using linear
digital actuators for frame selection

electrical power, and once a single error has been made with relative addressing
all frames will be incorrectly located. The problem is less acute when dealing
with older children or adults who are usually sufficiently sophisticated to realise
that something is wrong with the sequence of material being presented. If
relative addressing systems are used with younger or retarded children some
consistency check should be made from time to time in order to ensure that the
children are not subjected to extended periods of training on inconsistent
materials.

Logical control circuits are usually based on solid state devices (digital
transistor or integrated circuits) or electromechanical devices (relays, cam
operated microswitches etc.). The modular programming systems devised for
controlling psychological experiments are ideal for use as control logic in
experimental automated teaching systems. Two basic families of modular
programming equipment are manufactured: relay logic (Hetzel and Hetzel,
1969) and solid state logic. In general terms relay logic is best for small-scale,
simple systems and solid state logic is best for large, complicated systems.

When the control logic is very complex, involving say decisions based on an
analysis of the nature of the subject's past responses or on the type of errors, it is
probably worth considering the use of a computer to control the system. A

modern mini-computer can be purchased for a cost equivalent to that of a moderately large collection of modular programming equipment. This point will be taken up again in Section 5.5.1.

4.5 Knowledge of results

In systems designed for use with older children or adults, knowledge of results often takes the form of either a specimen answer when a constructed response is required (e.g. Figure 1.9) or it is included in the text along with the stimulus material in a branching programme (e.g. Figure 1.4). As discussed in Section 4.3 the former method is hardly suitable for our target population and the latter method is dependent upon the subject's comprehension being sufficiently developed. In most systems designed for young or retarded children explicit reinforcers have been used for knowledge of results. The reinforcer may take the form of a material reward, such as a sweet (M & M in the USA or Smartie in the UK), or it may be a sensory reinforcer, such as a flash of light or the chime of a bell.

Because of the week nature of the reinforcers available for use with children and the impracticability of instituting adequate deprivation regimes, rapid satiation presents a serious problem and much effort has been devoted to the development of durable reinforcers for experimental use with children. For a review of this topic, see Bijou and Baer (1966).

In the case of non-material reinforcers many of the techniques which have been described for stimulus presentation are suitable, the only difference being in the contingent nature of the control of reinforcement by the machine logic. However, there is a tendency for the stimuli used as reinforcers to contain more

Figure 4.28 An animated, talking puppet for studies of social reinforcement with young children (from Baer (1962))

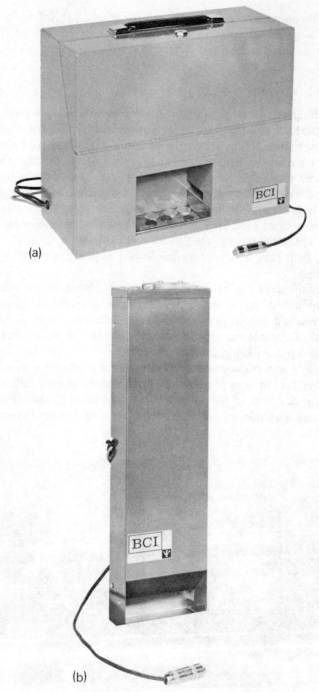

Figure 4.29 (a) Coin and (b) candy dispensers which can
be operated by remote contact closure

unpredictable or novel elements, presumably in an attempt to counter satiation. Devices which have been used as reinforcers and are not normally used for stimulus presentation include remotely controlled mechanised toys with interesting routines (Bijou and Baer, 1966) and an articulated puppet (Figure 4.28) with a mouth which moves as speech sounds are played through a loud-speaker (Baer, 1962). In many cases reinforcing material can be presented by tape or motion picture film without the same need to maintain control in relation to the material content as is usual in stimulus presentation. Thus Baer (1961) used movie cartoons as an ongoing state of positive reinforcement which could be terminated in the absence of a required response. The cartoons were of the 'Woody Woodpecker' type and were projected by means of an endless loop sound projector with integral rear-projection screen. Withdrawal of the cartoon reinforcer was accomplished automatically by operating a shutter in front of the projector lens and breaking the loudspeaker circuit. Jeffrey (1955) used taped music presented through earphones. St. James-Roberts (1973) used a series of rear-illuminated transparencies which built up to form a cartoon story in an operantly based audiometer for use with language disordered children (see Section 3.2.3).

When material reinforcers (e.g. tokens, candy, trinkets etc.) are used, some form of dispenser, such as those illustrated in Figure 4.29 is required. Many forms of dispensers suitable for a variety of materials are produced by manufacturers of control equipment for operant conditioning studies. They are usually operated by solenoid and merely require the switching of a suitable electricity supply for a minimum duration to actuate the dispensing mechanism. In our experience material reinforcers have been generally less effective than non-material ones. The former present mechanical difficulties in delivery, are less easy to vary and more liable to satiation effects. More importantly, material reinforcers carry little information content, i.e. simply that the preceding response was correct or incorrect. In contrast, by using non-material reinforcers a wide range of information in one or more modalities can be presented.

4.6 Monitoring performance

Some form of monitoring the subject's performance is required in any teaching system. At minimum it is necessary to know when the task has been completed to criterion, even if this only means reaching the last frame in the program. The completion criterion may be more complicated than this, for it may be specified in terms of response rate, probability of a correct response or some other performance measure. In these cases some form of instrumentation is necessary, though we would stress the need to specify the requirements in advance and to relate them to facilities for subsequent analysis.

Response data may be collected on an event recorder (Figure 4.30) in the form of a visible record in a moving chart. This allows a variety of analyses to be made and is particularly useful for analysing responses to a program with a view to remedying any unusually difficult or easy frames, or for recording

96

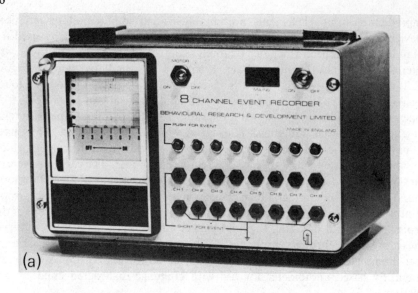

(a)

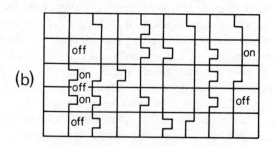

(b)

Figure 4.30 (a) An 8-channel event recorder. Each
channel can be operated either by a local pushbutton or by
remote contact closure. (b) A sample record

experimental data. However, if much work of this kind is envisaged it is probably worth collecting the data on punched tape or in some other machine
readable form for subsequent computer analysis (see Section 5.5.2).

In this section we are primarily concerned with techniques which allow
a decision to be made in real-time that a task has been performed to
criterion. Data recorders only help us to make decisions between sessions.
It is often useful to detect the attainment of criterion performance during
the session, since it is more economical of both the subject's and experimenter's time. Additionally, if the task is a prerequisite for some further stage
of training, the control over the subject's entry behaviour to the second stage is
improved. When the subject has mastered a task he is likely to satiate rapidly
and will be less willing to participate in further sessions with similar equipment.
Consider a typical colour matching-to-sample task. The experimenter may

specify as his criterion performance that ten consecutive responses are correct. The apparatus could consist of translucent response panels illuminated by coloured lamps. Modular programming equipment could be used to control an endless sequence of presentation and further modules could continuously monitor runs of correct responses. When a criterion run length is detected the experimenter can be automatically notified and the session terminated. Figure 4.31 shows a flow chart for a form of control logic which would provide performance monitoring of this kind. The use of real-time performance monitoring does not conflict with collection of response data. It is still possible to connect an event recorder to the apparatus for subsequent analysis.

Rather than expressing the criterion as a run length one might prefer to express it in terms of the probability of a correct response. If one is measuring a stable performance then the probability can be estimated by dividing the number of correct responses by the total number of responses. These totals can

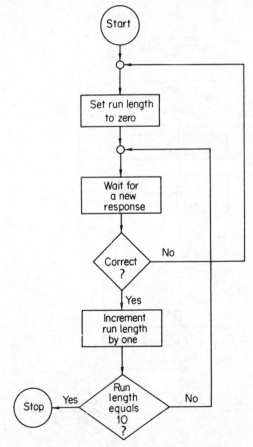

Figure 4.31 Flow chart for logic to stop training
when the criterion that ten successive responses
should be correct has been achieved

98

easily be counted using an electromechanical counter. However, as we are explicitly trying to change behaviour this is hardly a valid procedure for, if the training is effective, the indicated performance will be lowered by the subject's early high error rate. To calculate a running average in real-time requires the repeated division of the number of correct responses by the total number of responses and this could be achieved by on-line connection to a digital computer. An alternative procedure is to treat groups of say 50 responses and to calculate the proportion which is correct in each group. Continuous monitoring on this basis could be readily carried out using modular programming equipment and a suitable flow chart is shown in Figure 4.32. A print-out counter, which is an electromechanical counter with printing mechanism, could be used to give a

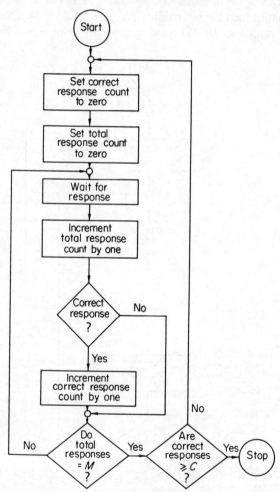

Figure 4.32 Flow chart for a logical procedure to test whether C or more correct responses have occurred in a series of M responses

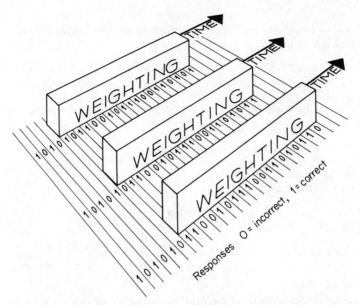

Figure 4.33 Representation of the method of computing a moving
average, equal weight being given to the last 19 responses

permanent record of the number of responses which were correct in each
group.

However, it is unsatisfactory to test performance after every so many responses have elapsed. Ideally one should check at every response. One solution
is to compute a moving average (Figure 4.33), that is to calculate the proportion
of correct responses in the last M responses as every new response occurs. This is
rather difficult to do automatically without a computer on-line to the experiment, for the subject's responses have to be stored in a way which preserves
sequential information. In addition, there is still persistent doubt about arbi-
trarily assigning the same weight to the Mth response back as one does to the
most recent response, but zero weight to the $(M + 1)$th response which is only
one response older.

When we calculate performance measures which are estimates of the current
probability of a correct response and, given that we have reason to think that
this probability is changing, we should assign the greatest weight to the most
recent response and gradually reduce the weights for the older responses. Our
best prediction will be based on the most recent response, but as we are dealing
with binary data (correct or incorrect, 1 or 0) we are forced to take a larger
sample than one in order to form any kind of estimate of the probability. The
exponentially weighted moving average (Figure 4.34) has desirable characteristics for this purpose. It gives greatest weight to the most recent response
and the weight given to older responses decreases geometrically with the age
of the response. If the weight given to the current response x_n is α, then the
weights given to successively older responses must be reduced by the factor

$(1 - \alpha)$ for each response. The subject's performance level $S(x)$ at the nth response will then be given by

$$S_n(x) = \alpha x_n + \alpha(1 - \alpha)x_{n-1} + \alpha(1 - \alpha)^2 x_{n-2} + \alpha(1 - \alpha)^3 x_{n-3} + \dots$$
$$+ \alpha(1 - \alpha)^r x_{n-r} + \dots + \alpha(1 - \alpha)^n x_1 \qquad (4.1)$$

Similarly if we had considered the performance at the $(n - 1)$th response it would have been

$$S_{n-1}(x) = \alpha x_{n-1} + \alpha(1 - \alpha)x_{n-2} + \dots + \alpha(1 - \alpha)^{r-1} x_{n-r} + \dots$$
$$+ \alpha(1 - \alpha)^{n-1} x_1 \qquad (4.2)$$

Rearranging Equation 4.1

$$S_n(x) = \alpha x_n + (1 - \alpha)\left[\alpha x_{n-1} + \alpha(1 - \alpha)x_{n-2} + \dots\right.$$
$$\left. + \alpha(1 - \alpha)^{r-1} x_{n-r} + \dots + \alpha(1 - \alpha)^{n-1} x_1\right] \qquad (4.3)$$

Substituting from Equation 4.2 in Equation 4.3 we have

$$S_n(x) = \alpha x_n + (1 - \alpha)S_{n-1}(x)$$

The practical importance of this result is that only one value, the performance level at the previous response, needs to be stored. At each response the performance level is computed by adding a proportion, α, of the value of the new response to a proportion $(1 - \alpha)$ of the value of the previous performance level. This operation smooths out variations in the responses and α is known as

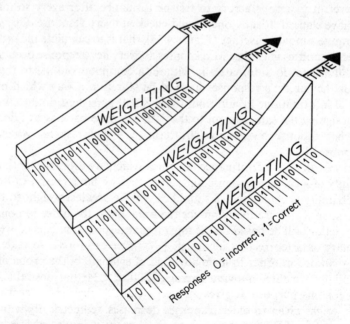

Figure 4.34 Similar representation of an exponentially weighted moving average. In this case $\alpha = 0.1$ and the smoothing effect is equivalent to the normal moving average of Figure 4.33

the smoothing constant. Exponential smoothing has been shown to provide an efficient estimation for the mean of a discrete time series (Brown, 1963) and is widely used in forecasting and statistical process control. Thus we have a measure which appears intuitively plausible, has well established properties and is computationally convenient.

Low values of α effectively give averaging over a large number of responses, that is greater smoothing, but a larger lag if the probability of a correct response is changing. High values of α reduce the lag but give less smoothing. If the smoothing effects of exponentially weighted and normal moving averages are compared, it can be shown that the equivalent length of the former is $\frac{2-\alpha}{\alpha}$ responses. Thus $\alpha = 0\cdot1$ has a smoothing effect equivalent to averaging over 19 responses and $\alpha = 0\cdot01$ is equivalent to averaging over 199 responses. Ideally α should be adjusted to suit the rate of learning expected from each subject. In practice a value of $0\cdot1$ is satisfactory, as few subjects show such a rate of learning that any appreciable lag is likely and the smoothing is sufficient for there to be a negligible chance of reaching a criterion performance of say $0\cdot9$ under conditions of random responding (Cleary and Packham, 1968).

Exponential smoothing is the performance measure which was used in the Touch-Tutor (Section 3.2.4). The circuit of the performance computer is relatively simple, being a form of analogue computer based on the controlled charge and discharge of a capacitor. The voltage across the capacitor represents the current performance level. The original circuit (Cleary and Packham, 1968) used a valve to provide the drive to a meter indicator. In the current version this is replaced by a field effect transistor. Apart from its use in the Touch-Tutor the performance computer is available as a module compatible with a range of modular programming equipment.

When performance can be computed on-line in this manner it is possible to use it to control the difficulty of the task. A series of experiments with the Touch-Tutor has been aimed at an investigation of the effects of varying the intensity of cueing in relation to the amount by which a child's current performance level falls short of some predetermined level. This has, in effect, represented an attempt to develop this machine into an adaptive system.

Two methods of cueing have been investigated, varying the visual intensity of the distractors and varying the intensity of the auditory stimulus which names the correct alternative. For the variable brightness experiment an electronic control unit was designed which allowed the optical transmission to be varied in proportion to the output of the performance computer and a preset performance level. For the audio-cueing an amplifier was constructed which could be controlled in a similar manner. In this case cueing was provided by naming of the stimulus prior to the child touching the response panel, the audio volume being determined by the current performance level.

In all 56 pre-school children were tested on a beginning reading program over eight sessions using these adaptive cueing techniques. The results indicated that auditory cueing was more effective than visual in raising the children's initial performance towards the predetermined level, although the overall rates of learning and final performance under the two conditions were very similar. The data suggested that training with auditory cueing may well be about twice as effective as training with visual cueing in the early stages. These techniques have not, however, yet been evaluated with handicapped children.

4.7 Summary

We reviewed the various devices which may be used as components in an automated teaching system giving special consideration to the requirements for experimentation with our target population. Figure 4.1 indicates the relationship between these components. For stimulus presentation devices we restricted our considerations to the visual and auditory modalities, as they are likely to cover the vast majority of applications. In discussing the detection of responses we gave main emphasis to the various types of touch detecting panels which can be incorporated into the stimulus display. The requirements of control logic and synchronisation of media were reviewed. For many purposes modular programming systems as used in psychological experimentation are suitable, but for sophisticated control problems mini-computers (Section 5.5.1) may be used. Knowledge of results will often be provided by the same kind of displays as are used for the presentation of stimuli, but dispensers are needed for material reinforcers. The problems of monitoring performance to allow decisions to be made during the training process were discussed. The collection of data for subsequent computer analysis will be considered in the next chapter.

CHAPTER 5

Computer Applications

5.1 The uses of computers in education

It is not necessary in this chapter to do more than give the flavour of the workings of a computer system. The reader who wishes to pursue computer applications seriously should consult a specialised text. Fields (1973) is a short, readable review of the workings and use of modern computer systems. A technical introduction to mini-computers and their use in scientific and technical work is given in Korn (1973). Books which cover applications related to psychology are Uttal (1967) and Apter and Westby (1973).

For our present pruposes it is sufficient to regard the computer as a device which is capable of carrying out at high speed a set of logical operations on the information it receives from various input devices, such as keyboards, punched card readers, laboratory instruments etc. The result of these logical operations may be directed to various output devices, such as printers, graphic displays, card punches etc. The computer will also have some form of internal data storage and retrieval, which on large machines may be of very great capacity.

The logical operations which the computer carried out on the data are determined by the computer program. This is stored in the memory of the computer and may be changed very easily. Thus the same machine can be used for varied purposes. It is also normal practice to use the computer to help write and develop these programs, so that progressively more powerful computer programs can be developed.

Let us briefly review the possible applications of computers in education. There are two general purpose applications which are common to many other disciplines, commercial data processing (e.g. accounting and record keeping) and scientific data processing (e.g. statistical and other mathematical analyses of data). Well established techniques exist in these areas and it matters little whether the subject matter is education or any other discipline. The third area is the use of computers directly to assist in the educational process itself. There are broadly two forms of approach here: (i) the use of the computer as a sophis- ticated teaching machine which presents the instructional material to the student and interprets his response, known as computer-assisted instruction (CAI), and (ii) the use of the computer to assist the teacher in managing the educational process by assessing the student's capabilities and prescribing a course of instruction, known as computer-managed instruction (CMI). In this chapter we will briefly review the development and future potential of CAI and

CMI and assess their possible application to early childhood education. We will also consider the use of mini-computers and data collection devices for experimental purposes.

5.2 Computer-assisted instruction

The use of computers for administrative and commercial purposes, such as invoicing and the payment of salaries will be familiar to most readers. The way in which computers can be used for CAI will not be so widely known and consequently it may be of value to review the way in which CAI systems operate.

Because of the very high speed of operation of the digital computer, it can switch rapidly between a number of different terminals, appearing to handle them simultaneously. This is known as time-sharing and is the mode of operation adopted in almost all large computer systems. In the case of CAI each student may be working at a different stage in a particular course or be taking a completely different course. In the simplest mode of operation, the student sits at a teletypewriter which is something like an electric typewriter. Messages are typed from the computer and the student types his responses on the keyboard. To augment a simple teletypewriter terminal, perhaps the next most important feature would be a device which could deliver audio messages under computer control. The next step might be to add a graphical and pictorial display such as a computer-controlled television terminal or slide projector. In most cases the terminal is restricted to a simple keyboard printer of the type shown in Figure 5.1. Terminals with audio and graphical facilities are not widely needed for normal computing purposes and do not benefit from the economies of large-scale production.

Thus the computer can be used to teach a large number of students. How is this different from a lecturer in the lecture theatre, film or television? The main argument in favour of CAI is its ability to provide individualised instruction. Children differ widely in their abilities. They work at different rates and with different levels of accuracy and comprehension. For obvious economic reasons conventional schools cannot offer courses of instruction tailored to meet the needs of each individual child. However, the computer, whilst simultaneously handling many students, can allow each to proceed at his own pace and level of achievement. As in the case of other automated teaching systems an important aspects of CAI is the provision of immediate knowledge of results. The system also demands the attention of the student during the entire session, just as would an individual tutor.

Three possible levels of interaction between student and the computer in a CAI system have been proposed by Suppes (1966): (i) drill-and-practice systems, (ii) tutorial systems and (iii) dialogue systems. Discrimination between these levels is not based on hardware considerations but rather on the complexity and sophistication of the student–system interaction. Thus the dialogue mode, involving the highest level of interaction, may be achieved with only a simple teletypewriter terminal, whilst for some purposes even the simplest drill-and-

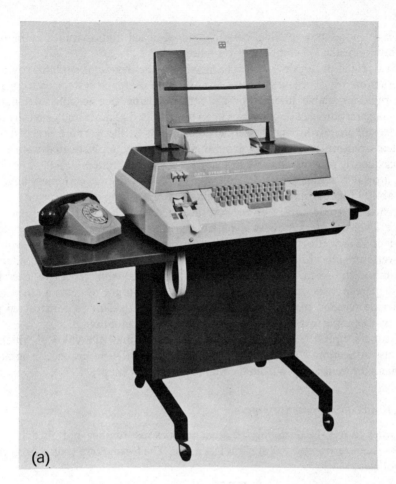

(a)

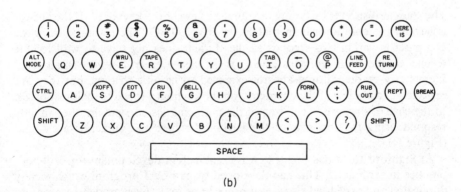

(b)

Figure 5.1 The ASR 390 teletypewriter (a). (b) shows a typical keyboard arrangement. Some of the special keys are intended for communications applications, but the extra keys are often used in computing

practice mode may involve, perhaps, a specialised audio-visual terminal and highly sophisticated computer programming.

At one end of Suppes's scale characterising the degree of student–computer interaction are dialogue systems. The aim with dialogue systems is to provide the richest possible interaction, the student being free to construct natural language responses, ask questions in an unrestricted manner and generally to be free to take control over the sequence of events in the learning process. Such systems require text analysis programs of a highly sophisticated nature and consequently progress in these systems has been very limited.

Tutorial systems, which lie midway between the two extremes, have the capability for real-time decision making and branching contingent on a single response or some subset of the response history. The aim is to provide the same level of interaction as a patient tutor would have with an individual student. Every effort is made to avoid an initial experience of failure with the slower student, whilst on the other hand the program should have sufficient flexibility to avoid boring the brighter students with repetitive exercises. Student responses are more restricted than in dialogue systems as they must either be selected from a prescribed set of alternatives or so constructed that relatively simple text analysis will suffice for their evaluation.

At the simplest level are drill-and-practice routines (the value of which we discuss in Section 7.1). Let us consider a typical drill-and-practice program in elementary mathematics from the Stanford project (Suppes, 1971).

5.2.1 A drill-and-practice program

In order to use the terminal, the student types his number and his first name. The system responds by typing his last name. The format of a simple problem is as follows:

$$8 \times 9 = \quad - \quad - \quad -$$

The student responds by typing the numeric keys of the keyboard. If the answer is wrong, the computer immediately types WRONG. The response from the computer is within two seconds so the student does not have to wait for the teacher to check his work, as usually is the case even with a very small class. Elementary-grade children are not expected to be able to type, but they are expected to use a few of the characters on the keyboard to make their responses. In the case of first-grade children in the mathematics curriculum, they mainly respond using the top row of the keyboard where the numerals are found (Figure 5.1).

At Stanford there has been extensive curriculum development for drill-and-practice in arithmetic. This had developed from a CAI program which merely duplicated and expedited classroom procedures for a given grade to a program which is intended to provide the most efficient drill for a given individual through all the grade levels. Thus instead of basing the problems on the individual's grade and the subject matter usually taught in that grade, the program keeps track of the concepts which the child has already mastered and determines those which should be learned next.

This attention to the learner rather than to the classroom resulted in the drill-and-practice programs being reorganised into ungraded strands, such as number concepts, vertical and horizontal addition, equations, fractions etc. The student works on several strands simultaneously, beginning at the bottom of a strand and moving upward as his performance on the strand improves. Since the movement along the strand depends on the student, the differing levels of performance on the various strands create different sets of problems for each student. Thus, unlike the traditional classroom exercises, each student will be solving a different set of problems, each set of problems containing problem types from each strand appropriate to the ability of the particular student.

The strand system consists of three major elements:

(1) *A curriculum structure.* This contains 15 strands, each of which includes all problem types of a given concept (e.g. fractions, equations) or of a major sub-type of a concept (e.g. horizontal addition, vertical multiplication) presented in grades 1–6. Within a strand the problems of a homogeneous type are grouped into an equivalence class. The strand contains either five or ten classes per half year with each equivalence class labelled in terms of a grade-placement level. In addition to this ordering of problems within a strand there is also provision for controlling the emphasis given on each strand at a particular point during the academic year. This is known as the curriculum distribution.

(2) *Rules for sampling the problems.* The curriculum distribution may be considered to reflect the proportion of problems from each strand which would be presented in a notional average textbook. If a student has an equal level of performance on all strands he will be given problems from each strand purely according to the emphasis dictated by the curriculum distribution. However, in order to take account of individual differences in performance, a sampling function has been defined to modify the curriculum distribution in those cases when there are differing levels of performance between strands. This function is calculated weekly and results in greater emphasis being given to those strands on which the student has a lower level of performance.

(3) *Progress through the strand structure.* The rate at which a student progresses through the strand structure depends on his performance on each strand. For the equivalence classes on each strand criteria are set such that after a defined number of problems on that class, he is advanced one equivalence class if more than a certain number are correct. If less than a certain number are correct he is moved down one equivalence class.

Suppes and Morningstar (1969) report that this CAI program gave average increases in grade-placement of 1·14 on the Stanford Achievement Test for experimental student over a three-month period, as compared with an average of 0·26 for control students.

108

5.2.2 Tutorial systems

The Stanford Tutorial System was developed under a contract between the university and IBM. Subsequent development by IBM resulted in the IBM 1500 instructional system which was commercially manufactured. The basic system (Figure 5.2) consists of a central process control computer with accompanying disc drives, tutor stations and an interface to 16 student stations. The central computer acts as an intermediary between each student and his particular course material which is stored on disc. A student terminal (Figure 5.3) incorporates a film projector, CRT display, light pen, keyboard and an audio system which can play pre-recorded messages under computer control.

The Stanford CAI reading program (Atkinson, 1968) provides an example of a tutorial program. The major response device used in this program is the light

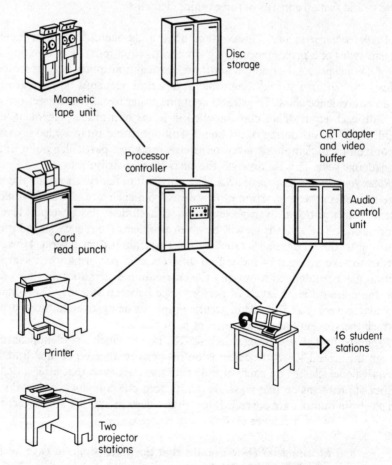

Figure 5.2 System configuration for the Stanford CAI tutorial system. (Copyright 1968, by the American Psychological Association. Reprinted by permission)

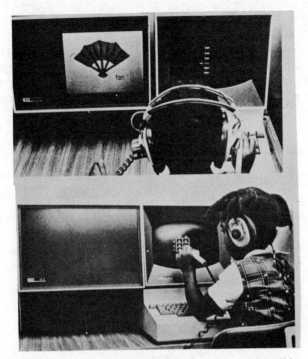

Figure 5.3 The IBM 1500 student station. The slide projection screen is on the left and the CRT display on the right

pen. This is a light sensitive probe which sends the coordinates of the point touched on the display screen to the computer.

The instructional materials are divided into eight levels each comprising about 32 lessons. Details of the curriculum materials are given in Wilson and Atkinson (1967) and Rodgers (1967). The lessons are designed so that an average student completes each one in about 30 minutes, depending on the amount of remedial material required. Within a lesson the various instructional tasks can be divided into three broad areas: (i) decoding skills, (ii) comprehension skills and (iii) games and other motivational devices. Decoding skills involve letter and letter-spring identification, phonic drill and related activities. Comprehension involves such tasks as having the computer present a short story about which the child is then asked a series of questions. Finally, many different games are included along with the other tasks primarily to encourage continued attention to the materials. The games are similar to those played in classrooms and are structured to evaluate the developing reading skills of the child.

A typical task from the decoding skills area is what Atkinson terms matrix construction. This task provides practice in learning to associate orthographically similar sequences with appropriate rhyme and alliteration patterns. Rhyming patterns are presented in the columns of the matrix and alliteration

110

patterns in the rows of the matrix as indicated in the criterion test frame of
Figure 5.6. The matrix is constructed one cell at a time. The initial consonant
of a consonant–vowel–consonant word is termed the initial unit, and the vowel
and the final consonant are termed the final unit. The interaction of an initial
unit row and a final unit column determines the entry in any cell. In the example
to be considered the initial units are f, r, c and the final units are at, an, ag.

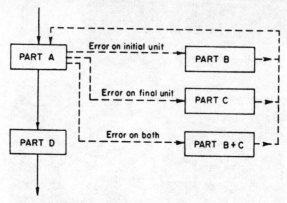

Figure 5.4 Flow chart for the construction of a cell in
the matrix construction task. (Copyright 1968, by the
American Psychological Association. Reprinted
by permission)

The problem format for the construction of each cell is divided into four
parts. Parts A and D are the standard instructional sections and parts B and C
the remedial sections. The flow chart in Figure 5.4 shows the relationship
between the parts. Remedial parts B and C are branches from part A and may
be presented independently or in combination.

In order to see how this works, consider the example shown in Figure 5.5.
The empty cell is first presented with its associated initial and final units and an
array of response choices. The student hears the audio message indicated by
RR 1 in part A. If the student gives the correct answer by touching 'ran' with his
light pen, he proceeds to part D where he sees the word written in the cell and is
given one more practice trial.

Part A is designed to identify three possible types of errors: (i) the initial unit
is correct but the final unit is not, (ii) the final unit is correct but the initial unit is
not and (iii) neither the initial unit nor the final unit are correctly identified.

If the student responds with 'fan' in part A he is branched to the remedial part
B which focuses on the initial unit of the cell. If the student is correct on part B,
he is returned to part A for a second attempt. However, if he gives a wrong
answer on part B, an arrow is displayed against the correct answer, which the
student is then asked to touch.

If the student responds to part A with 'rat', he is branched to the remedial
part C which gives additional instruction on the final unit of the cell and the
procedure is similar to that for part B. If the student responds with 'bat' he has

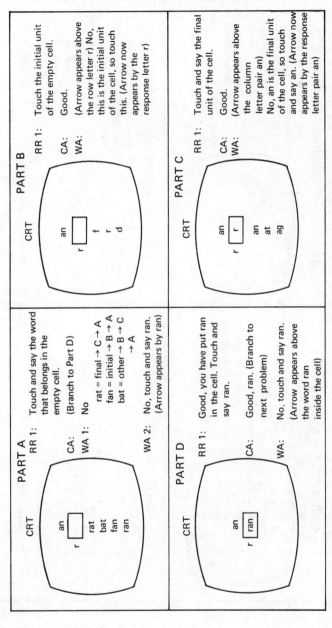

Figure 5.5 The first cell of the matrix construction task. RR = audio response request; CA = correct answer; WA = wrong answer. (Copyright 1968, by the American Psychological Association. Reprinted by permission)

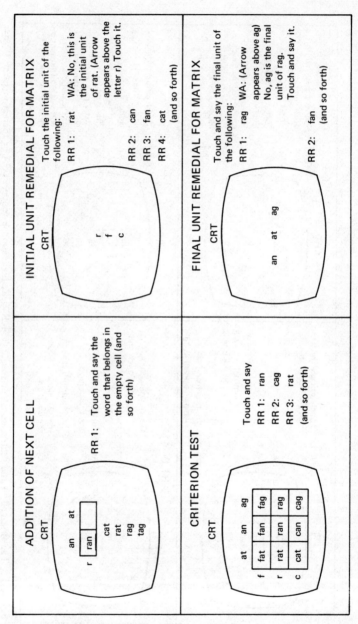

Figure 5.6 Continuation of the matrix construction task. (Copyright 1968, by the American Psychological Association. Reprinted by permission)

made an error in both the initial and final units and he is branched through both parts B and C.

When the student returns to part A after completing a remedial section, a correct answer will advance him to part D as indicated in Figure 5.4. If a wrong answer is given on the second pass, an arrow is set to point to the correct answer until the student makes the correct response.

When the student has successfully completed parts A and D, the program moves to the next word cell of the matrix using a format and sequence identical to that already described. The upper left-hand panel of Figure 5.6 shows the CRT display for adding the next cell of the example. The order in which row and column cells are added to the matrix is essentially random and the individual cell building continues until the matrix is complete.

The problems involved in translating curriculum materials into computer programs are considerable. Much effort has been devoted to writing special languages which are oriented to the problems of education, so that this translation will be simplified. The particular author language used for the Stanford reading program was Coursewriter II, developed by IBM. A coded lesson is a series of Coursewriter commands which, when executed, cause the computer to display and manipulate text on the CRT display, select and display a frame from the projector, position and play an audio message, accept and evaluate responses on the keyboard and light pen, update the performance record of the student and control the branching logic of the lesson.

A typical 30-minute lesson for the reading program would require more than 9000 Coursewriter commands.

A simple example will give some idea of the problems of coding a CAI lesson in Coursewriter. The example (Atkinson, 1968) is from a task designed to teach letter discrimination and word meaning. A picture illustrating the word to be taught is presented on the projector screen and three words, including the word illustrated, are presented on the CRT. An audio message is played asking the child to touch the word on the CRT which matches the picture on the projector screen. If the student fails to make a response within 30 seconds, he is told the correct answer, an arrow points to it and he is asked to touch it. If he responds before the time limit has expired, the area selected is compared with that defined as a correct answer. If the pen was placed on the correct answer, the student is told that he was correct and the next problem is presented. If the light pen was not placed on the correct answer, the area selected is compared with that defined for the wrong answers. If the pen was placed on a wrong answer, he is told that he was wrong, told the correct answer and asked to touch it. If his response was in an undefined area it is treated as a wrong answer, but the response is logged on the data record as undefined. The student is then allowed another attempt until he gives a correct answer, when he progresses to the next problem.

In order to prepare an instructional sequence of this kind, a programmer must write a detailed list of commands for the computer program. He must also prepare a filmstrip of the pictures and record the audio messages. The filmstrip

114

Table 5.1   Audio script and film strip with hypothetical addresses. (Copyright 1968, by the American Psychological Association. Reprinted by permission)

Address	Message
	Audio information
A01	Touch and say the word that goes with the picture.
A02	Good. Bag. Do the next one.
A03	No.
A04	The word that goes with the picture is bag. Touch and say bag.
A05	Good. Card. Do the next one.
A06	No.
A07	The word that goes with the picture is card. Touch and say card.
	Filmstrip
F01	Picture of a bag.
F02	Picture of a card.

and audio tape have an address for each frame or message and can be called in any order, although it is more efficient to prepare them in approximately the order in which they will occur.

Table 5.1 shows the audio messages and film pictures together with hypothetical addresses required for the problem which has just been described and next problem in the program which is of similar type. Table 5.2 details the Coursewriter commands required to present these problems and analyse and record the student's responses. On the right of the commands are comments which provide an explanation of each command. When a student is at a terminal, he may complete five or ten problems of this kind per minute. Clearly, if all the instructional material had to be prepared in the detail shown here, the programming task would be a almost impossible. The task can be simplified by the use of macro-instructions which allow for the repeated use of strings of commands which differ only in certain specified ways. The string can be defined once, given a two-letter name and then used by giving a one-line macro command. This use of macros greatly reduces the effort required to program many different but basically similar problems.

Finally, Holland and Doran (1974) have described an attempt to teach young children classification skills by a program which allows the arrangement of complex reinforcement contingencies. A low error rate is attained and the computer is used to determine whether the child has fulfilled the condition for reinforcement. Holland and Doran contrast this use of a computer with that of the examples we have just been discussing. The drill-and-practice programs (Suppes, 1966) use high error frequencies to differentially weight items for drill. The Stanford reading program, on the other hand, uses a basically linear program with remedial items for incorrect responses. Both these, argue Holland and Doran, only generate a need for a computer because they ignore good programming practice.

Table 5.2 Computer commands required to present two examples of the problem described in the text. (Copyright 1968, by the American Psychological Association. Reprinted by permission)

Commands	Explanation
PR	Problem: Prepares machine for beginning of new problem.
LD 0/S1	Load: Loads zero into the error switch (S1). The role of switches and counters will be explained later.
FP F01	Film Position: Displays frame F01 (picture of a bag).
DT 5,18/bat/	Display Text: Displays 'bat' on line 5 starting in column 18 on the CRT.
DT 7,18/bag/	Displays 'bag' on line 7 starting in column 18 on the CRT.
DT 9,18/rat/	Displays 'rat' on line 9 starting in column 18 on the CRT.
AUP A01	Audio Play: Plays audio message A01. 'Touch and say the word that goes with the picture.'
L1 EP 30/ABCD1	Enter and Process: Activates the light pen; specifies the time limit (30 s.) and the problem identifier (ABCD1) that will be placed in the data record along with all responses to this problem. If a response is made within the time limit the computer skips from this command down to the CA (correct answer comparison) command. If no response is made within the time limit, the commands immediately following the EP command are executed.
AD 1/C4	Add: Adds one to the overtime counter (C4).
LD 1/S1	Loads one into the error switch (S1).
AUP A04	Plays message A04. 'The word that goes with the picture is bag. Touch and say bag.'
DT 7,16/→/	Displays arrow on line 7, column 16 (arrow pointing at 'bag').
BR L1	Branch: Branches to command labelled L1. The computer will now do that command and continue from that point.
CA 1,7,3,18/C1	Correct Answer: Compares student's response with an area one line high starting on line 7 and three columns wide starting in column 18 of the CRT. If his response falls within this area, it will be recorded in the data with the answer identifier C1. When a correct answer has been made, the commands from here down to WA (wrong answer comparison) are executed. Then the program jumps ahead to the next PR. If the response does not fall in the correct area, the machine skips from this command down to the WA command.
BR L2/S1/1	Branches to command labelled L2 if the error switch (S1) is equal to one.
AD 1/C1	Adds one to the initial correct answer counter (C1).
L2 AUP A02	Plays audio message A02. 'Good. Bag. Do the next one'.
WA 1,5,3,18/W1 } WA 1,9,3,18/W2 }	Wrong Answer: These two commands compare the student response with the areas of the two wrong answers, that is, the area one line high starting on line 5 and three columns wide starting in column 18, and the area one line high starting on line 9 and three columns wide starting in column 18. If the response falls within one of these two areas, it will be recorded with the appropriate identifier (W1 or W2). When a defined wrong answer has been made, the commands from here down to UN (undefined answer) are executed. Then the computer goes back to the EP for this problem. If the response does not fall in one of the defined wrong answer areas, the machine skips from this command down to the UN command.

Table 5.2—*Contd.*

Commands	Explanation
AD 1/C2	Adds one to the defined wrong answer counter (C2).
L3 LD 1/S1	Loads one into the error switch (S1).
AUP A03	Plays message A03. 'No.'
AUP A04	Plays message A04. 'The word that goes with the picture is bag. Touch and say bag.'
DT 7,16/→/	Displays arrow on line 7, column 16.
UN	Undefined Wrong Answer: If machine reaches this point in the program, the student has made neither a correct nor a defined wrong answer.
AD 1/C3	Adds one to the undefined answer counter (C3).
BR L3	Branches to command labelled L3. (The same thing should be done for both UN and WA answers. This branch saves repeating the commands from L3 down to UN.)
PR	Prepares the machine for next problem.
LD 0/S1 ⎫ FP F02 ⎪ DT 5,18/card/ ⎬ DT 7,18/cart/ ⎪ DT 9,18/hard/ ⎭	These commands prepare the display for the 2nd problem. Notice the new film position and new words displayed. The student: was told to 'do the next one' when he finished the last problem so he needs no audio message to begin this.
L4 EP 30/ABCD2	Light pen is activated.
AD 1/C4 ⎫ LD 1/S1 ⎪ AUP A07 ⎬ DT 5,16/→/ ⎪ BR L4 ⎭	These commands are done only if no response is made in the time limit of 30 seconds. Otherwise the machine skips to the CA command.
CA 1,5,4,18/C2	Compares response with correct answer area.
BR L5/S1/1 ⎫ AD 1/C1 ⎬ L5 AUP A05 ⎭	Adds one to the initial correct answer counter unless the error switch (S1) shows that an error has been made for this problem. The student is told he is correct and goes on to the next problem. These commands are executed only if a correct answer has been made.
WA 1,7,4,18/W3 ⎫ WA 1,9,4,18/W4 ⎭	Compare response with defined wrong answer.
AD 1/C2 ⎫ L6 LD 1/S1 ⎪ AUP A06 ⎬ AUP A07 ⎪ DT 5,16/→/ ⎭	Adds one to the defined wrong answer area and the error switch (S1) is loaded with one to show that an error has been made on this problem. The student is told he is wrong and shown the correct answer and asked to touch it. These commands are executed only if a defined wrong answer has been made.
UN	An undefined response has been made if the machine reaches this command.
AD 1/C3 ⎫ BR L6 ⎭	Adds one to the undefined answer counter and we branch up to give the same audio, etc. as is given for the defined wrong answer.

The above two problems could be presented in macro format as follows:
Problem 1: CM PW] F01] bat] bag] rat] A01] ABCD1] A04] A02] A03] 7] 1,7,3,18] C1]
Problem 2: CM PW] F02] card] cart] hard]] ABCD2] A07] A05] A 06] 5] 1,5,4,18] C2]
The command to call a macro is CM and PW is an arbitrary two-character code for the macro involving a picture-to-word match. Notice that in problem 2 there is no introductory audio message; the ']]' indicates that this parameter is not to be filled in.

If CAI is to be used in early childhood education it seems fairly clear that the terminals used must have audio and pictorial capabilities. This demands a fairly sophisticated terminal and, if the computer were to service a number of such terminals distributed throughout the community, a means of two-way data transmission between the terminals and the central computer. At present two broad approaches seem possible. One is based on the use of interactive cable television and will be treated separately in Section 5.4. The other, a more conventional approach, is to use voice grade telephone lines with data adaptors or modems (Section 5.5.2) to allow computer terminals to be used remotely from the central installation. There are few problems when the terminal can be of the type normally used for standard time-shared computer systems, that is a teletypewriter or visual display unit. However, high quality audio and pictorial material cannot be transmitted over a telephone line in real-time and this problem is normally solved, as in the case of the IBM 1500 student station, by means of pre-recorded audio messages and projected transparencies. One of the most advanced terminals specially developed for CAI is that used on the PLATO (Programmed Logic for Automatic Teaching Operation) system at the University of Illinois (Bitzer and Skaperdas, 1973).

Work on the design of the current PLATO IV system started in 1968. Two important features of the system have established it as a particularly good prospect for development:

(1) The terminals (Figure 5.7) consist of a plasma panel for the display of

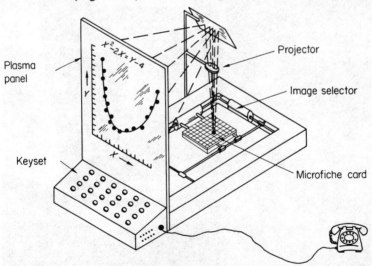

Figure 5.7 A schematic diagram of the PLATO terminal which uses a plasma display. A slide selector and projector allow static pictorial information to be projected together with computer-generated dynamic information. The projector is driven by digitally controlled pneumatic actuators. It contains a matrix of 256 images on an easily removable 4-inch square of microfilm and has a random access time of approximately 0·2 seconds

visual information, the associated electronics, a keyboard, a random access projector, connections to a telephone line and various optional extras, including a random access audio device and a touch panel which responds to a finger placed on any part of the visual display. The plasma panel, unlike a normal CRT can display graphic information permanently without the need for auxiliary storage, thereby simplifying the transmission of computer-generated graphics over telephone lines. It is of basically simple construction, consisting of thin glass sheets in which two fine wire grids are embedded. A gas, which is contained between the sheets, is ionised by a voltage applied to selected wires in the two grids. The ionised points are maintained by a smaller voltage applied across the whole grid. The graphic information is specified point by point, and a wide range of characters can be displayed (Figure 5.8). The panel is transparent and is combined with the rear-projection screen for the sheet film projector, so that information generated either by the computer or keyed in by the student can be superimposed on colour pictures.

(2) The powerful author language, TUTOR, can readily be used by people

Figure 5.8 A display generated by computer on the PLATO IV plasma panel. The display is approximately 12 inches square and contains 512 digitally addressed positions along each axis

with no previous computing experience. This has contributed greatly to the rapid acceptance of the system by the authors of lesson materials. PLATO allows both time-shared student use and simultaneous time-sharing authoring. This greatly facilitates program development, since there are no constraints on the times when authors can have access to the system and there is also minimal delay between writing a program and trying it out. This ready availability of the system with many terminals throughout the campus has resulted in a very large author population.

The cost of running a full PLATO system with 4000 terminals is estimated to be 34 cents per hour per student (Bitzer and Skaperdas, 1973). This cost is comparable to that of conventional elementary school education in the USA. For the two-year demonstration period which began in 1973, however, only a few hundred terminals are expected to be in operation, and so the initial costs will be higher. Also a large proportion of the cost is attributable to the terminals and with quantity production the unit cost would be substantially reduced. The cost of a basic terminal in quantity production is estimated to be $1900, approximately twice the cost of a basic teletypewriter.

PLATO has been used to present a wide range of courses. According to Hammond (1972) in one course for elementary school children, originally designed at the Massachusetts Institute of Technology, students using PLATO explore by trial and error the movements of a man balancing a stick, eventually discovering the effects of over-correction and the principles of dynamic balance. At the other extreme Hammond reports that organic chemistry students at the University of Illinois in an advanced laboratory course have used PLATO to 'pre-run' their experiments as computer simulations so that they will better understand the experiments before carrying them out in the laboratory. For all types of PLATO courses the system provides the teacher with the capability of monitoring the class performance, so that the teacher can see which tasks were taught efficiently, the number of errors which were made and the length of time which was required.

5.3 Computer-managed instruction

One of the most important potential uses of computers in education is as a means to individualise the educational process. Individualisation may be implemented by the kind of CAI systems we have discussed or, of course, by non-automated instruction. A third way is by CMI.

Cooley and Glaser (1969) of the Learning Research and Development Center at the University of Pittsburgh suggest the following general model for individualisation:

(1) The goals of learning are specified in terms of observable student behaviour and the conditions under which this behaviour is to be manifested.
(2) When the learner begins a particular course of instruction, his initial

capabilities—those relevant to the forthcoming instruction—are assessed.
(3) Educational alternatives suited to the student's initial capabilities are presented to him. The student selects or is assigned to one of these alternatives.
(4) The student's performance is monitored and continuously assessed as he learns.
(5) Instruction proceeds as a function of the relationship between measures of student performance, available instructional alternatives, and criteria of competence.
(6) As instruction proceeds, data are generated for monitoring and improving the instructional system.

Various degrees of automation can be used in the implementation of the model. It is possible to start without any automation at all. In fact a non-automated version, known as IPI (Individually Prescribed Instruction) was introduced at Oakleaf Elementary School, near Pittsburgh; but after a period of pilot work in this form, CMI was introduced to speed up the collection and analysis of data needed for the continuing development and improvement of the system. The CMI system is known as IPI/MIS. (IPI Management and Information System.)

The system uses the University of Pittsburgh IBM 360 model 50 computer with a remote 1050 card reading terminal at Oakleaf School and three 2741 typewriter terminals at the Learning Research and Development Center. The central processing unit has an extended memory, allowing up to 131,000 characters per on-line terminal and a 250 million byte disc and six tape drives also form part of the computer configuration.

The major aspects of IPI/MIS are summarised in Figure 5.9. The basic data are recorded by teachers, students and clerks on forms, which are designed to be processed by the optical scanner and output as punched cards. These cards are read by the computer terminal at the school and the edited data added to the student files stored on disc at the computer. When a student completes a unit, the data obtained during his work on that unit are written into a temporary file and at the end of the day a program updates the student tape from this file. The student tape contains all the instructional history available for each student, together with background data collected at the beginning of each school year, such as standardised test results, home background data, the student's sex and so on.

There are four major functions which the MIS can provide in an individualised school: (i) collection of data, (ii) monitoring of student progress, (iii) providing information as a basis for prescribing a course of instruction and (iv) the diagnosis of student difficulties. The objectives are to both increase the effectiveness of the model for individualising instruction and to increase the productivity of the teachers operating the IPI system. Such a system provides a highly suitable environment for the adoption of mastery learning strategies (Bloom, Hastings and Madaus, 1971) which are aimed at providing each student with the appropriate instruction to allow him to achieve mastery of the

125

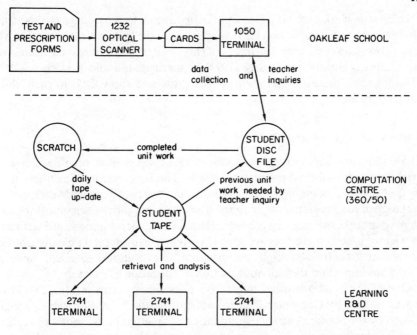

Figure 5.9 Diagram indicating the physical location of, and the relationship between, components of IPI/MIS. (Copyright 1969, by the American Association for the Advancement of Science)

subject. Briefly the model suggests that if students are normally distributed with regard to aptitude for some subject and they are all provided with the same instruction, then at the end of the instruction they will show a normal distribution on an appropriate measure of achievement, with a high correlation between aptitude and achievement. However it is argued that the vast majority of students, given the appropriate instruction, are able to master most educational objectives. Therefore if the kind and quality of instruction and the amount of time available for learning are made appropriate to the characteristics and needs of each student, they may be expected to achieve mastery of the subject and show almost zero correlation between aptitude and achievement.

Cooley and Glaser believe that the development and adoption of this kind of individualised model is a necessary prerequisite for bringing CAI from the laboratory into the classroom. They argue that CAI is unlikely ever to provide all the instruction for all of the students all of the time, and yet it is virtually impossible to incorporate CAI into traditional schools in which the classroom is the basis for instructional decisions and scheduling. It is, however, easy to incorporate CAI into IPI/MIS when lessons become available for solving specific instructional problems, since IPI/MIS already provides a computer with terminal capability, and the flexibility for individualisation within the school exists. Most importantly, they believe, IPI/MIS will have implemented a model for individualisation.

In Britain, work on CMI has mainly been directed to providing a cheap means of allowing teachers to obtain CMI support from the local education authority's data processing computer. Examples of this work, at secondary education level, are Gilligan, Hazelton and Kay (1971) in mathematics and Broderick (1972) in biology. No attempts seem to have been made to apply CMI to early childhood education.

5.4 Interactive television

The systems we have considered so far in this chapter have been developed to meet the needs of formal instruction in school and universities. The high capital cost, specialised communication methods and types of terminals used do not make them readily suited to use in the home and less formal organisations such as play groups and nursery schools. However the development of interactive television, based on the mass-produced colour television set, cable distribution system and centralised high performance mini-computers, could have an enormous impact on the individualisation of education at all levels.

One of the most advanced interactive television systems is TICCIT (Time-shared Interactive Computer-Controlled Information Television) which is being funded by the National Science Foundation in an attempt to evaluate a realistic working demonstration of such a system. It is being developed by the Mitre Corporation in collaboration with the University of Texas and Brigham Young University. Each TICCIT installation (Stetten and Volk, 1973) will deliver CAI and other information services to more than 1000 households. Its pair of mini-computers will be able to handle up to 100 active terminals simultaneously. It is assumed that the television sets will be used for the passive reception of conventional programmes for most of the time. The cost of leasing the cable, keyboard and the use of the central computer and other electronic facilities for the system is estimated to be about $12 per month, which brings the cost of CAI down to within the range for realistic consideration in early childhood education.

TICCIT lessons provide several optional ways of learning. It is possible, for example, to allow the choice of an initial overview of the material. They also allow considerable freedom of the order in which lessons are completed, the rate of progress and the handling of auxiliary material such as films. The TICCIT courses assume that the student's attitude is more positive when he has control over his own learning process and, following from the approach to television of the Children's Television Workshop (originators of *Sesame Street*), TICCIT courses attempt to increase the student's motivation and interest by the inclusion of cartoons, games and humorous items in the instructional materials.

The two mini-computers operate as a time-shared system and respond to a student's terminal within a fraction of a second. Terminals are attached to the computer through a cable television distribution system which can transmit signals to the television receivers and keyboard responses back to the

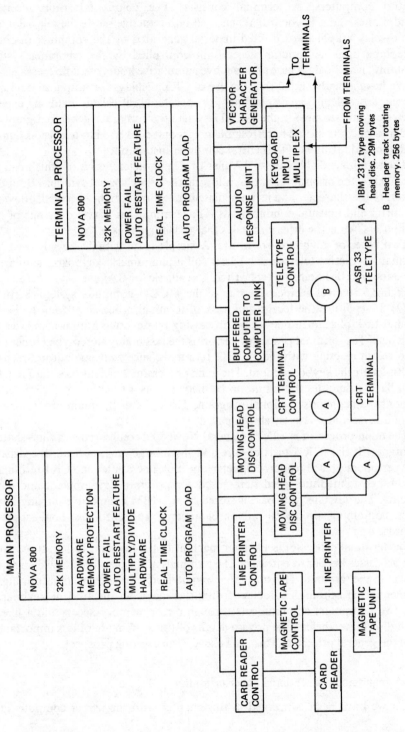

Figure 5.10 The TICCIT computer system

central computers. A terminal consists of a colour television receiver, headphones and a keyboard. When used in interactive mode the television set can display graphical or printed material generated by the computer or short videotape films. A random access unit controlled by the computer system contains an audio data base of about five cumulative hours of audio messages.

We have already stated that the use of CRT displays for graphical data can present a problem. The display must be repeatedly refreshed, involving expensive electronic storage. In the TICCIT system the computer-generated graphics and messages are stored in refresh memories and converted to television signals in the shared facilities of the central computer installation.

The terminals display up to 17 lines of 43 characters, each of which can be specified by the programmer, thus allowing the use of special symbols. Both the colour of the character and its immediate background can be specified, allowing colourful and unusual combinations. The terminals are serviced by one of the computers, while the other processes the student responses.

Two types of keyboard are in use. A simple form with 16 keys is used for normal interactive television, whilst a full alphanumeric keyboard, similar to the standard IBM Selectric typewriter, is available for CAI use.

Figure 5.10 gives a block diagram of the TICCIT computer system (Stetten, 1972). It separates the foreground task of terminal processing from the background task of algorithmic frame processing by devoting a mini-computer to each task. The terminal processor performs the fast highly stereotyped functions involved in reacting with the TICCIT terminals, such as frame outputting and multiplexing the keyboard input. The main processor, which utilises the TICCIT data base, assembles the frames to be displayed as a function of the student's responses and the instructional program. The tasks of the main processor are more diverse and relatively slowly paced.

The main processor is a Data General Nova 800, configured as a time-shared computer. It has 32K words of core and three large moving-head disc drives. The peripherals (card reader, magnetic tape unit, line printer and CRT terminal) are low cost, medium-speed items used for program development and data logging. The TICCIT data base is stored on two IBM compatible moving-head discs, containing almost 50 million characters. The third disc holds student records.

The terminal processor is a similar machine to the main processor. It receives and processes keyboard entries on the terminals and generates a new display to be sent to the terminal. This may be a computer-generated frame of information or merely the echoing characters for entries made on the student keyboard. The two computers communicate through direct memory access and a fixed-head disc. Nevertheless, the precise details of this system are of less importance than the general principle. This, we believe, is an exciting prospect.

5.5 Computers in educational experimentation

So far we have been concerned in this chapter with the use of computers to control the educational process. A particular system may have been experimental, but the long-term objective of the work is the development of viable systems for routine use in education. Another area of computer application which is of interest to us is their use as tools in educational research. There are two broad categories of such use. First, mini-computers may be used for the on-line control of laboratory experiments and second, data may be collected off-line during an experiment in machine-readable form for subsequent computer analysis.

5.5.1 On-line control of experiments

In this section we shall be concerned with experiments in which only one subject at a time is involved. The use of a computer rather than some other form of control equipment is determined in this case by convenience or cost or the need for high-speed decision making. The computer may already be available with facilities suited to the experiment, or the purchase of such a machine may be cheaper than constructing special purpose control equipment.

We mentioned in Section 4.4 that relay and solid state modules of the kind used in behavioural experiments provide a flexible means for controlling highly automated educational experiments. However, the problems of data collection and analysis remain. There are also cases when capital equipment needs to be shared between a number of users and here computers have the advantage of flexibility, for loading a new computer program can be much easier than manually changing the interconnections between a lot of modules. There are also some applications which require the computational power of a computer during the course of the experiment or need some special peripheral, such as a graphical display for the presentation of stimuli.

A typical mini-computer configuration would consist of the central processor with core memory, teletypewriter, paper tape reader and punch, CRT display and some mass storage device such as a disc or magnetic tape unit. Stimulus presentation and response detection devices of the type discussed in Chapter 4 are not readily connected by the average experimenter to such a system. The electronic circuits, through which links are made between any peripheral device and the central processor, are termed the interface of the computer. Making a connection between laboratory equipment and the interface of most computers requires specialist knowledge and experience. However, some machines have been specially designed for laboratory instrumentation and have interfaces which can be readily connected to laboratory instruments. One of the classic machines of this type was the LINC (Laboratory INstrument Computer) developed at the Lincoln Laboratories, MIT by a group of people who needed laboratory computers for biomedical research. Clark and Molnar (1965) gave as their objectives a machine (i) small enough for the individual laboratory, (ii) providing direct communication with the scientist via the console and the display, (iii) fast enough for on-line work, (iv) flexible with respect to the connection of external devices and (v) with an instruction set easy to learn and use. The laboratory interface of the LINC provides analogue to digital converters which allow the computer to measure external voltages, sense lines which can detect whether an external switch of pushbutton contact is open or closed, relay contacts which can switch on and off external devices and circuits to drive a remote CRT display. The modern successors to the LINC are manufactured by Digital Equipment Corporation and are based on the PDP-8. They are the PDP-12, which combines the instruction sets of the LINC and the PDP-8, and the LAB-8/E which does not have a LINC instruction set but is available with similar laboratory peripherals.

It is generally necessary to write on-line control programs in assembly language. This requires a fair measure of skill and is greatly facilitated by the availability of a large mass storage device and an operating system with a sophisticated text editor and assemblers. A system of this kind will also provide high level programming languages and mathematical subroutines which are useful for the analysis of the data which can be stored on the mass storage device. Some manufacturers provide special experimental control languages which are supersets of standard languages, with additional functions to operate specific laboratory peripherals. Both Digital Equipment and Hewlett–Packard offer such a version of BASIC and the former also have an advanced real-time FORTRAN IV which will run under their operating system OS/8 on suitable configurations of both the LAB-8/E and the PDP-12. A great advantage of using such languages for the control of experiments is that once the data collected during the experiment has been written into files, it can be easily accessed by analysis programs using the powerful arithmetic features of the same languages. An example of on-line control by computer is an experiment conducted with the Touch-Tutor in which the provision of auditory reinforcement was controlled by a LINC-8. The point of the experiment was to investigate the ease with which young children would be able to change their strategy. Once a certain performance level was achieved on a two-choice matching-to-sample task a reversal occurred so that the child was now correct if he non-matched. Subsequently a position strategy became correct. (This experiment is essentially similar to those on which Harlow based his notion of learning sets.) The speed of computation was a necessary feature of this experiment in order to relate stimuli and responses appropriately from moment to moment.

5.5.2 Off-line collection of data for computer processing

Although an experiment may not use a computer for on-line control, it may generate large quantities of data, which justify the use of a computer for their analysis. In such cases it is advisable to collect the data initially in a computer-readable form. This removes the possibility of errors being introduced during manual keypunching operations and can greatly reduce the time delay before the results of the analysis are available.

It is important to first check what forms of data input can be used on the computer which is to analyse the data. If a central computing facility is to be used, there will probably be well defined and inflexible rules. However, if the machine is in your own laboratory the situation is quite different, for one can even consider adding an extra peripheral in order to accommodate a particularly attractive recording medium.

The most common input medium for large data processing installations is the punched card. Unfortunately card punches are expensive devices and it is quite impractical to collect data in this form. If the data is collected manually, mark sense forms can be used and converted off-line into cards (cf. Section 5.3). Even if the installation does not have an optical scanner, many bureaux exist which can provide this conversion as a service.

The commonest way to collect data automatically is to use punched paper tape. This is the main input medium in mini-computers and is also acceptable data to many data processing installations. Standard paper tape is one inch wide and has an eight-hole format (Figure 5.11). Groups of holes are punched across the tape to represent defined symbols when read by the computer. The most common code is ASCII (American Standard Code for Information Interchange), which uses a 7-bit code (Figure 5.12), the 8th bit being available for

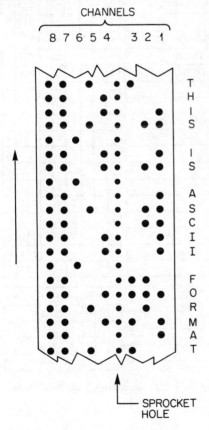

Figure 5.11 Data is punched on paper tape by groups of holes arranged in a definite format along the length of the tape. The tape is divided into channels, which run the length of the tape, and into columns, which extend across the width of the tape. The specimen of ASCII code shown here was prepared on a system which does not use parity check and so channel 8 is always punched

128

1 = HOLE PUNCHED = MARK
0 = NO HOLE PUNCHED = SPACE

MOST SIGNIFICANT BIT
LEAST SIGNIFICANT BIT

			Name	8	7	6	5	4	S	3	2	1
	@	SPACE	NULL/IDLE				0	0		0	0	0
	A	!	START OF MESSAGE				0	0		0	0	1
	B	"	END OF ADDRESS				0	0		0	1	0
	C	#	END OF MESSAGE				0	0		0	1	1
	D	$	END OF TRANSMISSION				0	0		1	0	0
	E	%	WHO ARE YOU				0	0		1	0	1
	F	&	ARE YOU				0	0		1	1	0
	G	'	BELL				0	0		1	1	1
	H	(	FORMAT EFFECTOR				0	1		0	0	0
	I	)	HORIZONTAL TAB				0	1		0	0	1
	J	*	LINE FEED				0	1		0	1	0
	K	+	VERTICAL TAB				0	1		0	1	1
	L	,	FORM FEED				0	1		1	0	0
	M	−	CARRIAGE RETURN				0	1		1	0	1
	N	.	SHIFT OUT				0	1		1	1	0
	O	/	SHIFT IN				0	1		1	1	1
	P	0	DC0				1	0		0	0	0
	Q	1	READER ON				1	0		0	0	1
	R	2	TAPE (AUX ON)				1	0		0	1	0
	S	3	READER OFF				1	0		0	1	1
	T	4	(AUX OFF)				1	0		1	0	0
	U	5	ERROR				1	0		1	0	1
	V	6	SYNCHRONOUS IDLE				1	0		1	1	0
	W	7	LOGICAL END OF MEDIA				1	0		1	1	1
	X	8	S0				1	1		0	0	0
	Y	9	S1				1	1		0	0	1
	Z	:	S2				1	1		0	1	0
	[	;	S3				1	1		0	1	1
	\	<	S4				1	1		1	0	0
Alt-mode	]	=	S5				1	1		1	0	1
	↑	>	S6				1	1		1	1	0
RUB OUT	←	?	S7				1	1		1	1	1

1	0	0	SAME
1	0	1	SAME
1	1	0	SAME
1	1	1	SAME

Figure 5.12 ASCII code. Channel 8 may be parity or always punched (always punched is shown in this figure)

parity check or it may always be punched. Parity checking is used to improve reliability when transferring data. For example, when punching the paper tape, the parity bit may be made to equal 1 if, and only if, the number of 1s in the seven information bits is odd. The computer reading in the paper tape can then check for even parity over all the eight bits on the paper tape. If an odd number of holes is detected an error can be signalled. Errors occurring in an even number of bits on the same character would remain undetected, but these are much less likely to occur than single-bit errors, which would always be detected.

Paper tape punches are available which operate at speeds ranging from about 10 to 100 characters per second. The higher speed punches are considerably more expensive than the lower speed devices, which are usually fast enough for the data rates likely to be generated in educational experiments.

If very large quantities of data or high data rates are being generated digital magnetic tape might be necessary. Standard or IBM-compatible tape units will be available at most data processing installations, but are rarely found on mini-computers. In order to use a conventional tape unit for data collection some form of electronic buffering is required. Incremental tape units, however, are available at a reduced cost; these are specifically designed for the collection of intermittent data. It is important to check carefully on the tape standards at the data processing installation before specifying the data recording tape unit.

Tape cassette or cartridge units are common on mini-computers and may be found in some data processing installations. They are slower than IBM-compatible tapes, but are considerably cheaper, usually being employed as a replacement for punched paper tape and employing similar codes. Unfortunately a wide variety of mechanical standards and tape formats exist and so, in order to preserve compatibility, one is usually restricted to using units made by the same manufacturer for collecting the data and reading in into the computer. However, the cost of these units can be so low that if a suitable mini-computer is already available for the data analysis, it might be well worth adding such a unit to provide a convenient medium for off-line data collection.

It is not necessary to provide a physical medium for the collection of data. It may be transmitted over a telephone line directly to the computer by a similar method to that used by time-shared computer systems. In order to transmit coded characters, it is necessary to arrange the elements in some agreed way at the transmitter and receiver. The ways in which this can be done may be classified broadly as serial data transmission and parallel data transmission.

In parallel data transmission, each element of the code has its own channel (Figure 5.13). In the case of paper tape this corresponds to the row of holes along the length of the tape (Figure 5.11). In electrical data transmission, each channel would require a separate circuit. Accordingly parallel data transmission is normally only used over short distances.

In serial data transmission (Figure 5.14) each element of the coded character is sent in turn rather than simultaneously. Thus multi-level codes, such as ASCII code, can be transmitted over a single channel, such as a telephone

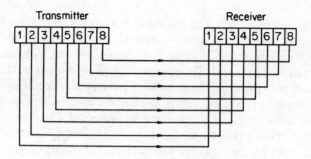

Figure 5.13 Parallel data transmission

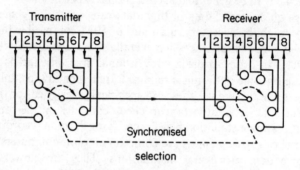

Figure 5.14 Serial data transmission

line. There are two basic forms of serial data transmission: synchronous and asynchronous. Synchronous data transmission is normally restricted to high-speed communication between computer installations and the like. Asynchronous serial transmission is the method which is used with devices such as teletypewriters. It is particularly suited to situations in which the data occurs intermittently and at times unrelated to the operation of the receiver. With this method each character consists of three parts: (i) a bit to define the start of the character, (ii) the data bits, normally an 8-bit ASCII character and (iii) a stop bit.

When this method is used to communicate with a local device, such as a teletypewriter, the value of the bits will be represented by the presence or absence of an electrical current. However, telephone systems are designed to transmit audio signals, and so the information must be converted into a suitable form before it can be transmitted over a telephone line. The conversion takes place in a device known as a modem (modulator–demodulator). In modems designed for transmission of data at teletypewriter speeds (about 10 to 30 characters per second) the modem converts the bits of value 0 or 1 to two different audio frequencies for transmission and performs the inverse operation for reception. Different pairs of frequencies are used for transmission and reception. Various modems are available, but one of the most convenient for casual use is the acoustic coupler modem. This needs no electrical connection to the telephone system and so avoids many of the stringent safety regulations.

The handset of the telephone is merely placed in a special chamber and the information is transmitted and received by acoustic coupling between the handset and the modem.

If data communications of this kind are used for data collection it is, of course, necessary to generate the appropriately coded signals in serial form. Specialist manufacturers can supply a variety of electronic modules which greatly facilitate the construction of systems of this kind.

For further reading on data communications Murphy and Kallis (1971) give an elementary introduction. Martin (1969) gives a more thorough treatment of the topic.

5.6 Summary

This chapter has reviewed the ways in which computers can be directly involved in education. Firstly computers may be used directly in the control of the educational process, either to present material directly to the student in computer-assisted instruction or to assist the teacher by assessing students and prescribing courses of instruction in computer-managed instruction. Secondly computers may be used in educational experimentation, both to control laboratory experiments and to process experimental data which has been collected off-line.

CHAPTER 6
Organising the Resources

6.1 The systems approach

The importance of the systems approach in educational technology no longer needs arguing. Indeed the recent report issued by CERI (Centre for Educational Research and Innovation, 1971) and based on a workshop entitled 'Educational technology—strategies for implementation' stated quite simply that 'recent thinkers have *conceived educational technology as a system approach* to the teaching–learning process centring around the optimal design, implementation and evaluation of teaching and learning' (our italics). We cannot, however, merely equate two different terms 'educational technology' and 'the systems approach' and assume that this has advanced our understanding of either. Another view was described by Romiszowski (1970), 'others see the whole concept of systems and "systems approach" as a new jargon, which has been conjured up to explain old ideas; invented (or at least promoted) by those who wish to obscure that they are substituting talk for action'. It seems that the systems approach is for educational technology what educational technology is for teachers. For some it provides a rationale, for others a mere diversion from what they regard as their proper activity. Since the systems approach undoubtedly now occupies a central position in thinking about educational technology, and since it appears to be subject to varying interpretations, we propose at this point to examine the origins, assumptions and applications of systems thinking and to consider what implications this holds for the kind of techniques we have been discussing so far.

The systems approach derives, not surprisingly, from the scientific study of systems. This study, still in its infancy, has produced a set of postulates and associated techniques which together comprise general systems theory. The starting point for most treatments of systems theory is to grope for an adequate definition of the term 'system'. This turns out to be an elusive concept which should surprise no-one since the major aim of systems theory is to provide a general description of all systems. One difficulty, of course, is that the term is employed in a non-technical sense when we speak freely of the solar system, political systems, the nervous system, systems for remembering names, systems for losing weight etc., or just 'the system'. DeGreene (1970) has suggested, not altogether frivolously, that the systems field would benefit from systemisation and has pointed to the need for the development of a basic language for communicating systems ideas across disciplines.

133

We may identify three main questions here:

(i) What distinguishes systems from non-systems? How may systems be described?
(ii) How can different systems be classified?
(iii) What do we know of, and how might we study, system behaviour?

Angyal (1941) defined a system as a holistic organisation and made a critical distinction between systems and aggregates. The parts that comprise a system are arranged (organised, interrelated) in some way that distinguishes them from a simple collection of objects. We might regard six people acting as a committee as a system, whereas we would probably want to say that six names chosen at random from a telephone directory or six tennis balls in a box constitute simple aggregates. The distinction can be made both in terms of the structure or organisation of the assembled parts and the function they perform. The parts (system components, constituents or elements) may, however, belong simultaneously to numerous different systems. The specification of a particular system is quite arbitrary and may exist only in relation to the viewpoint of the investigator. An example often quoted is that of a telephone system which can be considered at the receiver, local exchange, nationwide or worldwide level. At each level several subsystems can be identified and when the human operator is included as a component in the system its complication is considerable. Nevertheless such an example is a simple-minded one when compared with biological or social systems with immense complexity. In Beer's (1959) classification of systems, education and training are included in the category of exceedingly complex. Despite this complexity, however, it is instructive to consider features which the educational system shares with all other systems.

First, it has a boundary. At some point we have to decide what is inside a system and what is not. This is a conceptual aid since it permits the system to be viewed as a black box so that the behaviour of the overall system can be studied rather than that of particular subsystems. This is a most important concept. The level of explanation adopted by a science is a direct consequence of what it decides to regard as black boxes. Often these decisions are implicit, nevertheless this is largely all that separates one scientific discipline from another. Biochemists, physiologists and psychologists, for example, may sometimes study the same empirical phenomenon. What distinguishes their separate approaches is the assumption they make about the appropriate level of analysis, that is, what they are specifying as systems. Neil (1970) has pointed out that system boundaries are usually defined by existing discontinuities between processes. Viewed in this way it seems surprising, perhaps, that so much controversy should surround the assumptions of psychologists who treat the whole organism as a black box (since the organism–environment discontinuity seems one of the clearest of them all). The fact is, however, that systems theorists do not simply treat an identified system as a black box; they are also concerned to identify, in as fine detail as possible, the subsystems and links between components.

Social boundaries are among the most difficult of all to draw. This is partly because the components of social systems, people, belong at the same time to a variety of social systems and subsystems so that continuous interaction occurs at all levels. When it is considered that each component may adopt a variety of different states then the behaviour of the system appears unmanageably complex.

It is, however, partly the very complexity of systems that has led to the assumption, in general systems theory, that the whole is greater than the sum of its parts. That is to say, certain kinds of behaviour appear only to be exhibited by systems. Ashby (1964) suggested that this feature of systems really reflects our ignorance of the properties of system components. It is the case, nevertheless, that certain behaviour can only emerge when components are linked together to form a system. Learning, for example, depends on a system for transmitting information.

Certain system features are usually employed in the classification of systems. One such is whether a system is deterministic (when the sequence of states is fixed) or probabilistic (when the system output is, at any point in time, uncertain). Systems may also be discrete or continuous, open or closed. Biological systems are usually continuous open systems in that a constant relationship with the environment is maintained. Many attempts to draw up a general classification of systems have been made (e.g. Jones (1967)).

Our third question, the study of system behaviour, is largely the domain of cybernetics. Theoretical cybernetics is highly mathematical in treatment and includes, for example, information theory. Ashby's Law of Requisite Variety (which states that the variety in the control system must be as great as the variety in the system or parts that are to be controlled) is an example of the kind of principle which cyberneticians have proposed for the description of system behaviour. Von Bertalanffy's distinction (1950) between open and closed systems in terms of the principle of equifinality is another which has influenced thinking about both biological and social systems. In educational terms this principle might be used to clarify how a number of techniques can all lead to an objective of successful learning. Cybernetics can throw light on the control of learning by describing how feedback mechanisms can control system output. Related issues concern the description (by simulation) or self-organising systems, adaptive systems, automata and artificial intelligence. Recently a new discipline, known as bionics, has emerged. This represents an attempt to gain understanding of engineering principles through the study of biological systems.

It is also important to point out that in many cases the systems approach is not discussed in a way that a systems theorist would consider appropriate. Two usages which, strictly speaking, are inaccurate have involved the following:

(1) The systems approach has been equated with the application of principles of programmed instruction to curriculum design and development. The principles on which this approach is based are clearly stated by Mager (1962) and

essentially consist of the precise specification of behavioural objectives and the identification and evaluation of terminal behaviour.

(2) The systems approach has referred only to educational hardware. The CERI report, mentioned at the beginning of the chapter, suggests that this misconception has led to resistance from educators and disenchantment with the 'gadget approach'. In our view, there is adequate understanding both of the teaching–learning process and of the potential of existing technology, but the problem is matching the two in a real-life situation. A failure to implement the technology in fact.

The reader may by this point be wondering how a precisely defined systems theory can be related to education or indeed to problems in any real-world socio-technical system. Such confusion, as we have just seen, is well-founded since a large gap exists between general systems theory and what is often understood by the systems approach. The literature of systems theory is usually very mathematical while that of the application of systems thinking is more often than not on the level of 'make sure that the system boundaries are properly drawn'. However, the technique of systems analysis does attempt to offer some general purpose procedures in dealing with real systems. First it is necessary to define the system and identify the nature of the problem it poses. Next one proceeds both inwards into the subsystems and outwards into the environment by identifying the subsystems, their components and links and by generally attempting to build a model of the system structure. The feedback loops must be specified and finally the system input–output relationships described. Ideally one is then in a position to be able to predict the behaviour of the overall system. All this is considerably easier to state than to carry out. However, one consequence of attempts to model system structure is that the essentially hierarchical and interactive nature of most real-world systems is revealed.

Silvern (1968) has identified four stages of the systems approach, viz. analysis, synthesis, model-building and evaluation; the approach is represented schematically in Figure 6.1. In the analysis stage an attempt is made to describe the existing system, in synthesis previously unrelated elements are combined and a new model is produced which overcomes any problem existing in the original system. Finally the new model is evaluated in relation to the problem. This fourth stage may be effected by simulation, such as those conducted on eco-systems by the Systems Dynamics Laboratory at Massachusetts Institute of Technology (Forrester, 1971). Rowntree (1969) has made an analogy between these stages and the stages involved in scientific method. The analysis stage can be seen as the identification of a problem, the synthesis stage that of formulating a hypothesis while the evaluation stage may be viewed as testing the hypothesis with experimental data. This will remain as an analogy however until suitably rigorous tools for dealing with the problems posed by complex systems have been developed.

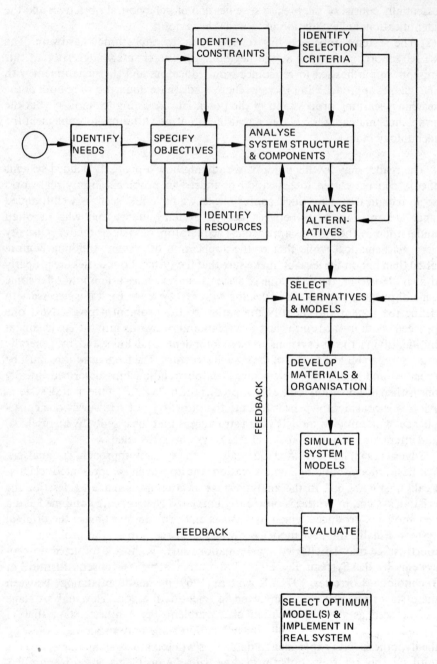

Figure 6.1 The systems approach to education (from Hodge (1970a))

6.2 Case studies

A good illustration of a systems application in education is provided by Neil's (1970) discussion of the setting up of the Open University. This is a particularly interesting example because at the outset no system existed and the planners were able to adopt a systems approach in both the creation and subsequent development of an innovative educational system. The various stages of decision and action which derived from this approach are illustrated in Figure 6.2.

Neil regards this largely as a systematic approach with only hints of the true systems approach. 'In our present state of limited knowledge about the applications of general systems theory in practice, a total systems approach is always a severe compromise between the desirables, the acceptables and the practicables.' Notwithstanding this, the system designers of the Open University began constructing a model which would relate the various functions to be performed by the system. From this they derived the more detailed model for the preparation and dissemination of learning materials and for relating these materials to the associated support activities (see Figure 6.3). One essential task was seen to be the creation of a system for the optimum use of educational technology. Neil and his colleagues identified four main subsystems: (i) the course team; (ii) a design subsystem; (iii) a television and radio technical subsystem and (iv) a 'business activities' subsystem. A further stage involved the modelling of control mechanisms which 'must arise from a subsystem superordinate to those subsystems for which the mechanism has been devised'.

The basic approach here was described by Neil as follows: 'the process of designing a new system, using a systems approach, is not linearly sequential, but iterative and evolutionary'. First, the process involves outlining a functional model, recognising primary functional activities and defining subsystem boundaries. As one advances it becomes possible to improve the functional model by specifying more clearly primary functional activities and modifying initial boundaries. The first step must always be a preliminary specification of primary purposes and objectives. In the case of the Open University these were derived from the Planning Committees Report, the Vice-Chancellor and from the few members of staff in post at the time. The next stage was the setting up of working parties to provide much more detailed examinations of the University's educational concerns and practical procedures. 'Therefore, whilst working towards the achievement of preliminary objectives it becomes possible to continually refine and extent them and to assess how good we are at achieving them and to learn from our experience.'

The achievement may, perhaps, be gauged by considering the subsystem for the production of Open University course units. This has recently been described by Rowntree (1971) and might be regarded as illustrating the essential features of a systematic approach to learning. Firstly, of course, the setting of behavioural objectives is emphasised. Authors have been persuaded to go beyond a first statement of aims 'to then produce a set of objectives, describing what the student is expected to be able to do as a result of the author's efforts'. Next the

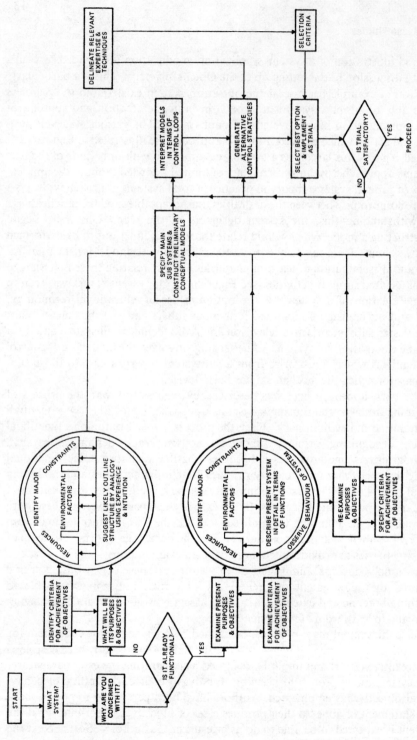

Figure 6.2 An example of stages of decision and action derived from the systems approach

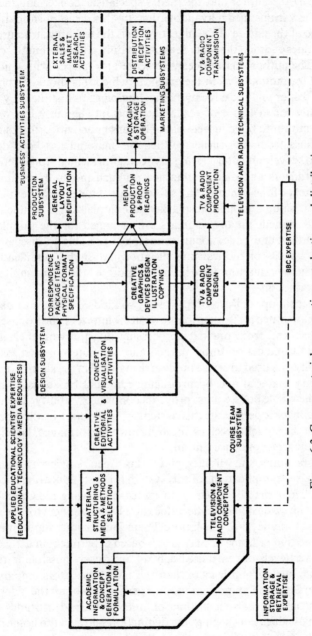

Figure 6.3 Course materials preparation, production and distribution

author is encouraged to devise a structure for his teaching material by indicating the relationships among the concepts to be taught. At this stage a joint decision is required, by the author and the media specialists, concerning the role to be played by the various media available. Ideally this decision should follow as a consequence of the nature of the objectives and the teaching structure, although Rowntree does admit that at present mainly rule-of-thumb criteria are employed. The author then proceeds to write his material with guidance from educational technologists as to the extent to which this should be programmed for student response. 'The educational technologist, as a student by proxy, will look not only for evidence of readability and intelligibility but will also encourage the author to build in frequent questions or activities to get some kind of active response from the learner.' When the material has been drafted it is subjected to developmental testing by being presented to a representative sample of students and data is obtained on such measures as time taken to achieve mastery of the concepts and subjective estimates of student interest and difficulty. The sample group is also asked to complete an assignment based on the material learned. Finally seminars are arranged for the sample group at which the author and educational technologist are able to discuss with them any further aspects of the learning situation. After the modifications which result from these evaluations have been incorporated the course-unit is ready for full-scale production.

The feedback loops in this system are of two kinds. Firstly, a course monitoring system is operated: 'information flows in from tutors and counsellors, from students direct and from our data processing division with their analyses of students' performances on tutor-marked and computer-marked assignments'. This information is used to revise the course material in the short term by adding supplementary material and by producing remedial broadcasts while, in the long term, the whole course must prove its continued viability. The other sense in which feedback operates in this system is, of course, in the knowledge of results which the student receives about his own performance, largely achieved by individual correspondence tuition.

Before concluding our discussion of the Open University example it is important that the implications of this system for early education should not be overlooked. There may be much to be gained by viewing the Open University not simply as an extension of higher education but as a model for the organising of resources at any level of education. There are óbvious similarities with the *Sesame Street* kind of home or play group based experiment in early education, although lower levels of centralised control are clearly possible in the case of, say, voluntary play group leaders than the part-time tutors employed by the Open University. The important point, perhaps, is that the adoption of a systems approach reveals that some of our established attitudes about the organisation of education, such as the distinction between the home and school environments, may actually represent a barrier to the optimal organisation of our available resources.

Although the Open University represents the only really large-scale imple-

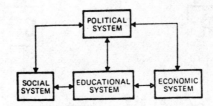

Figure 6.4 General system environment

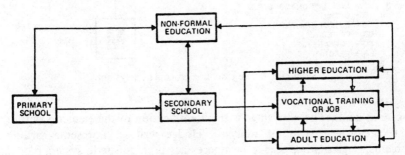

Figure 6.5 Immediate environment of Secondary School subsystem

mentation of the systems approach to education, there have been other attempts to apply systems theory, most of which have not proceeded beyond the analytic stage. One such study is that of Hodge (1970b) who attempted a systems theory analysis of secondary education. Figures 6.4 and 6.5 illustrate Hodge's view of the secondary school system as a subsystem of the whole educational system, and the relation of the latter to other systems. Hodge adapts Coombs' (1968) analysis of the components of the educational system and arrives at the following list of subsystems: aims, management, teachers, content, structure and schedule, measuring instruments, learning aids, physical facilities. The input to and output from the system are measurable characteristics of the students (see Figure 6.6). Hodge assumes that the system objectives can be clearly stated and this is in many cases a big assumption. He points to the contribution of programmed learning in showing how short-term objectives can help in defining

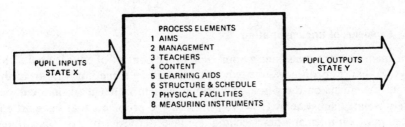

Figure 6.6 The secondary subsystem

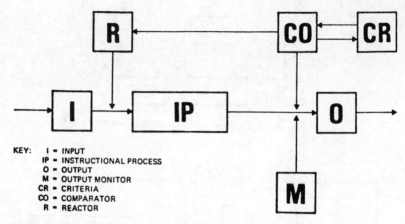

Figure 6.7 The teaching process as a system

long-term goals. The next stage is the identification of the elements within the eight categories. 'Such an analysis', Hodge writes, 'represents formidable problems, but would appear to be a necessary prerequisite to system modelling and simulation at a practical level'. Hodge then goes on to discuss the application of general systems concepts to the secondary school instructional system but draws attention to the dangers inherent in using models as though they themselves were the systems under study. Examples of this are seen in attempts to quantify parameters when no quantification techniques exist or in the use of a static model to represent a dynamic system.

Hodge then proceeds to model the instructional process at an intermediate level of complexity. This is shown in Figure 6.7. The instruction system is seen to be an open one with a closed loop subsystem controlling the system output. 'This regulator mechanism consists of measurement (in the form of tests, examinations etc.), a set of criteria or objectives which define output standards, and a comparator device (either human or mechanical) which compares the results obtained from measurement with the 'ideal' criteria established by the school or examinations board.'

Hodge also draws attention in his paper to several of the problems that a successful application of general systems theory to an instructional system would need to confront.

6.3 Problems of implementation

The main value of the systems approach, in the context of educational technology, is that it encourages one, when implementing some innovation, to think about the effects on the whole educational system rather than on a comparatively isolated subsystem. However, most of the problems that have arisen in attempts to implement new techniques have derived from the fact that no agreed strategy for implementation exists within education. Agreed objectives have not emerged because the various groups concerned in the implementation process have tended to operate on the basis of their own separate short-term objectives. Inevitably following from this has been a failure to find an appropriate method of evaluation. The problems boil down to the question posed by Cumming and Dunn (1970), viz. what kind of information does the decision maker want about effectiveness? Since the answer to this is in doubt, decisions within the educational system are more often than not taken without any systematic evaluation of empirical data at all. Again, we can identify three relevant topics here:

(i) Practical problems of developing new technology and implementing new learning systems.
(ii) Assuming that objectives can be stated, what measurements for evaluation are available?
(iii) How can we assess effectiveness?

The CERI report suggests that seven stages arise before a new system is ready for large-scale production and implementation. These are: (i) statement of objectives; (ii) description of target population; (iii) decision on content; (iv) initial preparation of material; (v) trial and revision; (vi) large-scale production and continuing revision of materials; (vii) implementation (see Figure 6.8).

Quoting from the report, 'Educational technology in the widest sense cannot be grafted on to existing systems but will lead to fundamental changes whose purpose is the provision of a better education'. The difficulty of objectives is described as follows:

Although for example we know what is meant by a better motor car, it is not easy to define what is meant by a better education. The performance of a car can be measured but the objectives of new learning systems that are easiest to measure are often the least important.

The implementation of the kind of systems discussed in Chapter 3 poses more and different problems from those involved in implementing, say, an individualised technique for teaching mathematics. This is because they also involve the development and evaluation of, as it were, a 'better motor car'. In a sense we can only speculate about the problems posed by these new systems since none of those discussed has yet been fully implemented. At the time of writing two of the systems discussed, the Talking Typewriter and the Talking Page, have recently been withdrawn from the UK market. The superficial reason is that sales or hiring revenue has not been maintained at a level sufficient to support further development or even manufacture. Of course, one view of this is that these systems were simply not meeting a need (or did not do what the manufacturers claimed, or were too expensive for what they did achieve, or just were not good enough). The fact is, however, that these systems have been withdrawn without any systematic evaluation at all (except by purely

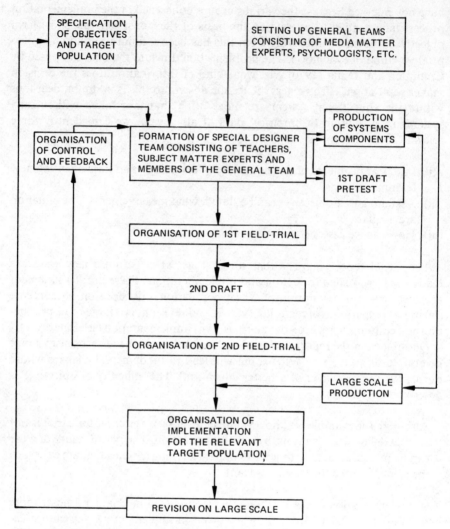

Figure 6.8 Flow chart showing the requirements to be met prior to the large-scale implementation of a learning system

commercial criteria). These remarks must, of course, be restricted to the UK situation. One is tempted, however, to speculate on the prospects of systems such as these being implemented in educational systems even less affluent than our own (which, presumably, includes a large majority of the world's children, particularly those who are most in need of some benefit from the educational technology 'revolution').

It is somewhat ironic to note that over the next few years developing countries may implement educational technology more effectively than our own. Unlike the developed countries where, for example, programmed instruction materials have been for the most part distributed widely by the private sector to further commercial interests (sometimes at the expense of educational objectives), in the developing countries the private sector is often unable or too conservative to take such initiatives. In these countries also, there is often more direct control over education by government and, given stable and continued administrative support, the prospects for implementing relevant aspects of educational technology can be good. Conversely in this country it is difficult to persuade the government to make resource investments.

The reasons for this state of affairs are complicated but in our view essentially stem from the lack of coordination between the producers and implementers of innovating technology in education; lack of the systems approach, in fact. Kay, Dodd and Sime (1968) point out that there is surprisingly little continuity in post for central government personnel, either political or administrative, who are responsible for educational innovation. An additional factor is that our educational system is a labour-intensive rather than a capital-intensive one. The capital outlay necessary to develop new hardware systems is available, under the present arrangements, only to the largest of our commercial producers. The need for closer liaison between designers, developers, researchers, planners and teachers within the educational system as a whole is a prerequisite if we are to do anything other than pay lip-service to systems ideas. The CERI report makes just this point: 'An extension of the principle of partnership between the private and public sectors is likely to be educationally desirable and should be encouraged'. This puts it moderately. So long as they function as separate subsystems then the objectives of researchers, manufacturers and users seem likely to remain disparate. Only control of the overall system can ensure that these subsystems operate towards a single objective.

A concept that has in recent years assumed importance in relation to the control or management of complex systems is that of accountability. Davies (1971) defined accountability in the context of education and training: 'As a result of the responsibility and authority delegated to them, a teacher and his students are judged on how well each student achieves his agreed learning objectives'. It is presumed that in the case of young or handicapped children the accountability for early education rests solely on the educator. The concept should not be identified with responsibility or authority (which concepts Davies considers refer to the planning and leading functions, respectively), but rather with the controlling or managing function. Educators should be accountable to society for both the objectives they set and the degree to which these are achieved. Again then, we can discern the influence of systems thinking. Educators are to be accountable for the system output. The difficulty with such a concept is again one of agreeing objectives. How can an underpaid, harassed primary school teacher be simultaneously accountable for the achievement of objectives set by her headmaster, local authority, parents and society, to say nothing of her own and those of her pupils? One possible solution to this problem has been termed performance contracting, whereby an independent commercial organisation tenders for an educational contract and agrees to implement instruction to a specified performance level. This scheme is discussed further in Section 7.3.

6.4 Criteria of success

This brings us to the whole question of criteria for success. By what process can we make judgements and come to decisions about the success of learning systems? Immediately we are faced again with a circle of definitions. What do we mean by success? Perhaps effectiveness. If so, effectiveness for what? Effectiveness in attaining objectives. Objectives for what? At the risk of labouring the point it must again be stated that evaluation techniques must be determined by the nature of the objectives. Objectives, moreover, also require value judgements. Mager (1962) points out that instructional objectives are frequently phrased in ambiguous and imprecise phrases such as 'to know' or 'to appreciate'. Such objectives can only be evaluated on the basis of subjective or even anecdotal evidence. If evaluation is to be precise and capable of generalisation then both objective and evaluation must be defined in terms of a performance measure and this implies the availability of an appropriate measuring instrument. It is evident that there is no point in employing a measuring instrument whose sensitivity is less or greater than that required by the objective.

Payne (1968) classifies performance tests as:

(i)   informal (teacher-made) or standardised (specialist-made);
(ii) oral or written (we would need to extend this to include other performance tasks, such as matching-to-sample);
(iii) mastery (of basic knowledge and skills), survey (of general achievement) or diagnostic (of specific disabilities and deficiencies);
(iv) speed (in responding to items of approximately equal difficulty) or power (in responding to items of increasing order of difficulty);
(v)   verbal, non-verbal or performance (referring to assumptions about the underlying skills or knowledge being tested).

An important point about the interpretation of test scores is that the same tests are often employed both to evaluate the effectiveness of materials or techniques (either employing pre-test and post-test measures on a sample of the target population or by using them to compare two or more techniques) and to assess individual learners. These two uses require tests with different features. Roebuck (1971) has argued that most tests do not reveal adequate information about the specific skills required. The usual index of learning is some kind of gain measure. Roebuck points out the following assumptions underlying the derivation of gain scores: (i) that the scale units are uniform throughout the range of possible gain scores for a given test; (ii) that the tests that are used to measure pre-test and post-test proficiency can be equivalent; (iii) that observed gain scores rank examinees in the same order as would the best estimate of true gains; (iv) that the observed scores are appropriate estimates of the true scores. Each of these assumptions is questionable.

It is helpful to make the general distinction between criterion-referenced and norm-referenced tests. This distinction was drawn originally by Glaser (1963) and recently has been discussed by, among others, Ward (1970) and Moxley (1974). Norm-referenced tests depend on relative rankings between individuals while criterion-referenced tests are based upon mastery of a specified performance on a particular task. Moxley argues that the selection of one or the other emphasises a particular source of variability. The selection of a norm-referenced measure depends on the existence and maintenance of variability between individuals, whilst that of a criterion-referenced measure essentially looks for variability in the environment and emphasises similarities rather than differences between individuals. It is evident then that criterion-referenced tests will be sensitive to the differences produced by an instructional technique. Such tests can be designed so that they are difficult when administered before the training and easy afterwards. Given this, it is perhaps surprising to note that several attempts to evaluate the systems discussed in Chapter 3 have employed norm-referenced tests. The Touch-Tutor, however, has a built-in criterion measure which, in a sense, provides continuous evaluation. If the objectives are defined in terms of the instructional material actually employed then such a system guarantees successful attainment as long as the individual child is capable, eventually, of learning with that system. Such an interpretation of evaluation may appear somewhat weak. It does however show conceptual advantages in that it avoids many of the problems and assumptions associated with employing independent tests of performance.

The other general sense in which evaluation is employed is common to all technology. That is, is system A better than system B for achieving some objective? Both systems may demonstrably train a student to a criterion. The evaluation question may still be, 'which system does it more effectively?', in which case we must redefine our objectives so that it is possible to discriminate between the systems on some other criterion, such as retention. On the other hand we may wish to pose the question as, 'which system does it most efficiently?'. One way to interpret this is in terms of cost-effectiveness.

There is currently much interest in the question of whether cost-effectiveness techniques can be applied directly in education. Certainly there is general agreement that, as CERI puts it:

It is necessary first that accounting practices should be altered so that the required data are produced in a meaningful form . . . it is not generally realised that in most advanced countries no more than 4% of their large educational budgets is devoted to books, equipment, instructional materials etc. while 60% is spent on teachers' salaries.

Some attempts have been made to compute a rate-of-return analysis of education. Schultz (1968), for example, has estimated this for US college education on the basis of the difference in income between college and high-school graduates. Few, if any, would agree that the aims of education can be measured in this way. Cumming and Dunn (1970) have produced a blueprint for cost-effectiveness studies in educational technology, although neither this, nor anything like it, has yet been employed. The principle is simply one of estimating total costs in attaining a particular instructional objective by various methods and employing various media. Again, however, we come up against the obstacle of having to identify and measure a successful learning outcome.

6.5 Promoting collaboration between specialists

Our final concern in this chapter is to draw attention to the need for an inter-disciplinary approach to educational technology. Systems thinking has given technologists a new status and the distinction between a system scientist and a technologist is becoming very blurred. Nevertheless complex systems analysis and systems development require a multidisciplinary approach. No one special-ist can hope to solve the new kind of problems thrown up by complex systems. The systems approach has arisen precisely because the specialist sciences have not proved able to provide answers to the most pressing problems, most of which derive from the nature of complex systems. Systems theory may be regarded as a kind of meta-science, rather like philosophy, which cuts across the traditional boundaries of scientific enquiry. Man–machine systems, for example, demand expertise in physiology, psychology and engineering. Most learning systems should probably be viewed in this way; certainly it is our belief that the design and development of systems in beginning education requires collaboration between specialists, coordinated by an analysis of the overall system. Unfortunately the manner in which such research and development is currently conducted rarely exhibits these features, except in an informal way. It is instructive to note how many educational technologists are people trained in more than one specialist discipline.

It is, however, one thing to pay lip-service to the desirability of an inter-disciplinary or, perhaps, metadisciplinary approach to education and quite another to put forward constructive suggestions about how this might be achieved, given the constraints of our present system and attitudes. Let us briefly consider, then, some of the practical issues involved here. In the first place it is necessary to consider what proportion of available funds should be directed principally for organising resources. A system must be developed for applying systems thinking and this, in itself, will require a significant part of the available support. What is the optimum structure for such a system? At least two possibilities seem to require consideration. Firstly a central agency consist-ing mainly of system designers should be accountable for all technological development in education, and its successful implementation. The essential task of such a central body would be to coordinate and, through the allocation of funds earmarked for particular pieces of research or technical development, to control the activities of the various small units that now exist. It would be particularly important that this central agency should be the sole body account-able to society for the successful development and implementation of educational technology. The implications of this are radical. Not only would this body have control over research priorities, but also, through being the sole placer of orders for hardware, a large measure of control over the commercial producers. There are several objections to this proposal since it violates some of the assumptions and attitudes inherent in our present system. The dangers of centralised control are now well known in other contexts. It leads more often than not to bureaucracy and inertia and leaves the individual feeling isolated from the decision making process with a consequent lack of identification and personal commitment. But this, surely, is nothing if not a systems problem? The basic problem, which is by no means limited to the educational system, may be stated as follows. How can we achieve sufficient control over both research and technological development so that our resources are truly being organised while at the same time encouraging the kind of individual flair and originality which is normally associated with work in small and autonomous units?

The idea of a central coordinating body has the practical merit of maintaining the small units which currently exist. A second possibility is that support should only be available for a few large centres of excellence where all aspects of educational technology may be pursued in an interdisciplinary fashion. The argument here is that there is a minimum size of teaching/research unit below which an interdisciplinary approach becomes impossible both in the development and implementation stages. Without resources on a fairly sizeable scale the approach is bound to be piecemeal. It is significant that of the few implementations of a systems approach to educational technology so far reported, such as the Open University example we have quoted, all have involved fairly large-scale organisations. It is, nevertheless, undoubtedly the case that most educational technology is currently being developed in small-scale, fragmented units. Given this, the central agency suggestion may be both cheaper and more simple to implement since existing units could be maintained by the allocation of specific tasks. Certainly the implication of both these ideas is a degree of centralisation that might be regarded as threatening the independence of the specialist. That, however, we believe is the consequence of organising the resources.

In conclusion we would emphasise again that in our present system not all activities are directed towards the same goal. This fact may stem from a fundamental distinction between science and technology in terms of willingness to make decisions. The scientist's primary role is to provide explanations and it is in the nature of science that an adequate explanation is always at least one more experiment away. This is probably true even for the applied scientist whose role requires him to specify the effects of real-world, as opposed to laboratory, variables. The technologist, on the other hand, is required to solve immediate problems in the best way possible and can rarely afford the luxury of waiting until entirely appropriate data is available. It must be the 'systems man' who bridges the gap since in theory it is he who is in a position to evaluate the consequences, for the overall system, of making decisions on varying degrees of evidence at particular points in time. In short, the 'systems man' must be the decision maker. The reader may, at this point, be forgiven for a certain scepticism about all this since the kind of 'system man' we are describing at present barely exists and could be regarded as little more than a projection of a felt need. What we are saying then, is that we probably need to train a new kind of educational technologist. He must be primarily a system technologist. The level at which he should be trained as such is open to debate although it seems plausible to suggest that in the long term this will best be effected by first degree courses in systems technology followed by postgraduate specialisation in education.

6.6 Summary

In this chapter we have tried to show how the problems of organising educational resources and implementing decisions may benefit from an approach based loosely on systems theory. Although a direct application of the techniques of systems analysis has yet to be adequately demonstrated in the field of early education nevertheless some conceptual clarification of the problems has resulted from this approach. An example is the distinction between the stages of analysis, synthesis, model-building and evaluation. Two case studies, the setting up of the Open University and Hodge's (1970b) analysis of secondary education, have been discussed as illustrations of the systems approach. The problem of implementation has been viewed as a problem of agreeing objectives. It is argued that failure to implement available educational technology will continue as long as researchers, producers and users work towards different, and even incompatible, objectives, and as long as there is confusion about what constitutes a successful outcome. Only the development of a systems technology of education seems likely to bridge the wide gap between research and implementation.

CHAPTER 7

Prospects

7.1 Educational technology and the young child

So far we have described some existing techniques for those who wish to utilise them in early or special education. We have also attempted to indicate research trends for the kind of systems we have been describing and we have tried to set these within a more general educational context. In this chapter we propose to consider some of the outstanding problems and issues inherent in the general approach we have been supporting and to assess the prospects for future progress.

One general criticism that still persists is based on the false premise that the sort of technology we have been discussing would be employed as the sole teaching medium and may actually usurp the role of the parent, teacher or other interested adult. As we have tried to make clear earlier their role is changed when educational technology is used, but in no sense does it become less important. If anything the reverse is true. Educational technology brings with it increased control over the progress of the individual child and with increased control comes increased, or at least clearer, responsibility for the outcome.

Far more serious objections are levelled against the whole approach derived from operant conditioning, which provides a major theoretical basis for much of the technology discussed here. These objections range from arguments that the principles of reinforcement and the technology derived from them are simply irrelevant, to those imputing a positively harmful effect. The latter kind of argument suggests that the external manipulation of reinforcers leads to a reduction in intrinsic motivation. In other words, if you expect a child to learn solely in order to obtain rewards, you may teach a cynical attitude to learning which is incompatible with the aim to which most educators would subscribe, namely a self-motivated desire for learning *per se*. We suspect that, though this danger cannot be disregarded, it is unlikely to prove very potent in the field of early and special education. The empirical evidence about the nature of the effects of using operant techniques with young children is, despite the large research effort that has been mounted in recent years, inconclusive. In particular it is not clear how far the reinforcement of particular responses will generalise to encompass attitudes on learning sets. Certainly spontaneous interest can be rewarded as a step towards the shaping of a general approach to learning in such a way that this becomes self-reinforcing. Yet how far this can be achieved is an empirical question; to come down firmly on one side or the other at present requires something of an act of faith. From current evidence it is already difficult to deny that operant techniques can achieve limited and specific teaching goals or that they conveniently lend themselves to precise control. On balance we believe that it is irresponsible to forgo practical advantages in order to lessen the risk of future failure or to protect a favoured theoretical position.

By now it should be clear that in our view the most sensible way to proceed is by attempting to evaluate the technology in the light of the objectives of the overall system. It should also be clear that pure deduction will not provide the answers. The systems approach, like educational technology itself, consists of techniques which will only be effective if we are first clear about priorities. Let us take an example. One issue on which educators are still divided is the question of the value of repetition. Most teaching machines are particularly suitable for drill-and-practice routines and the value of developing these will depend on the weight given to the need for this kind of teaching in the first place. If, as for example Nordberg (1965) has argued, teaching machines that employ repetition also tend to discourage creativity then a judgement is required about the probable long-term effects. In the context of early and special education it seems to us important to allow sufficient repetition of, for example, graded discrimination problems in order to achieve mastery. This is a limited teaching goal for which it seems entirely appropriate to make use of automated techniques.

In a sense though this is avoiding the issue. Many studies in developmental and cognitive psychology make it clear that the learning process is not a simple matter of passively recording a variety of external events but depends on an active process of construction and interaction between previous and new experiences. One common objection to teaching machines is that they place too great a limitation on the opportunities for such active processes. This is certainly a valid criticism of most teaching machines currently in use. However this cannot be an objection in principle unless one wants to argue against the use of any kind of control of the child's environment. It is an objection to the adequacy of the available technology rather than to the principle of automated instruction. In any case the potential flexibility now being incorporated into some of the automated systems will reduce the force of this kind of objection.

There is an undeniably strong case for the use of automated techniques in special education. Here the need for repetition and, if you like, patience in taking careful account of every response is well met by the facilities of most teaching machines. In fact some aspects of the way in which young normal children learn argues for the use of simple repetition techniques in early education generally. Flavell (1970) in summarising several developmental studies of mediated memory suggests that children do not develop the use of verbal rehearsal as a strategy until the age of about six. Interestingly, in one experiment (Keeney, Cannizzo and Flavell, 1967) it was demonstrated that children, who did not spontaneously rehearse and were trained to do so, afterwards showed a clear tendency to return to their non-rehearsing mode given free choice. For applied purposes, then, it may be inappropriate to attempt to train such strategies in young children. In general it seems that young children are less responsive to social pressures to learn and less able to utilise instructions than older children; in short their learning is largely incidental rather than intentional. Repetition provided by teaching machines may then serve to compensate for the lack of spontaneous rehearsal and also allow substantial opportunities for incidental learning. Simple drill-and-practice routines can have an important function in early education.

Throughout most discussions of educational technology, and this book is probably no exception, there is a tendency to overemphasise the importance of the physical technology at the expense of the underlying behavioural principles, perhaps because the latter are relatively imprecise and undeveloped. We should emphasise therefore that the use of programmed instruction or (to use the parallel terminology) a behaviour modification schedule does not necessarily involve the use of automated techniques. Apter, Boorer and Thomas (1974) have recently reviewed the use of materials involving both machine and non-machine presentation. They also attempted to distinguish between examples where operant techniques have been used with young children and those using linear programmed instruction (they could find no examples at all of branching programs written for use in early childhood education). They propose that the main difference lies in the assumption that with programmed instruction the child has some linguistic competence, though not necessarily the ability to read or write. The point here seems to be that the decisions about whether or not to try to automate a teaching situation and whether to opt for programmed instruction procedures or a pure operant conditioning schedule (probably involving the dispensing of material reinforcers of some kind) are generally taken on the basis of assumptions about the initial level of competence of the pupil. Part of this book has been concerned with attempts to design a physical technology for children who have an initially low level of linguistic competence. It is, however, important not to confuse the evaluation of these attempts with an evaluation of the behavioural technology or educational theory underlying them.

In assessing the prospects for an educational technology based on detailed and precise behavioural specifications there seems little reason for optimism. We have argued that serious advances need the combined efforts of a team comprising design and production engineers, educationalists and psychologists (and probably even marketing specialists). Yet even among educational technologists there is a reluctance to admit the interplay between developments in programming techniques and physical technology. The problem is how to combine improvements in both at the design stage. At present it is difficult to see how any behaviourally based system can get fair consideration since industry tends, quite reasonably, to be organised around products involving a particular physical technology. Psychologists and educationalists are more likely to be involved in evaluating a new product after its initial design features have been laid down. The result is that the physical technology then places undue limitations on the preparation and nature of the learning material. It is evident that just as pre-production equipment is subjected to environmental testing and the

154

designs modified where necessary, so a behaviourally based product should be subjected to behavioural testing.

7.2 Educational technology and compensatory education

The term 'compensatory education' implies some kind of attempt to improve the educability of children who for one of a number of possible reasons might be in a disadvantageous position for learning basic skills in school. One general assumption is that intervention to compensate for the disadvantage, whatever it is, is more likely to be successful the earlier it is started and the longer it can be maintained. But even this assumption can be questioned. As far as 'the earlier the better' is concerned this is not universally true for human learning and for some skills the principle of equifinality (see Section 6.1) may apply. Stanley (1973) suggests that a child who precociously attains skills that would not normally develop until later might instead have spent some of his time and energy doing something else that would have been more fun or more permanently effective. Nevertheless the main rationale for compensatory education rests on the assumption that certain kinds of disadvantage will lead to a permanent decrement unless intervention takes place.

For our present purposes the main link between educational technology and compensatory education is due to the emphasis in both on student based or individualised instruction. Since the range of possible disadvantages is so vast, including specific mental and physical handicaps and social and intellectual deprivations of all kinds, a blanket approach to intervention may be doomed to comparative failure. The principle of individualised instruction could, if fully implemented, obviate the need for separate compensatory programs entirely. Each individual child should get the education he needs, whatever his starting point and whatever his rate of learning. There are, of course, several difficulties here. The obvious one is in the phrase 'if fully implemented'. Not least among the problems of implementing an educational technology based on the needs of the individual child is the organisation of formal education as we presently understand it in the school context.

There is certainly no shortage of suggestions about the radical restructuring of formal education. Stanley (1973), for example, suggests the complete abolition of school grades and the establishment of longitudinal teaching teams spanning the whole range of skills from birth onwards. This means removing the emphasis on age-related achievements (norm-referenced), to one of criterion-referenced achievement regardless of age. It seems clear that educational technology, with its learner centred approach, would facilitate such restructuring.

Even given such radical reorganisation, however, financial resources will always limit the extent to which formal education can meet the needs of the individual child. In this context it is encouraging to note the recent emphasis placed on non-formal education programmes. Such programmes are based in the home or the community (e.g. Halsey (1972) and Midwinter (1972)) and often make use of an existing social organisation, such as a trade union or play group, with support through the media from a centralised agency. Non-formal education takes place outside the graded school system, but is nonetheless planned and systematic. It should be further distinguished from informal education by, for instance, the example and precept of elders and from incidental education resulting from the natural observation of society and the world around the learner (Michigan State University, 1973). Such distinctions can provide a useful conceptual framework for relating needs and resources. In the developing countries non-formal education can be an effective means of social change and is being applied to objectives which are met by formal education in the developed countries. Its main application in the developed countries is to a population outside the age range of the formal educational system.

The best existing model of this kind is in the use of television as an educational medium by the *Sesame Street* project mentioned in Section 1.2. The project was the result of collaboration between an impressively wide range of specialists: educational researchers, child psychologists, pre-school teachers and television specialists. Behavioural objectives for both cognitive and social skills were formulated although these were, as Ball and Bogatz (1970) point out, in fact somewhat more limited than those of a good nursery school. *Sesame Street* was primarily aimed at disadvantaged children, at home, without benefit of formal educational experience. The major conclusion from the study was that children who viewed the programme most often showed the highest gains and that this was independent of other factors such as social class, IQ and previous achievements. Younger children gained as much as older children and, if they viewed the programme as much, the disadvantaged gained as much as the advantaged. The trouble unfortunately, was that the disadvantaged did not view the programme as much as the advantaged. Worse still, within the disadvantaged group as a whole it was the most disadvantaged who viewed least.

The results from the *Sesame Street* project already seem to have raised some fairly fundamental questions about how priorities should be assigned for different groups of pre-school children. The strategy of the Children's Television Workshop in making proposals for television aimed at pre-school children was to allow universal rather than selective coverage. It was not initially recognised very clearly that the interests of the advantaged and disadvantaged could conflict. The *Sesame Street* evaluation has shown that educational television, like some other forms of intervention, may be effective in teaching large numbers of children but it might at the same time widen rather than narrow the gap between the advantaged and the disadvantaged. Perhaps it should be recognised that a universal coverage by television is bound to fail if the objective is essentially a compensatory one. Educationally-rich homes will provide a better environment for the child to view the programme at all and also for providing better general support for the child who does view.

One approach to this problem is to intervene more directly in the individual home environment. From various pilot projects related to *Sesame Street* it seems likely that involving parents or volunteer helpers could be valuable.

Home based intervention can be justified not only on the grounds of economy but it also provides the pervasive type of intervention required to stand a real chance of success. Nevertheless, the more direct the intervention the more acute are the problems created by the intervention itself. There is in all this approach an implied approval of certain (middle class) cultural values and a complementary suggestion of cultural deficiency on the part of the disadvantaged. This means that the manner of offering help may be unacceptable because of the social stigma attached to it. In addition there may well arise clashes of interest between subgroups of advantaged and disadvantaged. Providing some measure of compensatory education for particular subgroups will alter their position relative to the remainder. One relevant factor here is that parents of socially disadvantaged children are apparently less able and willing to acknowledge educational problems than their counterparts whose children are physically and mentally handicapped. Such attitudes are likely to be reduced if the intervention is of a non-formal nature. Research recently initiated at the Hester Adrian Research Centre, University of Manchester (Mittler, 1974), is indicative of the trend. Parents of mentally handicapped children between two and five years old will be able to observe their children interacting with specialists at the centre and they will be involved in recording behaviour and in planning, carrying out and evaluating teaching programmes.

7.3 What next?

Firstly, there seem to be two broad areas in which *theoretical* developments are likely to make an impact on the advancing technology of early education. One of these will concern theories underlying educational technology in general, and theories about child development and learning in particular; the other will concern models which specify procedures for evaluating educational research. The psychology of learning is not currently short of theoretical models; what it lacks are models which give adequate indication of the elements of a pre-school curriculum which could benefit later development. The outstanding exception is that of Piaget and it is highly probable that a major area of progress will see the merging of Piagetian and other cognitive models of human development together with the techniques of educational technology as discussed in Section 2.2.2. Parallel with this the behaviour modification approach seems certain to be further developed in the context of early and special education. The divisions between these approaches are likely to become less clear-cut.

Experimental psychology can also be expected to make an impact in other ways. To take an example from the study of human memory, it is now possible to specify the precise conditions under which auditory presentation will lead to superior recall of the same information presented visually. It will be necessary for the designers of audio-visual presentation devices to take account of reliable phenomena of this kind even though the cognitive models to account for such effects are constantly changing. Smith (1974) has recently reported the results of a survey in which a series of questionnaires was given to a panel of 50 selected psychologists. The questionnaires required predictions about future developments in psychology and the area of likely application and when these were likely to occur. The general picture that emerges is that psychology will develop rapidly into applied areas and that psychologists will increasingly adopt a role as an interface between the planners and the planned. It is interesting to note that the estimates of when computer-assisted learning, tape–slide packages and tutoring in small groups will become the standard mode of education is around the turn of the century. At that time, however, it is envisaged that the present theories of learning will still be with us. It is not the case that a complete theory of learning is a necessary prerequisite for tackling the development of a theory of instruction. Indeed it may be argued that commitment to large-scale general theories actually discourages attempts to obtain modest improvements by the application of evidence obtained in the applied situation.

We devoted a substantial part of the last chapter to a discussion of the influence of the systems approach to educational technology and this approach will probably continue to grow in influence. At the moment, however, one can do little more than emphasise that in early childhood education the system is particularly complicated. The developing child can be viewed as one of a set of complex units, subject to a host of variable influences over time. As Messick and Barrows (1972) have pointed out, 'this system is composed of differentiated but overlapping subsystems that embrace the child, the family, the community and the various peer groups as well as the school, the teachers and the programs'. They specify a broad range of measurement domains in detail and indicate that, since alteration to one part of this system can produce unexpected consequences elsewhere, a straightforward analysis of a particular experimental treatment may fail to detect a wide range of other possible effects.

Using analogies from medicine and engineering Messick and Barrows stress the advantages of the 'medical' model for use in educational research. This entails taking into account not only the comparison of gain scores for each experimental treatment but also side-effects produced by the individual's own characteristics and his interaction with his environment. Furthermore the analogy with say, drug testing, implies that reactions should be sampled from time to time and not merely at a single pre-test and post-test occasion. In contrast, this latter form of summative evaluation is typical of the literature of programmed instruction over the last decade: it is characterised by experimental reports comparing traditional teaching methods with new materials and is based on an 'engineering' model which seeks to specify input–output differences, often in relation to cost. Whether statistical significance is achieved is regarded as of greater importance than the magnitude of the effect, though often a small effect will be of little use for practical purposes. Apart from the limitations of the comparisons this approach is particularly open to various sources of bias, especially the effects of novelty favouring the new method or experimenters themselves unwittingly acting as important determinants of performance. Hopefully, then, we will see less of this kind of research in educational technology in the future and more in the way of frequent evaluation of ongoing longitudinal studies, conforming to the medical model.

Even so, a continuing problem will be in decision making about whether the present time is opportune for implementing the results of research or whether another series of studies is necessary. It is rarely the case that both short-term and long-term solutions are compatible and proceed together. The difficulty of forward planning is acute when both physical and behavioural technology change rapidly and unsuspected developments may significantly affect the reception and value of an innovation. Since decisions have to be made, more attention needs to be given to techniques which attempt to quantify all the relevant factors involved and their relevant importance. The techniques occasionally used at present are crude but nevertheless very helpful. Smith's (1974) study, mentioned earlier, employed the Delphi technique, pioneered by Helmer and used in the development of weapons systems. Allan (1973) has developed an intuitive method involving the systematic weighting of 15 factors likely to influence decision making about the use of eight possible media of instruction. This is illustrated in Tables 7.1. and 7.2.

It is, of course, easy to disagree with the details but the main point is that some basis is provided for trying to clarify the decision making process about the selection of media and, indeed, for the planning of research and development strategy in general.

Turning now to the general problem of implementation let us consider the recent experiment of performance contracting. The principle of performance contracting in education is a straightforward one but it raises some interesting questions about the future strategy of educational technology and, incidentally, so far seems to have provided some disturbing answers. The principle is that an education authority signs a contract with an independent (usually commercial) organisation both to produce and implement an instructional system leading to the attainment of mutually agreed behavioural objectives. Since such a system can only operate when standardised measuring instruments are available for assessing the extent to which the specified performance has been achieved, its use at present is restricted to the learning of specific skills such as reading. The contractor is paid by an agreed formula on actual student performance on criterion tests at the completion of the program. Thus a salient feature is that the performance of individual pupils is allowed to influence the success or failure of the entire system.

Now, opponents of performance contracting argue that many key factors cannot be measured by pay-off tests. It is not accepted that a succession of discrete items, designed to separate individuals on a standardised scale, can properly assess mastery of the material and affective components in learning. In addition, performance contracting may be particularly abhorrent to those who see it as the introduction of the profit motive directly into education. It is the case, however, that this motive is already firmly entrenched in the sense that the producers of almost all educational resources are commercial organisations. Nevertheless, performance contracting can be viewed as an attempt to apply reinforcement theory to the practitioners of educational technology themselves. As Page (1972) has put it, 'it is main-line, established reinforcement theory put into action'. Another way of looking at it, perhaps, is to suggest that it serves

Table 7.1 List of variables with rating scale and weighting for Table 7.2

	−2	−1	0	+1	+2	Weighting
1. Availability	almost unavail-able	to very limited extent	moderately	easily	completely	× 5
2. Cost	very expensive	expensive	moderately	cheap	very cheap	× 5
3. Convenience for class use	very in-convenient	fairly	a little	con-venient	very con-venient	× 1
4. Convenience for individual use	very in-convenient	fairly	a little	con-venient	very con-venient	× 1
5. Participation potential	very low	low	moderate, interested	high	very high	× 3
6. Control of class	very weak	weak	moderate	fairly strong	very strong	× 3
7. Quantity and variety of messages available	very small	fairly small	moderate	fairly large	very large	× 4
8. Capacity for communica-ting complex conceptual thinking	very low	low	moderate, interested	high	very high	× 2
9. Capacity for demonstra-tion	very low	low	moderate, interested	high	very high	× 3
10. Perceptual range and variety	very small	fairly small	moderate	fairly large	very large	× 2
11. Affective power	very weak	weak	moderate	fairly strong	very strong	× 1
12. Control of time of use	almost none	very little	reasonable	very con-siderable	complete	× 3
13. Control of pace of delivery	almost none	very little	reasonable	very con-siderable	complete	× 2
14. Programmed feedback	none	very little	moderate	consi-derable	very con-siderable	× 3
15. Free feedback	none	very little	moderate	consi-derable	very con-siderable	× 3

Table 7.2 Weighted comparison of different factors affecting the selection of media for education 1973/1978

	Live teacher Now 1978		Print Now 1978		Audio B/C recorded Now 1978		B/C ETV Now 1978		Film Now 1978		Tape/ slide Now 1978		CAI Now 1978		Recorded A-V Now 1978	
1. Availability × 5	+10	+10	+10	+10	+5	+10	+5	+5	0	0	+5	+5	−10	−10	−10	+5
2. Cost × 5	−10	−10	+5	+5	+5	+5	+5	+5	−5	−5	−5	0	−10	−10	−5	0
3. Convenience for class use × 1	+2	+2	+1	+1	+1	+1	+1	+1	−1	−1	0	0	−2	−2	0	0
4. Convenience for individual use × 1	+2	+2	+2	+2	+1	+1	+1	+1	−1	−1	−1	−1	+2	+2	+2	+2
5. Participation potential × 3	+6	+6	0	0	0	0	0	0	0	0	0	0	+6	+6	0	0
6. Control of class × 3	+6	+6	−6	−6	−6	−6	−6	−6	−6	−6	−6	−6	−6	−6	−6	−6
7. Quantity and variety of messages × 4	+4	+4	+8	+8	0	0	0	0	−4	−4	0	+4	−4	+4	−8	+1
8. Capacity for conceptual thinking × 2	+2	+2	+4	+4	+2	+2	0	0	0	0	0	0	+4	+4	0	0
9. Capacity for demonstration × 3	+3	+3	−3	−3	−3	−3	+6	+6	+6	+6	+3	+3	0	0	+6	+6
10. Perceptual range and variety × 2	−2	−2	−4	−4	−4	−4	+4	+4	+4	+4	+2	+2	−2	−2	+4	+4
11. Affective power × 1	+1	+1	+1	+1	+1	+1	+2	+2	+2	+2	+1	+1	−2	−2	+2	+2
12. Control of time of use × 3	+6	+6	+6	+6	+6	+6	−6	−6	+3	+3	+3	+3	+3	+6	+6	+6
13. Control of pace of use × 2	+4	+4	+2	+2	+2	+2	−4	−4	0	0	+2	+2	+4	+4	+2	+2
14. Programmed feedback × 3	+6	+6	−6	−6	−6	−6	−6	−6	−6	−6	−6	−6	+6	+6	−6	−6
15. Free feedback × 3	+6	+6	−6	−6	−6	−6	−6	−6	−6	−6	−6	−6	−6	−6	−6	−6
+	+58	58	39	39	23	28	24	24	15	15	16	20	25	32	22	31
−	−12	12	25	25	25	25	28	28	29	29	24	19	42	38	41	18
Score	46	46	14	14	−2	+3	−4	−4	−14	−14	−8	+1	−17	−6	−19	13

Rank order of scores	Use now	Use in 1978
Live teacher	1	1
Print	2	2
Audio (B/C and recorded)	3	4
ETV (B/C)	4	6
Tape/Slide	5	5
Film	6	8
CAI	7	7
Recorded audio-video	8	3

mainly to match the objectives of the resource producers with those of the educational planners, which is certainly not the case in the traditional system.

By 1971, performance contracting had been introduced into at least 25 American school systems (Davies, 1971). Early reports seemed encouraging and such was the enthusiasm generated that the US Office of Economic Opportunity mounted a large-scale experiment which Page has described as the most impressive ever mounted in education. Thirty-one educational contractors put in bids and contracts were signed with six of these. Of the six at least three eventually went out of business, apparently as a result of the project.

The experiment involved 18 US school systems with over 25,000 children participating in either experimental or control groups. A wide range of age-levels was covered and the experiment included children 'across every major low-achieving ethnic group, from poor urban Anglos to Alaskan Eskimos' (Page, 1972). From each school the 100 pupils performing lowest at each age-level served as subjects. Great care was taken to avoid the usual criticism of performance contracting, namely that the system encourages teaching methods aimed specifically at getting the students through the particular assessment tests employed, to the detriment of more generalised learning. In this experiment any attempt by the contractors to discover what tests were to be used for assessing performance was to be sufficient cause for the termination of the contract.

The contracts specified that payment was to be made only for a student who gained one school year of growth between the autumn pre-test and the spring post-test. Page, in asking why such ambitious goals were set, given the likely growth of perhaps 0·7 of a year in a year of normal schooling for these low-achieving children, concludes that the office of Economic Opportunity, the schools and the contractors 'really believed that the lagging pupils were disadvantaged only in their prior experience; that the schools were terribly ineffective teachers; and that the application of the usual psychological principles would cause extraordinary leaps in achievement'.

The results of this study were almost uniformly disappointing. Not only were the contractors in all kinds of financial trouble as a result of the children's failure to achieve the performance criteria but, even worse, the experimental subjects showed no more gain than the controls who had simply continued to receive normal school instruction. During the study both experimental and control subjects slipped further behind the average performance for their age-levels.

On the present evidence, then, the conclusion must be that performance contracting seems very unlikely, in itself, to provide much of an answer to the general problem of educating the disadvantaged. It is not entirely clear, however, whether failure should be attributed to the system of performance contracting or whether a more fundamental criticism of the instructional techniques employed is implied here. The really disturbing point is that a system which was supposed to encourage the use of the best and most up-to-date educational technology should have failed to make any impact at all on learning rate. It would be necessary to look more closely at the actual techniques employed before accepting this as a failure of technology, but Page at least interprets the results as necessitating a fundamental reappraisal of many of our practices and assumptions about school learning and its evaluation.

A different but no less important pressure could involve an attempt to alter attitudes on the cost of education. Robens (1970) stresses the point that the accountant's classification of education as a revenue cost is incorrect. It would be more realistic to view education as an investment for human and non-human resources used now in order to provide a return later. 'It is not a poetic fancy to talk of it [education] as an investment in the country's future, but a strict economic truth.' He puts forward a specific proposal in line with his conception, that of building an experimental school in an educational priority area: a school where every classroom would be equipped with teaching aids, a school with its own computer and, not least important, a school with maximum flexibility of structure which could be adapted to changing requirements. Such a school would be in a position to evaluate new methods against one another, rather than against traditional methods thus minimising potential sources of bias; it would be able to carry out evaluation trials over a protracted period instead of an inadequately short duration; it would be able to test, so to speak, the whole system rather than attempting to make estimates of the effects of the sum of the parts; its scale of operation should make possible cost benefits and estimates of cost-effectiveness, not previously available.

In more general terms this argument amounts to a plea to stop regarding education as a totally distinctive, independent social process. Whilst still accepting the traditional view that in a sense no price is too high to pay for education, Richmond (1969), in justifying the title of his book *The Education Industry*, insists that it is both legitimate and necessary to think of educational services in industrial terms. Unless educationalists do so, he feels that the initiative and ultimately the control of these services may be taken over by a combination of management specialists and commercial entrepreneurs. Moreover he considers the distinction between agencies providing vocational training or purveyors of entertainment and educationalists is a misleading one. 'In so far as they are all in the information business they all have a part to play, and their impact (which is inescapable) is not to be minimised simply because it does not fall within the existing framework of schools and colleges.' In all, the conclusion is difficult to resist that, whether educationalists like it or not, the accumulation of industrial experience will be increasingly brought to bear on educational problems. Because of the traditional independence and conservatism of approach, it is very probable that there will then be widespread resentment and resistance.

Finally, let us look briefly at some specific proposals for developments in the field of early education. We will consider them in order of an increasing time-span for development which happens to coincide with ascending order of cost. First, the potential for educational toys seems to have been rather neglected within the present context. Of course manufacturers have always had a ready sale of toys of all kinds to relatives and friends of young children but a consequence of this is that comparatively little attention has been paid to their specifically educational features. It is interesting to ask when does a toy become a teaching machine. The word toy seems to imply a non-specific use since play behaviour would not on the face of it seem to be directed in the manner required for the operation of a teaching machine. Yet a little thought leads one to the conclusion that the distinction is an entirely arbitrary one. Suffice it to say that operating teaching machines or, indeed, using any kind of educational technology should be as much fun for the child as playing with a toy. If not then it may be argued that the technology is somehow missing out an important element in early learning. Nevertheless, there is undoubtedly a great deal of scope for the imaginative development of educational toys. Perhaps the main point is that by regarding them as important tools in the educational technologist's repertoire they will be subjected to more rigorous behavioural evaluation.

A thorough study of the effects of an educational toy has been undertaken by Olson (1970) who developed three versions in investigating the acquisition of diagonality. He acknowledges that there is no theory of educational toys but puts forward three relevant considerations: (i) a toy should make a measurable contribution to a specified educational objective; (ii) informal experience with a toy may underlie ability to profit later from formal instruction; and (iii) this experience may be more critical for some children than others. As a result of successful demonstrations of his experimental toy's value, Olson identifies four attributes of any educational toy which he considers to be relevant to its effectiveness. Briefly, it should offer a suitably graded intellectual challenge, it should possess intrinsic interest, it should provide relevant information and the knowledge and concepts gained should transfer to other situations. It is worth pointing out that these are essentially similar to attributes we listed earlier for teaching machines. Figure 7.1 shows the final version of Olson's toy.

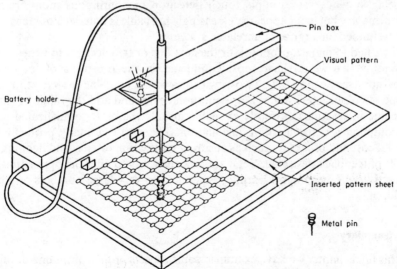

Figure 7.1 The electrical version of Olson's educational toy

The sequence of operation is that, if the stylus is inserted into a hole corresponding to a position on the model to be copied, the light will come on but this is not so for any inappropriate positions. Programming is by means of pattern sheets which are interchangeable. The toy thus allows a child to copy the model of the diagonal as well as a large set of other spatial models. It can also be used in memory and problem solving tasks where locating and using information is relevant. As Olson points out, the toy has the virtue of 'portability, durability, versatility and economy'. In the wider context we feel that it is unfortunate that only a fraction of the potential value of toys in intellectual development has so far been appreciated.

The main practical differences between educational toys and automated teaching systems relate to the mechanical complexity, sophisticated modes of presentation and response and the facilities for providing response records possessed by the latter. A frequent line of argument is that the cost of teaching machines should be reduced by omitting or degrading certain facilities offered. Thus Hegarty (1973), after carrying out an extensive survey of the potential of the Touch-Tutor with severely subnormal children, proposes a simpler and less costly alternative. We would not wish to prejudge the likelihood of success of his proposal in the field of special education but in general we want to make the argument in the opposite direction. In our view there is an increasingly clear dichotomy between short-term low-cost and long-term high-cost, without a satisfactory middle way between. Toys fall into the first category and automated systems into the second. An implication of the dichotomy is that apart from restricted areas of application, such as various research purposes and perhaps special education, the development of separate automated systems should be integrated with the long-term strategy of introducing computer-controlled learning systems. Such systems may well make use of elements of existing systems, for example touch detection or continuous monitoring of performance, but what appears decreasingly probable is that development work can be funded for a range of unrelated systems.

If we had to make a proposal for the next one or two decades to benefit early education, we would have most confidence in the prospects of interactive television (see Section 5.4). Two-way cables would combine the versatility and scope of colour television as a presentation device and add the range of child–machine interactions currently available in only the most sophisticated types of computer-assisted learning installation. There will be many problems: of capital cost and of factors such as ensuring motivation to view and defining the kinds of feedback desirable. Yet it seems a clear way to offer the opportunity of attractive and meaningful learning experience to very large numbers of young children.

7.4 Summary

In this final chapter we have examined some aspects of the continuing development of educational technology that seem likely to be of importance. It is envisaged that progress in experimental psychology will be incorporated into the further development of a behavioural technology, with the current divergence of approach narrowing as theories of learning and instruction merge. We see a continuing but restricted role for medium cost devices but in general the development of automated systems will be directed towards the long-term aim of implementing computer-controlled systems. In the short term more attention should be paid to the potential for educational toys. It is also suggested that automated systems, with their potential for individualised instruction, have an important role to play in the context of compensatory and special education. Despite the great problems of implementation, which performance contracting seems unlikely to solve, we remain hopeful.

References

Alford, R. W. (1971) Home-oriented pre-school education, *Report ED 060 742 ERIC Research in Education*, US Department of Health, Education and Welfare, Washington, DC.

Allan, T. S. (1973) Educational selection of media with particular reference to ETV, in R. Budgett and J. Leedham (Eds.), *Aspects of Educational Technology VII*, London: Pitman.

Angyal, A. (1941) *Foundations for a Science of Personality*, Cambridge, Mass: Harvard University Press.

Apter, M. J., Boorer, D., and Thomas, S. (1974) Programmed instruction with pre-school children: an appraisal, *Programmed Learning and Educational Technology*, **11**, 74–86.

Apter, M. J., and Westby, G. (Eds.) (1973) *The Computer in Psychology*, London: Wiley.

Ashby, W. R. (1964) *Introduction to Cybernetics*, London: Methuen.

Atkinson, R. C. (1968) Computerised instruction and the learning process, *American Psychologist*, **23**, 225–239.

Atkinson, R. C., and Wilson, H. A. (1968) Computer assisted instruction, *Science*, **162**, 73–77.

Baer, D. M. (1961) Effect of withdrawal of positive reinforcement on an experimental response in young children, *Child Development*, **32**, 67–74.

Baer, D. M. (1962) A technique for the study of social reinforcement in young children. Behavior avoiding reinforcement withdrawal, *Child Development*, **33**, 847–858.

Ball, S., and Bogatz, G. A. (1970) *The First Year of Sesame Street: An Evaluation*, Princeton, NJ: Educational Testing Service.

Beasley, N. A., and Hegarty, J. R. (1970) The use of the Touch-Tutor with s.s.n. children, *Journal of mental Subnormality*, **16**, 113–118.

Beer, S. (1959) *Cybernetics and Management*, London: English University Press.

Békésy, G. von (1967) *Sensory Inhibition*, Princeton, NJ: Princeton University Press.

Bernstein, B. B. (1971a) *Class, Codes and Control*, Vol. 1, London: Routledge and Kegan Paul.

Bernstein, B. B. (1971b) Language and socialization, in N. Minnis (Ed.) *Linguistics at Large*, London: Baylis and Son.

Bertalanffy, L. von (1950) The theory of open systems in physics and biology, *Science*, **111**, 23–29.

Bijou, S. W., and Baer, D. M. (1966) Operant methods in child behavior and development, in W. K. Honig (Ed.) *Operant behavior: Areas of Research and Application*, New York: Appleton-Century-Crofts, pp. 718–789.

Bijou, S. W., and Orlando, R. (1961) Rapid development of multiple scheduled performances with retarded children, *Journal of the experimental Analysis of Behavior*, **4**, 7–16.

Bitzer, D., and Skaperdas, D. (1973) The design of an economically viable large-scale computer-based education system, *CERL Report X-5*, Computer-based Education Research Laboratory, University of Illinois, Urbana, Illinois.

Blackwell, F., and Jackman, M. (1971) *Sesame Street*, Report by the Primary Extension Programme of the National Council for Educational Technology, 38 Grovelands Road, Purley, Surrey.

Bloom, B. S. (1956) *Taxonomy of educational objectives: the classification of educational goals*, Handbook 1 *Cognitive domain*, New York: McKay.

Bloom, B. S. (1964) *Stability and Change in Human Characteristics*, New York: Wiley.

Bloom, B. S., Hastings, J. T., and Madaus, G. F. (Eds.) (1971) *Handbook on Formative and Summative Evaluation of Student Learning*, New York: McGraw-Hill.

Bowlby, J. (1953) *Child Care and the Growth of Love*, Harmondsworth: Penguin.

Broderick, W. R. (1972) A system for computer managed instruction, in K. Austwick and N. D. C. Harris (Eds.), *Aspects of Educational Technology VI*, London: Pitman.

Brown, N. (1972) The use of an audio-visual reading programme, *Remedial Education*, **7**, 24–26.

Brown, R. C. (1963) *Smoothing, Forecasting and Prediction of Discrete Time Series*, Englewood Cliffs, NJ: Prentice-Hall.

Bruner, J. S. (1966) *Toward a Theory of Instruction*, Cambridge, Mass: Harvard University Press.

Buiten, R., and Lane, M. L. (1965) A self-instructional device for conditioning accurate prosody, *International Review of applied Linguistics*, **3**, 205–219.

Bushell, D., Wrobel, P. A., and Michaelis, M. L. (1968) Applying group contingencies to the classroom study behavior of pre-school children, *Journal of Applied Behavior Analysis*, **1**, 55–61.

Carroll, J. (1963) A model of school learning, *Teachers College Record*, **64**, 723–733.

Centre for Educational Research and Innovation (1971) *Educational Technology. The design and implementation of learning systems*. Paris: OECD (Organisation for Economic Cooperation and Development).

Clark, W. A., and Molnar, C. W. (1965) A description of the LINC, in R. W. Stacy and B. D. Waxman (Eds.), *Computers in biomedical research*, Vol. 2, New York: Academic Press.

Cleary, A., and Packham, D. (1968) A touch-detecting teaching machine with auditory reinforcement, *Journal of applied Behavior Analysis*, **1**, 341–345.

Cooley, W. W., and Glaser, R. (1969) The computer and individualised instruction, *Science*, **166**, 574–582.

Coombs, P. H. (1968) *The World Educational Crisis: A System Analysis*, London: Oxford University Press.

Cowles, J. T. (1937) Food tokens as incentives for learning by chimpanzees, *Comparative Psychology Monographs*, **14**, no. 5.

Cox, M., and Somerfield, M. (1970) *The final report of the Coventry primary schools reading project*, Nuffield Foundation, Resources for Learning Project, Nuffield Lodge, Regents Park, London, NW1 4RS.

Crouch, E. (1966) The Language Master in the classroom, *Visual Education*, February, **1966**, 3–4.

Crowder, N. A. (1959) Automatic tutoring by means of intrinsic programming, in E. H. Galanter (Ed.), *Automatic Teaching: the State of the Art*, New York: Wiley.

Crowder, N. A. (1960) Automatic tutoring and intrinsic programming, in A. A. Lumsdaine and R. Glaser (Eds.), *Teaching Machines and Programmed Learning*, Washington: DAVI-NEA, pp. 286–298.

Cumming, C., and Dunn, W. R. (1970) The application of cost-effectiveness techniques to educational technology, in A. C. Bajpai and J. F. Leedham (Eds.), *Aspects of Educational Technology, IV*, London: Pitman.

Davie, R., Butler, N., and Goldstein, H. (1972) *From Birth to Seven*, London: Longmans.

Davies, I. K. (1971) Developing accountability in instructional systems technology, in D. Packham, A. Cleary, and T. Mayes (Eds.), *Aspects of Educational Technology V*, London: Pitman.

Davies, W. J. K., and Needham, M. (1971) Programmed assessment of learning difficulties in sub-normal and normal children, in D. Packham, A. Cleary, and T. Mayes (Eds.), *Aspects of Educational Technology V*, London: Pitman.

168

DeGreene, K. B. (Ed.) (1970) *Systems Psychology*, New York: McGraw-Hill.

Denenberg, V. H. (1970) Introduction, in V..H. Denenberg (Ed.), *Education of the Infant and Young Child*, New York: Academic Press.

Douglas, J. B. (1964) *The Home and the School*, London: MacGibbon and Kee.

Dudley, H. (1939) The vocoder, *Bell Lab. Record*, **17**, 122–126.

Dunn-Rankin, P. (1968) The similarity of lower-case letters of the English alphabet, *Journal of verbal Learning and verbal Behavior*, **7**, 990–995.

Elton, L. R. B. (1970) The use of duplicated lecture notes and self tests in University teaching, in A. C. Bajpai and J. F. Leedham (Eds.), *Aspects of Educational Technology IV*, London: Pitman.

Evans, K. (1971) A role for television in compensatory education, in M. Chazan and G. Downes (Eds.), *Compensatory Education and the New Media*, Swansea: Schools Council.

Experimental Development Unit, NCAVAE (1970) Technical reports: Bell & Howell Language Master Model 701, *Visual Education*, April, **1970**, 13–14.

Fellows, B. J. (1968) *The Discrimination Process and Development*, Oxford: Pergamon.

Fields, C. (1973) *About Computers*, Cambridge, Mass: Winthrop Publishers.

Fitzhugh, R. J., and Katsuki, D. (1971) The touch-sensitive screen as a flexible response device in CAI and behavioral research, *Behavior Research Methods and Instrumentation*, **3**, 159–164.

Flavell, J. H. (1963) *The Developmental Psychology of Jean Piaget*, Princeton: Van Nostrand.

Flavell, J. H. (1970) Developmental studies of mediated memory, in H. W. Reese and L. P. Lipsitt (Eds.), *Advances in Child Development and Behavior*, Vol. 5, pp. 181–211.

Fletcher, S. (1971) Towards a standard code of practice for pulse track operation of $\frac{1}{4}''$ and cassetted tape in audio-visual and auto-instructional devices, in D. Packham, A. Cleary, and T. Mayes (Eds.), *Aspects of Educational Technology V*, London: Pitman, pp. 101–104.

Forrester, J. (1971) *World Dynamics*, Cambridge, Mass: M.I.T. Press.

Freemont, N. (1968) Programmed Learning in an infant school, *Visual Education*, October, **1968**, 35–39.

Gedye, J. L. (1967) A teaching machine programme for use as a test of learning ability, in D. Unwin and J. Leedham (Eds.), *Aspects of Educational Technology I*, London: Methuen.

Gedye, J. L., and Miller, E. (1970) Developments in automated testing systems, in P. Mittler (Ed.), *The Psychological Assessment of Mental and Physical Handicaps*, London: Methuen.

Gellermann, L. W. (1933) Chance orders of alternating stimuli in visual discrimination experiments, *Journal of genetic Psychology*, **42**, 207.

Gilligan, J., Hazelton, W., and Kay, W. (1971) The Ridgeway School computer-managed instruction system, in D. Packham, A. Cleary, and T. Mayes (Eds.), *Aspects of Educational Technology V*, London: Pitman.

Glaser, R. (1963) Instructional technology and the measurement of outcomes: some questions, *American Psychologist*, **18**, 519–521.

Glynn, E., Pearce, J. P., and Willott, A. S. (1969) A simple mobile feedback classroom, in A. C. Bajpai and J. F. Leedham (Eds.), *Aspects of Educational Technology IV*, London: Pitman.

Halsey, A. H. (1972) *EPA problems and policies. Educational Priority 1*, London: HMSO.

Hammond, A. L. (1972) Computer-assisted instruction: two major demonstrations, *Science*, **176**, 1110–1112.

Hansel, C. E. M. (1971) Optimum specification teaching machine design, in D. Packham, A. Cleary, and T. Mayes (Eds.), *Aspects of Educational Technology V*, London: Pitman.

Harlow, H. F. (1959) Learning set and error factor theory, in S. Koch (Ed.), *Psychology, a study of a Science*, Vol. 2, New York: McGraw-Hill.

Harlow, H. F., and Harlow, M. K. (1965) The affectional systems, in A. M. Schrier, H. F. Harlow, and F. Stollnitz (Eds.), *Behavior of Nonhuman Primates*, Vol. II, New York: Academic Press.

Harlow, H. F., and Harlow, M. K. (1969) Effects of various mother-infant relationships on rhesus monkey behaviour, in B. M. Foss (Ed.), *Determinants of Infant Behaviour 4*, London: Methuen.

Harlow, H. F., and Harlow, M. K. (1970) Developmental aspects of emotional behavior, in P. Black (Ed.), *Physiological Correlates of Emotion*, New York: Academic Press.

Harper, R., Cleary, A., and Packham, D. (1971) An automated technique for the training of retarded children, *Programmed Learning and Educational Technology*, **8**, 1–9.

Hebb, D. O. (1947) The effects of early experience on problem-solving at maturity, *American Psychologist*, **2**, 306–307.

Hegarty, J. R. (1973) Some experiments in the use of the Touch-Tutor with severely subnormal children, unpublished Ph.D. thesis, University of Keele.

Hegarty, J. R., and Beasley, N. A. (1971) Some experiments with a teaching machine for severely mentally handicapped children, paper read at the *International Seminar on Mental Retardation, University of Tubingen, Germany, July 1971*.

Hetzel, M. L., and Hetzel, C. W. (1969) *Relay Circuits for Psychology*, New York: Appleton-Century-Crofts.

Hill, J. R. W. (1970a) The Edison Responsive Environment: its development and its use, *Programmed Learning and Educational Technology*, **7**, 29–42.

Hill, J. R. W. (1970b) The preparations of programs for the Edison Responsive Environment, *Programmed Learning and Educational Technology*, **7**, 288–299.

Hill, J. R. W. (1971) An experimental validation of the Edison Responsive Environment, *Programmed Learning and Educational Technology*, **8**, 97–110.

Hill, J. R. W., and Cavanagh, P. W. W. (1968) Some explorations of the use of the E.R.E. as an aid to teaching reading to adults, in W. R. Dunn and C. Holroyd (Eds.), *Aspects of Educational Technology 2*, London: Methuen.

Hills, P. J. (1971) Self teaching systems in university courses, in D. Packham, A. Cleary, and T. Mayes (Eds.), *Aspects of Educational Technology V*, London: Pitman.

Hindley, C. B. (1965) Stability and change in abilities up to 5 years: group trends, *Journal of Child Psychology and Psychiatry*, **6**, 85–99.

Hively, W. (1960) An exploratory investigation of an apparatus for studying and teaching visual discrimination using pre-school children, in A. A. Lumsdaine and R. Glaser (Eds.), *Teaching Machines and Programmed Learning*, Washington: DAVI-NEA.

Hively, W. (1962) Programming stimuli in matching to sample, *Journal of experimental analysis of Behavior*, **5**, 279–298.

Hively, W. (1964a) A multiple-choice visual discrimination apparatus, *Journal of experimental Analysis of Behavior*, **7**, 387–389.

Hively, W. (1964b) Confessions of an experimental analyst of early reading behavior, Paper read at *American Educational Research Association, February 1964*.

HMSO (1967) Children and their primary schools, *Report of the Central Advisory Council for Education (England)*, referred to as the *Plowden Report*.

HMSO (1972) *Education: a framework for expansion*, Cmnd, 5174.

Hodge, P. (1970a) Systems structures and strategies for a technology of education, in A. C. Bajpai and J. F. Leedham (Eds.), *Aspects of Educational Technology IV*, London: Pitman.

Hodge, P. (1970b) The application of general systems theory to secondary education, in A. J. Romiszowski (Ed.), *The Systems Approach to Education and Training*, London: Kogan Page.

Holland, J. G. (1960) Teaching machines: an application of principles from the laboratory, *Journal of the experimental Analysis of Behavior*, **2**, 275–283.

Holland, J. G., and Doran, J. (1974) Teaching classification by computer, in R. Ulrich,

T. Stachnik, and J. Mabry (Eds.), *Control of Human Behavior, III*, Glenview, Illinois: Scott Foresman.

Holland, L. (1956) *Vacuum Deposition of Thin Films*, London: Chapman and Hall.

Huskisson, J. A. (1971) Programmed techniques for investigating the visual discrimination skills required for reading in young and handicapped children, unpublished M.Sc. thesis, University of Newcastle-upon-Tyne.

Huskisson, J., Packham, D., and Cleary, A. (1969) Pre-reading experiments with the Touch-Tutor, in A. P. Mann and C. J. Brunstrom (Eds.), *Aspects of Educational Technology III*, London: Pitman.

Israel, B. L. (1968) Reponsive Environment Program. The Talking Typewriter, Brooklyn, New York, *Report of the New York City Board of Education*.

Jeffrey, W. E. (1955) New technique for motivating and reinforcing children, *Science*, **121**, 371.

Jones, J. C. (1967) The designing of man-machine systems, in W. T. Singleton, R. S. Easterby, D. Whitfield (Eds.), *The Human Operator in Complex Systems*, London: Taylor and Francis.

Kamii, C. K. (1971) Evaluation of learning in pre-school education: socio-emotional, perceptual-motor, cognitive development, in B. S. Bloom, J. T. Hastings, and G. F. Madaus (Eds.), *Handbook on Formative and Summative Evaluation of Student Learning*, New York: McGraw-Hill.

Karlsen, B. (1966) Teaching beginning reading to hearing impaired children, using a visual method and teaching machines, University of Minnesota, *Report No. HCY-1204*.

Kay, H., Dodd, B., and Sime, M. (1968) *Teaching Machines and Programmed Instruction*, Harmondsworth: Penguin.

Keeney, T. J., Cannizzo, S. R., and Flavell, J. H. (1967) Spontaneous and induced verbal rehearsal in a recall task, *Child Development*, **38**, 953–966.

Korn, G. (1973) *Minicomputers for Engineers and Scientists*, New York: McGraw-Hill.

Krathwohl, D. R., Bloom, B. S., and Masia, B. B. (1964) *Taxonomy of educational objectives: the classification of educational goals*, Handbook 2 *Affective domain*, New York: McKay.

Kuder, G. F., and Richardson, M. W. (1937) The theory of the estimation of test reliability, *Psychometrika*, **2**, 151–160.

Leedham, J. F. (1965) Learning to read by programme, in J. F. Leedham and D. Unwin, *Programmed Learning in the Schools*, London: Longmans.

Leith, G. O. M. (1963) Programmed learning and special education, *Special Education*, **52**, 17–23.

Levinson, F. (1970) The value of automated techniques in exploring the learning problems of severely subnormal children, *Behavioural Technology*, **2**.

Levenstein, P. (1971) Mothers as cognitive trainers, *Report ED 059 786 ERIC Research in Education*, US Department of Health, Education and Welfare, Washington, DC.

Lewis, B. N., and Pask, G. (1966) The theory and practice of adaptive teaching systems, in R. Glaser (Ed.), *Teaching Machines and Programmed Learning II*, Washington: DAVI-NEA, pp. 213–266.

Lombard, A., and Stern, C. (1967) An instrument to measure visual discrimination of young children, US Department of Health, Education and Welfare, *Report No. ED-015-510*.

Lorenz, K. (1966) *On Aggression*, London: Methuen.

Mager, R. F. (1962) *Preparing Instructional Objectives*, California: Fearon Publishers.

Maling, R. G., and Clarkson, D. C. (1963) Electronic controls for the tetraplegic (POSSUM), *Paraplegia*, **1**, 161–174.

Martin, J. (1969) *Telecommunications and the Computer*, Englewood Cliffs, NJ: Prentice-Hall.

Martin, J. H. (1964) *Freeport public schools experiment on early reading using the Edison Responsive Environment instrument*, Englewood Cliffs, NJ: Publication of the Responsive Environments Corporation.

Maxwell, J. C. (1867) On governors, *Proceedings of Royal Society, London*, **16**, 270–283, Taylor and Francis.

Messick, S., and Barrows, T. S. (1972) Strategies for research and evaluation in early childhood education, in I. J. Gordon (Ed.), *Early Childhood Education*, the 71st Yearbook of the National Society for the study of education, Chicago: NSSE.

Mialaret, G. (1966) *The Psychology of the Use of Audio-Visual Aids in Primary Education*, London: Harrap.

Michigan State University (1973) *Discussion papers 1–6*, USAID Grant csd 3297, Program of Studies in Non-formal Education, Michigan State University.

Midwinter, E. (1972) *Projections: an Educational Priority Area at work*, London: Ward Lock.

Mittler, P. (1974) A rationale for parental partnership, *Bulletin of the British Psychological Society*, **27**, 174.

Moore, O. K. (1966) Autotelic responsive environments and exceptional children, in O. J. Harvey (Ed.), *Experience, Structure and Adaptability*, New York: Springer Publishing Co.

Morgenstern, F. S. (1969) *The Talking Typewriter. Data and case studies*, London: Publication of Rank-R.E.C. Ltd.

Morris, D. (1967) *The Naked Ape*, London: Cape.

Moseley, D. V. (1969) The Talking Typewriter and remedial teaching in a secondary school, *Remedial Education*, **4**, 196–202.

Moseley, D. V. (1971) A remedial program for severely sub-normal pupils with and without the Talking Typewriter, in D. Packham, A. Cleary, and T. Mayes (Eds.), *Aspects of Educational Technology V*, London: Pitman.

Moseley, D. V., and Sowter, D. (1972) The Hansel Training Machine: a new aid to (over) learning, in K. Austwick and N. D. C. Harris (Eds.), *Aspects of Educational Technology VI*, London: Pitman.

Moxley, R. A., Jnr. (1974) A source of disorder in the schools and a way to reduce it: two kinds of tests, in R. Ulrich, T. Stachnik, and J. Mabry (Eds.), *Control of Human Behavior*, III. Glenview, Illinois: Scott Foresman.

Murphy, D. E. and Kallis, S. A., Jnr. (1971) *Introduction to Data Communications*, Maynard, Mass: Digital Equipment Corporation.

Mylrea, K. C. (1966) A sixteen-unit projector with microsecond turn-on time, *American Journal of Psychology*, **64**, 314–317.

Neil, M. W. (1970) A systems approach to course planning at the Open University, in A. J. Romiszowski (Ed.), *The System Approach to Education and Training*, London: Kogan Page.

Newman, E. A., and Scantlebury, R. A. (1967) Teaching machines as intelligence amplifiers, *Report No. 31*, Autonomics Division, National Physical Laboratory, Teddington, Middlesex.

Nordberg, R. (1965) Teaching machines—six dangers and one advantage, in J. S. Roucek (Ed.), *Programmed Teaching*, London: Owen.

Oldfield, R. (1971) Gita 'talks' for the first time in her fifteen years, *Enfield Gazette*, 26th February.

Olson, D. R. (1970) *Cognitive Development: the Child's Acquisition of Diagonality*, New York: Academic Press.

Olson, D. R., and Bruner, J. S. (1974) Learning through experience and learning through media, in D. R. Olson (Ed.), *Media and Symbols: the Forms of Expression, Communication and Education*, the 73rd Yearbook of the National Society for the Study of Education, Chicago: NSSE.

172

Orr, N. W., and Hopkin, V. D. (1968) The role of the touch display in air traffic control, *The Controller*, **7**, 7–9.

Packham, D. M. (1974) Aspects of play and social experience in four year old pre-school children, unpublished M.Ed. thesis, University of Durham.

Page, E. B. (1972) How we ALL failed in performance contracting, *Educational Psychologist*, **9**, 40–42.

Pavlov, I. P. (1927) *Conditioned Reflexes*, London: Oxford University Press.

Payne, D. A. (1968) *The Specification and Measurement of Learning Outcomes*, Waltham, Mass: Blaisdell.

Philips Industries (1970) The PIP audio viewing unit, *Eduology*, **1**, 12–16.

Premack, D. (1959) Toward empirical behavior laws. I. Positive reinforcement, *Psychological Review*, **66**, 219–233.

Pressey, S. L. (1926) A simple apparatus which gives tests and scores—and teaches, *School and Society*, **23**, 373–376.

Pressey, S. L. (1963) Teaching machine (and learning theory) crisis, *Journal of applied Psychology*, **47**, 1–6.

Pressey, S. L. (1964) A puncture of the huge 'programming' boom, *Teachers College Record*, **65**, 413–418.

Pringle, M. K. (1974) *The Needs of Children*, London: Hutchinson.

Raggett, B. (1970) Breakthrough in storage heralds videodisc, *Electronics Weekly*, July 1st.

Reese, H. W. (1963) Discrimination learning sets in children, in L. P. Lipsitt and C. C. Spiker (Eds.), *Advances in Child Development and Behaviour*, Vol. 1, New York: Academic Press.

Richmond, W. K. (1969) *The Education Industry*, London: Methuen.

Robens, Lord (1970) Realising the potential of educational technology, in A. C. Bajpai and J. F. Leedham (Eds.), *Aspects of Educational Technology IV*, London: Pitman.

Rodgers, T. S. (1967) Linguistic considerations in the design of the Stanford computer-based curriculum initial reading, *Technical Report III*, Stanford University, Institute for Mathematical Studies in the Social Sciences.

Roebuck, M. (1971) Floundering among measurements in educational technology, in D. Packham, A. Cleary, and T. Mayes (Eds.), *Aspects of Educational Technology V*, London: Pitman.

Romiszowski, A. J. (Ed.) (1970) *The System Approach to Education and Training*, London: Kogan Page.

Rosewood State Hospital Education Dept. (1970) *The Rosewood 'Talking Typewriter' Project*, Owing's Mills, Maryland: unpublished report.

Rowntree, D. G. F. (1969) The systems approach to educational technology, *Yearbook of Educational and Instructional Technology*, London: Cornmarket Press.

Rowntree, D. G. F. (1971) Course production in the Open University, in D. Packham, A. Cleary, and T. Mayes (Eds.), *Aspects of Educational Technology V*, London: Pitman.

Rutter, M. (1972) *Maternal Deprivation Reassessed*, Harmondsworth: Penguin.

St. James-Roberts, I. P. (1973) The development of multimodality assessment procedures for use in audiological testing of children, unpublished Ph.D. thesis, University of Newcastle-upon-Tyne.

Salisbury, G. R. (1971) The 'Talking Page' machine, *Visual Education*, May **1971**, 12–13.

Schaefer, E. S. (1970) Need for early and continuing education, in V. H. Denenberg (Ed.), *Education of the Infant and Young Child*, New York: Academic Press.

Schultz, T. (1968) Education and economic growth, *Readings in the Economics of Education*, Paris: UNESCO.

Scriven, M. (1967) The methodology of evaluation, *AERA Monograph series on curriculum evaluation*, **1**, 39–83.

Seltzer, R. A. (1971) Computer-assisted instruction—what it can and cannot do, *American Psychologist*, **26**, 4.

Serrell, R., and Kling, F. R. (1968) Response apparatus for teaching machines, *US Patent* 3382588.

Silvern, L. C. (1968) Systems approach—what is it?, *Educational Technology*, **16**, 5–6.

Skinner, B. F. (1953) *Science and Human Behavior*, New York:Macmillan.

Skinner, B. F. (1954) The science of learning and the art of teaching, *Harvard Educational Review*, **24**, 2.

Skinner, B. F. (1957) *Verbal Behavior*, New York: Appleton-Century-Crofts.

Sluckin, W. (1964) *Imprinting and Early Experience*, London: Methuen.

Smith, F. V. (1969) *Attachment of the Young*, Edinburgh: Oliver and Boyd.

Smith, K. U., and Smith, M. F. (1966) *Cybernetic Principles of Learning and Educational Design*, New York: Holt, Rinehart and Winston.

Smith, M. (1974) When psychology grows up, *New Scientist*, **64**, 90–93.

Smith, M. S., and Bissell, J. F. (1970) Report analysis: the impact of Head Start, *Harvard Educational Review*, **40**, 51–104.

Spates, D. B., Alessi, G. J., Gutmann, A., Ellesworth, S., Mueller, K. L., and Ulrich, R. E. (1974) An educational day-care program for infants, in R. Ulrich, T. Stachnik, and J. Mabry (Eds.), *Control of Human Behavior, III*, Glenview, Illinois: Scott Foresman.

Spiker, C. C. (1959) Performance on a difficult discrimination following pretraining with distinctive stimuli, *Child Development*, **30**, 513–521.

Stanley, J. C. (1973) *Compensatory Education for Children, ages 2 to 8*, Baltimore: Johns Hopkins.

Stetten, K. J. (1972) Toward a market success for CAI, *Report M72–73*, The Mitre Corporation, 1820 Dolley Madison Blvd., McLean, Va. 22101.

Stetten, K. J., and Volk, J. L. (1973) Interactive television, *Report M72–200*, The Mitre Corporation, 1820 Dolley Madison Blvd., McLean, Va. 22101.

Stolurow, L. M. (1966) Programmed instruction and teaching machines, in P. H. Rossi and B. J. Biddle (Eds.), *The New Media and Education*, New York: Aldine.

Suppes, P. (1966) The use of computers in education, *Scientific American*, **215**, 206–221.

Suppes, P. (1971) Technology in education, in S.M. Brownell (Ed.), *Issues in Urban Education*, New Haven, Conn: Yale University Press.

Suppes, P., Jerman, M., and Brian, D. (1968) *Computer-assisted Instruction: Stanford's 1965–66 Arithmetic Program*, New York: Academic Press.

Suppes, P., and Morningstar, M. (1969) Computer-assisted instruction, *Science*, **166**, 343–350.

Thompson, D., and Johnson, J. D. (1971) Touch-Tutor at Hawksworth Hall, *Special Education*, **60**, 11–12.

Thorndike, E. L. (1913) *The Psychology of Learning*, New York: Teachers College.

Tinbergen, N. (1972) Foreword, in N. Blurton Jones (Ed.), *Ethological Studies of Child Behaviour*, London: Cambridge University Press.

Turing, A. M. (1950) Can a machine think?, *Mind*, **59**, 433–460.

Ulrich, R. E., Alessi, G. J., and Wolfe, M. (1971) The Learning Village: An alternate approach to traditional education, in D. Packham, A. Cleary, and T. Mayes (Eds.), *Aspects of Educational Technology V*, London: Pitman.

Uttal, W. R. (1967) *Real-Time Computers: Techniques and Applications in the Psychological Sciences*, New York: Harper and Row.

Waite, C. (1971a) Equipment: a brief survey of current trends in projectors, recorders and players, in M. Chazan and G. Downes (Eds.), *Compensatory Education and the New Media*, Swansea: Schools Council.

Waite, C. (1971b) Stories, picture books, and the new media and their place in compensatory education, in M. Chazan and G. Downes (Eds.), *Compensatory Education and the New Media*, Swansea: Schools Council.

Ward, J. (1970) On the concept of criterion-referenced measurement, *British Journal of educational Psychology*, **40**, 314–323.

174

Weisberg, P., and Fink, E. (1966) Fixed ratio and extinction performance of infants in the second year of life, *Journal of the experimental Analysis of Behavior*, **9**, 105–109.

Weisblat, J., and Weisblat, G. (1966) *Report on the Children's Caravan*, Weston, Connecticut: Children's Caravan.

Wiener, N. (1948) *Cybernetics*, New York: Wiley.

Wilson, H. A., and Atkinson, R. C. (1967) Computer-based instruction in initial reading: progress report on the Stanford Project, *Technical Report No. 119*, Stanford University, Institute for Mathematical Studies in the Social Sciences.

Zimmerman, E. H., Zimmerman, J., and Russell, C. D. (1969) Differential effects of token reinforcement on instruction—following behavior in retarded students instructed as a group, *Journal of applied Behavior Analysis*, **2**, 101–112.

Zinn, K. (1967) Computer technology for teaching and research on instruction, *Review of educational Research*, **37**, 618–634.

Zucker, M. H. (1969) *Electronic Circuits for the Behavioural and Biomedical Sciences*, San Francisco: W. H. Freeman.

Glossary

achievement
The performance of a student on a test of knowledge or skill. See also *summative evaluation*.

adaptive system
A system which continuously monitors its own behaviour and which, by adjusting its parameters, is able to modify its behaviour to suit a changing environment.

analogue computer
Analogue computers are machines designed to perform arithmetical functions upon numbers, which are represented in the machine by a continuously variable physical quantity, such as electrical current or voltage. They are widely used in scientific and industrial work to simulate complex physical systems. They are to be contrasted with *digital computers*.

aptitude
Traditionally defined as the capacity to acquire proficiency with a given amount of training. The consequent implication of a causal relationship between aptitude and *achievement* has led advocates of *mastery learning* to redefine aptitude as the amount of time required by the learner to achieve mastery (Carroll, 1963).

artificial intelligence
A term used to describe the use of computers in such a way that they perform operations analogous with human thinking and decision taking.

audiometry
The measurement of the acuity of hearing. An audiometer can produce tones at various frequencies in the audible range and at different intensities above the normal absolute threshold. Measurements of hearing loss are expressed in terms of the difference between the observed threshold and the normal absolute threshold for each frequency tested.

author language
A computer program which simplifies the problems for non-specialists in writing CAI teaching programs.

automation
The control of a process on a routine or production basis by automatic devices.

behavioural objectives
See *objectives*.

bionics
The study of the functions and characteristics of living systems especially in their relations to electronic systems.

bit
A contraction of binary digit. An element which can take either of two valves, as in the binary number system. See also *bits of information, digital computer*.

bits of information
A bit is a unit of measurement of information and uncertainty. When the two binary digits 0 and 1 are equally likely, a binary digit conveys exactly one bit of information. In general the formula for information content of such events is $\log_2 n$ bits, where n is the number of possible events.

branching programming
A method of (teaching) program construction, also termed intrinsic programming, in which the sequence of material is organised to

176

provide gradual progress and remedial teaching if incorrect responses are made. In contrast to *linear programming*, the learner has usually to pick one alternative from a set of possible answers to the questions which follow each step.

CAI See *computer-assisted instruction.*

cathode ray tube (CRT) An electronic tube in which a beam of electrons can be controlled to produce a spot of light on the tube face. The spot can be deflected in the X and Y directions to produce a visual display as in a TV set or a *visual display unit.*

classical conditioning A simple form of learning which occurs when a conditioned stimulus (e.g. a bell) is presented with or just before an unconditioned stimulus (e.g. food). After repeated trials the conditioned stimulus becomes a signal for the unconditioned stimulus and can elicit a similar response even if presented alone.

closed-circuit television A television system in which the television camera, receiver and the controls are directly connected by cable and no aerials are employed for transmission and reception.

CMI See *computer-managed instruction.*

computer See *analogue computer, digital computer.*

computer-assisted instruction (CAI) The use of a computer system to present an instructional program to an individual student and interpret his response. CAI requires the use of an *on-line* computer terminal and should be distinguished from *computer-managed instruction.*

computer-managed instruction (CMI) The use of the computer to help the teacher manage the educational process by assessing the student, suggesting a course of instruction and monitoring his progress. To be distinguished from *computer-assisted instruction.*

constructed response The answering of a question, solving of a problem or completing of a sentence by the student as in *linear programming*. The form of the response is determined by the student and is to be contrasted with a *multiple choice response.*

criterion-referenced tests Tests which provide information on the extent to which learners have achieved a criterion based on instructional content. It is important to specify such criteria prior to the instruction or relate these tests clearly to the original *objectives*. For a comparison of *norm-referenced tests* and criterion-referenced tests, see Roebuck (1971).

CRT See *cathode ray tube.*

cue See *prompt.*

cybernetics The attempt to derive principles of control and communication from the study of biological and machine systems. Especially important in the context of educational technology is the principle of feedback control, which is described in Section 1.3.

Delphi technique A method for the prediction of likely developments in technology. A series of questionnaires is administered to a panel of technical experts who estimate the date by which specific technological predictions will be realised. At each round of the questionnaire the experts are given the results of the previous predictions of the panel.

digital computer A digital computer is a machine capable of performing operations on data represented in digital form, i.e. in the form of discrete elements coded to represent numbers. In most digital computers the binary system is used and each element can adopt either of the values 0 or 1. Although the basic processes performed by a digital computer are simple, they can be performed at extremely high speeds so the computer can be programmed to undertake highly complex tasks. An electronic digital computer usually consists of input devices, a central processor, backing stores and output devices. To be contrasted with *analogue computer*.

discovery methods A rather ill-defined term covering a range of teaching procedures and learning processes in which very little prompting is provided for the learner, e.g. learning by trial and error or similar hypothesis-testing situations. There is disagreement as to the validity of claims made for such methods at various levels of education.

discrimination Responding differently to two or more related but different stimuli.

drive A term implying an impetus to behaviour, usually directed toward a goal. Primary drives are unlearned and physiologically based (e.g. hunger) whereas secondary drives are learned (e.g. ambition).

educational technology A broad term which covers not only the use of teaching machines or similar devices in education but increasingly refers to the application to education of scientific principles and approaches derived from a wide variety of disciplines.

EEG See *electro-encephalogram*.

electro encephalogram (EEG) A record of electrical fluctuations in the brain, usually obtained by placing electrodes on the skull.

entry behaviour The behaviour, relevant to the instructional objectives, which the student brings with him. The instruction should bridge the gap between entry behaviour and *terminal behaviour*.

equifinality A principle derived from Bertalanffy's distinction between open and closed systems. In closed systems only one path leads to the final equilibrium state. In an open system however the end state can be reached by a number of different routes and from different starting conditions. An example of this occurs in child development when a temporary illness slows down growth rate for a while. Afterwards the child catches up by growing faster than the normal rate.

ergonomics The design of effective man–machine systems. Ergonomics is usually concerned either with the design of furniture and other aspects of the environment to maximise human performance or with the design of displays and manual controls.

error rate The percentage of errors made by the learner in completing a chapter or similar unit of programmed material. Writers of linear programs have advocated low error rates (10% or less) but there is disagreement generally as to the value of making errors while learning. This may well vary with the nature of the material and the individual characteristics of the learner.

event recorder An instrument which records the occurrence of event in time, usually by deflecting a pen which is tracing the record on a motor driven paper roll. See Figure 4.30.

fading A technique developed with *linear programming*, whereby help given in the early stages of a program is gradually reduced by successive steps. See also *prompt*.

feedback A technique from control engineering whereby part of the output of a system is redirected to the input. Positive feedback decreases the stability of a system and tends to produce oscillations, but negative feedback, in which the feedback signal tends to oppose changes in the output, reduces errors and tends to produce a more stable system (see Section 1.3). In programmed learning the term is applied to the sentence or paragraph at the head of a frame which provides *knowledge of results* for the previous response.

feedback classroom A system which enables all the learners in a class to make independent and overt responses at the same time, usually in the context of giving answers to multiple choice questions; they are subsequently given information feedback on the correctness of the choice.

formative evaluation The evaluation of a curriculum, teacher or learner *during* the preparation of instructional material or ongoing instruction, initiated with a view to diagnosing learning difficulties (see Scriven (1967)). To be contrasted with *summative evaluation*.

frame or **item** That material which is presented to the student in programmed form at any one time. It may vary in size from a simple match-to-sample task to a full page of text, but it will generally require a response to be made before the student is allowed to proceed to the next frame.

Gellermann series Sequences for the presentation of items in visual discrimination experiments, devised by Gellermann (1933) such that stereotyped choice behaviour, e.g. *perseveration* will result in a rate of reinforcement equal to that obtained by chance after a set of trials.

generalisation Making a response which has been learned to a specific stimulus to a wider set of similar stimuli.

GSR Galvanic skin response. The electrical reaction of the skin, either the potential developed across the skin or, more usually, the resistance of the skin. A reduction of skin resistance (skin resistance response) is often considered to indicate an emotional response. The skin resistance level is also considered to indicate the state of arousal.

incidental learning Learning which takes place without any intention on the part of the learner. Two types of experimental procedure have been differentiated (i) where no instructions to learn are given and the learner is misled as to the purpose of the experiment and (ii) where the instructions given are incomplete or irrelevant to the nature of the retention task.

item See *frame*.

knowledge of results A report to the student on the appropriateness of his response. The report may take a verbal form 'right' or 'wrong', or it may take the form of lights or buzzers signalling one of these results. In some cases (e.g. in most linear programs) knowledge of results is effected by presenting the student with a specimen correct response. Since knowledge of results has been shown to facilitate learning it is usually considered to be a form of *reinforcement*.

linear programming A method of teaching program construction, derived from studies of discrimination learning in animals. The learning material is split up into very small steps, each of which require the learner to make a response, usually by completing one or two words omitted from a sentence. Errors are kept to a minimum and immediate knowledge of results is given after each response. See also *fading, shaping*, and contrast with *branching programming*.

macro-instruction A single statement, which when included in a computer program, will generate several machine instructions. The use of macros simplifies the task of programming, particularly when a series of repetitive tasks is involved.

mastery learning An approach to education which emphasises the individualisation of instruction with the aim of enabling the vast majority of students to achieve mastery of the educational objectives. *Formative evaluation* is used for diagnostic purposes and *criterion-referenced tests* are used for *summative evaluation* to determine mastery. See also *aptitude*.

microteaching A technique developed in the Education School at Stanford University, whereby student teachers are provided, via *closed-circuit television*, with a semi-permanent audio-visual record of their teaching. Such records would subsequently be used for discussion purposes by the supervisor.

multiple choice response The student's selection of an answer from two or more alternatives as in the case of matching-to-sample tasks or as used in *branching programming*.

non-formal education Education which takes place outside the formal school system, but is still planned and systematic unlike incidental education, resulting from the natural observation of the world around the learner, and informal education by, for example, the precept and example of elders. Non-formal education often employs existing social organisations with support from a central specialised agency.

normal distribution A bell-shaped frequency distribution, also called the normal-probability curve, which is approximated by distributions obtained in such areas as psychology and education. The distribution is derived mathematically from a model in which the values of variable are observed when the numbers are infinite and the variation is chance.

norm-referenced tests Tests which provide information regarding the performance of each learner relative to the rest and the relative position of a particular group relative to the remainder of the population. To be compared with *criterion-referenced tests*.

objectives The aims or goals of instruction which may be specified on a continuum ranging from very broad and general statements (e.g. to understand the principles of the number system) to very precise behavioural terms (adding together correctly up to three single digits without external assistance). From its specification it should be possible to test whether or not an objective has been attained.

off-line A part of a computer system is off-line when it is not directly under the control of the central processor, i.e. it is not *on-line*.

on-line A part of a data processing system is on-line if it is able to communicate with or is controlled by a computer. For example the student terminal in a CAI installation is on-line to the computer system, but punched cards could be prepared on *off-line* card punches as part of a CMI system.

operant A class of behaviours which are defined in terms of the *reinforcement* they provide rather than the detailed nature of the response itself, e.g. key-pressing behaviour.

operant conditioning A simple form of learning situation in which rewards are made contingent upon operant behaviour, e.g. rats pressing levers to obtain food. An analogy has been drawn between such laboratory studies and responding by humans to programmed instruction: its validity has been disputed. See also *reinforcement* and Sections 1.4 and 1.5.

orienting response A response requirement that is intended to check that the child has attended to all of the material in a display and can therefore be presumed to be making a genuine attempt to match a response alternative to the sample (the actual orienting response may involve pressing the sample panel first), rather than simply guessing between alternatives or some arbitrary choice.

perseveration The tendency exhibited by young children to respond exclusively to a particular object or position, irrespective of the requirements of a discrimination task. Hence stimulus perseveration (e.g. always choosing red) and position preference (e.g. responding always to the central panel of three). Similar sources of error among non-human primates have been observed by Harlow (1959).

photocell or photoelectric cell An electronic device containing a light sensitive semiconductor, usually selenium, germanium, silicon or cadmium sulphide. Depending on the design of the cell the light level either alters the resistance of the cell or generates a voltage.

plasma panel Plasma refers to the glow of ionised gas in a cold cathode discharge tube. The plasma panel is a replacement for the *cathode ray tube* and contains a matrix of fine wires driven by electronic circuits so that a picture can be constructed by the discharges selectively produced at the wire–wire intersections. It is used in the PLATO CAI terminal (Figure 5.8) which also employs the panel as a rear-projection screen for photographic material.

POSSUM devices POSSUM is an acronym for Patient Operated Selector Mechanism. This system, which was devised at Stoke Mandeville Hospital, allows severely physically disabled patients to control electric and electro-mechanical devices. For example an electric typewriter or tape recorder may be controlled by means of mouth suction or pressure.

primary reinforcement The presentation of a stimulus which provides *reinforcement* without any need of prior training, e.g. food to a hungry animal. Contrast with *secondary reinforcement*.

programmed learning A method of self-instruction achieved by a series of carefully designed items, which require responses from the learner and then provide information as to the accuracy of the response. See also *linear programming* and *branching programming*.

Project Head Start The title given to a large American child and family development programme, designed to provide compensatory early education for the disadvantaged children.

prompt or cue A means by which the probability of obtaining a correct response is increased. Skinner classified prompts used in *linear programming* into two major types: (i) formal prompts which provide knowledge about the form of the expected response, such as the initial letter or sound pattern, perhaps by a rhyme; (ii) thematic prompts which depend upon meaningful associations which make it more likely the student will produce the correct response.

reinforcement In *classical conditioning* the presentation of the unconditioned stimulus with the conditioned stimulus: in *operant conditioning* the presentation of a reward consequent upon the desired response being made. See Section 1.4 for a discussion of further distinctions. Compare with *knowledge of results*.

reinforcement schedule The specification which relates the emission of responses to the occurrence of *reinforcement* in *operant conditioning*. Thus a one to one relationship produces continuous reinforcement and intermittent reinforcement can be arranged on the basis of time intervals or number of responses required.

reliability The extent to which a test is consistent in placing students in the same relative position on repeated occasions. A number of formulae have been presented to estimate the reliability coefficient related to the difficulty of the test, the number of items completed etc., see Kuder and Richardson (1937).

resource centre A centre which provides educational technology support to neighbourhood schools. The support may be of one or more kinds (i) software library, (ii) equipment for use or for loan, (iii) technical services such as reprographic facilities or equipment repair, (iv) media production, (v) teacher training in educational technology, (vi) self-instructional facilities for students. The centre may be located in a school or may be housed separately for use by schools and possibly by the general public.

response A term used for specific elements of behaviour, usually consequent upon stimulation. It may involve simple selection of alternatives by pressing buttons or keys as with a *multiple choice response* or the production of speech or written text for a *constructed response*.

scrambled text A term sometimes used for a branching program in book form. The pages are not read consecutively, but the answer selected by the student at the end of each *frame* determines which page should be read next. The number of pages to turn is often randomised so that it does not provide a *cue* to the correct answer.

secondary reinforcement Any stimulus which provides *reinforcement* by virtue of prior training, e.g. verbally confirming a correct response. Contrast with *primary reinforcement*

servo system An automatic control system, designed so that the output follows the input to the system as closely as is required. It has at least one *feedback* loop which provides an input signal proportional to the difference between the actual output and the desired output (i.e. the error).

shaping The use of a series of small steps to teach a particular response. The *reinforcement* of each component response of a final complex response is often referred to as a method of successive approximations.

significance level The level of probability at which the hypothesis of no difference is rejected and accordingly results are considered statistically significant. By statistical convention the null hypothesis is not usually rejected unless the result could have occurred by chance less than 1 in 20 times ($p < 0.05$).

stimulus Any object, energy or change in energy in the environment which excites a sense organ. The term is sometimes restricted to those sensory stimuli which are meaningful to the recipient. For example, although printed material would be a meaningful stimulus for most adults, this would not be so in the case of infants.

summative evaluation The type of evaluation made about a curriculum, teacher or learner after instruction has taken place. Contrast with *formative evaluation*.

synchronising pulse A signal recorded together with auditory information which when replayed can be detected and used to initiate the operation of automatic equipment at a defined time in relation to the audio information. For example a tape–slide show would use synchronising pulses to operate the automatic slide projector. The pulses are preferably recorded on a separate track from the audio message, although it is possible to use low frequency signals on the same track as the audio message and to filter out the synchronising pulses on replay.

systems approach Usually refers to attempts to structure the learning situation so that techniques and theories are integrated into a meaningful whole, which embodies both function and control. For a more detailed discussion of its derivation, see Section 6.1.

target population That group of learners for whom a particular set of programmed materials or a particular device is intended.

teaching machine A mechanical or electrical device for the presentation of teaching programs. The machine displays one *frame* at a time and requires a response before it will display the next frame.

teletypewriter An input-output device for use with a *digital computer*. When used as an *on-line* terminal the mechanical keyboard sends data to the

182

computer which echoes back the characters on the printer. The computer output is also printed on the paper roll. A teletypewriter is sometimes replaced by a *visual display unit*. See Figure 5.1.

terminal behaviour The behaviour which a student is expected to have acquired by the end of a training sequence. The evidence that such behaviour has been acquired is usually obtained by requiring successful responses to terminal items in the program or performance on a criterion test.

token economy A system operated within a community, such as a school or mental hospital, whereby children or patients obtain tokens for specified behaviour and can later trade the tokens to acquire objects or take part in events of their choice.

transfer This process refers to the effects of prior learning on the efficiency of performance in some current learning task. Such effects can range from facilitation (positive transfer) to interference and confusion (negative transfer). Broadly speaking, the extent and type of transfer depends on the similarity between the stimuli and responses in the two situations.

validity The extent to which a test measures the process or ability for which it was designed.

VDU See *visual display unit*.

video tape recorder (VTR) A tape recorder which allows television sound and vision signals to be recorded and replayed. The signals may be a broadcast programme or generated locally by a camera and microphone. In order to record the very high frequencies in the vision signal a VTR uses a method of helical scanning on the tape. This process has produced a number of different recording standards for the low cost machines which use half-inch tape. This lack of standardisation does not apply to broadcast quality VTR and so recordings made on these machines are interchangeable. Recently an international standard for half-inch tape has been introduced.

visual display unit (VDU) A replacement for a *teletypewriter* using an electronic keyboard and a *cathode ray tube* instead of printed paper output. See Figure 4.8.

VTR See *video tape recorder*.

Author Index

Page numbers in italics indicate authors' appearances in the References.

Subject Index